THE POWER OF PLACE

THE POWER OF PLACE

Geography, Destiny, and Globalization's Rough Landscape

Harm de Blij

OXFORD
UNIVERSITY PRESS

OXFORD
UNIVERSITY PRESS

Oxford University Press, Inc., publishes works that further
Oxford University's objective of excellence
in research, scholarship, and education.

Oxford New York
Auckland Cape Town Dar es Salaam Hong Kong Karachi
Kuala Lumpur Madrid Melbourne Mexico City Nairobi
New Delhi Shanghai Taipei Toronto

With offices in
Argentina Austria Brazil Chile Czech Republic France Greece
Guatemala Hungary Italy Japan Poland Portugal Singapore
South Korea Switzerland Thailand Turkey Ukraine Vietnam

Published by Oxford University Press, Inc.
198 Madison Avenue, New York, NY 10016

www.oup.com

First issued as an Oxford University Press paperback, 2010

Oxford is a registered trademark of Oxford University Press

Library of Congress Cataloging-in-Publication Data
De Blij, Harm J.
The power of place : geography, destiny,
and globalization's rough landscape / Harm de Blij.
    p.   cm.
Includes bibliographical references and index.
ISBN 978-0-19-975432-8
1. Human geography.   2. Globalization.   I. Title.
GF41.D42 2008
304.2—dc22   2007052451

7 9 8

Printed in the United States of America
on acid-free paper

To
E. James Potchen

CONTENTS

PREFACE

Numerous books and articles published in recent years argue, explicitly as well as implicitly, that the human world today is so mobile, so interconnected, and so integrative that it is, in one prominent and much-repeated assessment, "flat." Ancient and durable obstacles are no more, interaction is global, free trade rules the globe, migration is ubiquitous, and the flow of ideas (and money and jobs) is so pervasive that geography, in the perspective of more than one observer, "is history." The notion that place continues to play a key role in shaping humanity's still-variegated mosaic is seen as obsolete, even offensive and deterministic. Choice, not constraint, is the mantra of the new flat-world proponents. Join the "forces of flattening" and you will enjoy the benefits. Don't, and you will fall off the edge. The option is yours.

But is it? From the vantage point of a high-floor room in the Shanghai Hyatt, the Mumbai Oberoi, or the Dubai Hilton, or from a business-class window seat on Singapore Airlines, the world seems flat indeed. Millions of world-flatteners move every day from hotel lobby to airport limo to first-class lounge, laptop in hand, uploading, outsourcing, offshoring as they travel, adjusting the air conditioning as they go. They are changing the world, these modern nomads, and they are, in many ways, improving it—depending of course on one's definition of progress. But are they invariably agents of access and integration? Are they lowering the barriers to participation or raising the stakes against it? Have their influence and impact overpowered the imperatives of place, so that their very mobility symbolizes a confirmed irrelevance of location?

Not yet. The Earth, physically as well as culturally, still is very rough terrain, and in crucial ways its regional compartments continue to trap billions in circumstances that spell disadvantage. The power of place and the fate of people are linked by many strands ranging from physical area and natural environment to durable culture and local tradition. This book, therefore, views a world in which progress toward convergence is countered by stagnation, even setbacks. Various constituencies of the comparatively prosperous global core are walling off their affluent realms from intrusion by poorer globals, hardening a division between core and periphery that exacerbates contrasts and stokes conflicts. The near-global diffusion of various forms of English as a first or second language is promoting a cultural convergence, but the radicalization of religions has the opposite effect. The distribution of health and well-being shows troubling signs of inequity and reversal. Because people continue to congregate in places of high environmental risk, especially in the crowded periphery, hundreds of millions find themselves in continuing jeopardy (as the 2004 tsunami, in the absence of coordinated warning systems, tragically confirmed). Inevitably, places of costly historic and current conflict take their toll as the "international community" stands by without effective intervention, another form of jeopardy that afflicts the destinies of millions. And males and females in the same locales have widely varying experiences, their destinies diverging in sometimes agonizing ways. Even in the world's cities, where the "rising tide lifts all boats" promise of globalization should be especially evident, power creates a high-relief topography of privilege and privation. Nor is the world's divisive political stockade likely to be flattened anytime soon. Even as states try to join in unions and associations, their provinces and regions nurture nationalisms working the other way. The power of place still holds the vast majority of us in its thrall.

Of course, the question is not whether the world is flat. Thomas Friedman, who coined the phrase, concedes that he realizes "that the world is not flat. Don't worry, I know…I have engaged in literary license in titling [my] book to draw attention…" (Friedman, 2005). It is the *process* of "flattening" on which Friedman wants to focus through his provocative title, "the single most important trend in the world today," that is at issue. And in certain respects the global playing field *is* leveling, but in other ways the reverse appears to be true. Notions of a flat world raise expectations of growing access and increasing opportunity that are mantras of globalization but are all too often at variance with reality. Powerful forces, natural as well as human, slow the flattening process in a contest that will determine the future of the planet. Globalization may hold the promise its proponents proclaim, but it also inevitably creates inequities that can bring out the worst in human nature. When a group of disadvantaged and disaffected rebels can converge in remote mountain caves and have a realistic chance of securing destructive means once monopolized by superpowers, it is time to assess the prospects.

This book ranges over natural as well as cultural landscapes to assess the role of place in enabling as well as obstructing the world's march toward integration, mobility, and interconnection. For all the liberating changes that have already occurred, place of birth still has a powerful influence over the destinies of billions. For all our heralded mobility, the overwhelming majority of us will die relatively close to the place where we were born. For all the "flattening" perceived and relished by globals, the world still is dauntingly rough terrain for many more locals. From personal safety to public health, from compulsory religion to coercive authority, the world remains a mosaic of places presenting widely varying combinations of challenges to their inhabitants. What makes this power of place and how it can be mitigated are the interlocked themes of the discussion that follows.

ACKNOWLEDGMENTS

For the travels, readings, correspondence, conversations and other motivations and encouragements that led to my writing down these thoughts I owe an enormous debt of gratitude to many friends, colleagues, acquaintances, and even strangers willing to share their views, and I could not possibly thank them all (and some remained anonymous). Lori Maarschalk first drew my attention to geographic implications of flat-world notions during a trip to Cornwall in 2006. Jay Harman's insights and encouragements were indispensable. Dick Robb circulated an early draft of this book with good effect, for which I am very grateful. Jim Newman, Alan Best, Eileen Shapiro, Rich Earle, Antoinette WinklerPrins, Jan Nijman, Chris Rogers, and Tanya de Blij read all or part of the manuscript and made numerous recommendations and suggestions. When I ran up against data problems I had enormous help from Peter Muller, Alec Murphy, Ian MacLachlan, Don Larson, and Ab Brandt. I also thank Stan Brunn, Richard Carnovale, Iraphne Childs, Pinkie Christensen, Harrison Coerver, Roy Cole, Ken Corey, James de Blij, Ben Eaves, Julie Fiore, Ed Grode, Kim Honey, Dick Houk, Gene Jacobs, Tom Jeffs, Ted Kandle, Patti McCulley, Carol Milne, Jim Mosman, Gertjan Perdaems, Paul Peters, Ross Robbins, Eunice Rutledge, Jeff Sachs, Al Shuster, Marjorie Winters, and Marijke Wissen van Staden for their tangible interest. None of these acknowledgments implies endorsement by anyone of the views expressed in this book, and all errors and other shortcomings remain, of course, my responsibility. The maps were drawn by Mapping Specialists of Madison, Wisconsin, whose superb four-color cartography also graces my geography textbooks.

I am also grateful to the staff of Oxford University Press who produced this handsome book. The acquisitions editor, Ben Keene, always was a source of encouragement, and Niko Pfund, vice president and publisher of the Academic/Trade Division, was an early advocate for this project. The production editor, Keith Faivre, expertly coordinated this always-complicated process. The jacket design was by Jim Bricker, and the creative layout of the book is the work of SPI Publisher Services. I also appreciate the work of Megan Kennedy, the marketing director; Jamie Taratoot, the event coordinator; and Betsy DeJesu, the publicity director.

As always my greatest debt is to my wife, Bonnie Doughty, whose powers of observation and sound judgment leave me in no doubt as to the meaning of "better half."

Harm de Blij

THE POWER OF PLACE

1

GLOBALS, LOCALS, AND MOBALS

Earth may be a planet of shrinking functional distances, but it remains a world of staggering situational differences. From the uneven distribution of natural resources to the unequal availability of opportunity, place remains a powerful arbitrator. Many hundreds of millions of farmers in river basins of Asia and Africa live their lives much as their distant ancestors did, still remote from the forces of globalization, children as well as adults still at high personal risk and great material disadvantage. Tens of millions of habitants of isolated mountain valleys from the Andes to the Balkans and from the Caucasus to Kashmir are as bound to their isolated abodes as their forebears were. Of the seven billion current passengers on Cruiseship Earth, the overwhelming majority (the myth of mass migration notwithstanding) will die very near the cabin in which they were born.

In their lifetimes, this vast majority will have worn the garb, spoken the language, professed the faith, shared the health conditions, absorbed the education, acquired the attitudes, and inherited the legacy that constitutes the power of place: the accumulated geography whose formative imprint still dominates the planet. The regional impress of poverty continues to trap countless millions who are and will be born into it and who, globalization notwithstanding, cannot escape it. The "wealth gap" between the fortunate and the less fortunate, still largely a matter of chance and destiny, evinces a widening range resulting from the perpetuation of privilege and power in the so-called global "core" and its international tentacles. Those disparities, represented at all levels of scale, will entail increasing risk in a world of rising anger and weapons of growing destructive efficiency.

At the same time, the notion that the world, if not "flat," is flattening under the impress of globalization is gaining traction. As noted in the preface, the idea that diversities of place continue to play a key role in shaping humanity's variegated mosaic tends to be dismissed by globalizers who see an increasingly homogenized and borderless world. "Flatness" is becoming an assumption, not merely a prospect, as implied by the titles of numerous books and articles of recent vintage (Fung et al., 2008).

And indeed, certain global playing fields are leveling, but there is a danger in assuming that the benefits are within everyone's reach. All of us are blessed as well as burdened by the baggage of place—our place of birth, our mother tongue, of belief systems and conditions of health, of environmental norms and political circumstances. The same place presents different opportunities and challenges to males as compared to females. In our current rush to embrace the rewards of global "flattening," it is worth reminding ourselves that point of entry continues to matter when it comes to opportunities in reach.

This book, therefore, focuses on the rugged terrain of the world's environmental, cultural, social, economic, and political geographies. It proposes that the confines of place continue to impose severe limits on human thought and action, engendering (and, in some cases, still intensifying) inequalities affecting individuals and families at one end of a continuum that has communities and regions at its other end, disparities so evident that no flat-world or melting-pot postulations can wish them away. These differences reflect a still-pervasive power of place. They may be diminishing in some ways in certain areas, for example, in the nodes and channels of globalization that have cast a cloak of conformity over high-rise skylines, multilane highways, office "parks," and shopping malls from Minneapolis to Mumbai, but elsewhere such disparities persist and are even worsening. In China, the Pacific Rim triumph of free-market capitalism—of which Shanghai is a symbol—stands in sharp contrast to the tragedy of the rural interior, where poverty and entrapment condemn hundreds of millions to a penurious existence from which escape is not easy. In India, the much-publicized employment opportunities in the burgeoning high-tech industries of Bengaluru (Bangalore), Gurgaon (outside Delhi), and even Kolkata (Calcutta), may attract hundreds of thousands of qualified workers but remain essentially irrelevant to tens of millions of landless peasants in the remote reaches of the lower Ganges Basin. In Africa, thousands of desperate emigrants climb into unseaworthy boats every year, seeking to reach the European mainland; this has been going on for decades, with immeasurable cost in lives and misery. To these and countless others testing the obstacles, notions of a flat world remain essentially irrelevant. Yes, the world is flattening—for the fortunate minority in control of, in the path of, or with access to the mainstreams of modernization. But a minority it is, and population projections indicate that humanity's coming expansion, before stabilization sets in toward the end of the century, will magnify the numbers in the world's poorest regions. This means that *locals* (those who are poorest, least mobile, and most susceptible to the impress of place) will increasingly outnumber the fortunate *globals* to whom the world appears comparatively limitless.

If this argument seems to counter economic models projecting an ever richer China and India and a burgeoning of the middle class virtually everywhere, it is important to consider demographic projections as well. In our divided world, the populations of the rich countries are growing at a collective 0.25 percent annually, but poor countries at 1.46 percent (Cohen, 2003). It is a matter of common knowledge, and growing concern, that populations in the richest regions of the world, for example Japan and Germany, are declining. But the four dozen most poverty-stricken countries on the planet, representing some 700 million inhabitants, are growing at an explosive 2.4 percent. And *within* major nations whose overall statistics suggest a sustained decline of the rate of natural increase, certain areas—usually the poorer ones—continue to mushroom even as others, better off economically, are stabilizing. In India, for example, the 2001 census reported that the State of Uttar Pradesh, one of the country's poorest and most populous, was growing at the fulminant rate of 2.55 percent (Bihar and Jharkhand were growing faster still) even as the growth rate in Kerala and Tamil Nadu hovered around 1.0 percent. Projections suggesting that the Earth's human population will continue to grow at a declining rate of increase, to stabilize at around 10 billion by the end of this century, must be tempered by the prospect that the bulk of this growth will occur in countries and provinces that currently rank among the poorest of the poor. The overwhelming majority of the three billion people who will be joining Cruiseship Earth will embark as locals, and but a tiny minority as globals.

MOBALS AND MOTIVES

In the best-case scenario, a comparatively fast-growing number of these locals will be enabled to join the latticework of globalization, and to do so by choice rather than out of desperation. The argument rages today whether textile-industry sweatshops in low-wage countries should be seen as providing women the opportunity to escape their stultifying social environs or as exploitive corporate monstrosities, but either way they constitute the corridor out of the inside cabin to the privileged view from the deck. These (and other) harsh employments engender social and fiscal mobilities that should ultimately enhance choice, but studies are showing that they also widen wealth gaps and expose employees to cultural dislocation. All the same, globalization and mobility are synonymous, and even the toughest assembly lines make *mobals* out of locals. The same hope that sends a Bangladeshi villager to a textile factory propels a Chinese farmer toward the Pacific Rim and a Brazilian peasant toward São Paulo.

Mobals are the risk-takers, migrants willing to leave the familiar, to take a chance on new and different surroundings, their actions ranging from legal migration to undocumented border crossing, their motivations from employment to asylum. They move as highly trained professionals and as unskilled workers, as doctors and domestic servants, as bankers and bricklayers. Mobals are transnational migrants; that is, they cross international borders—they are agents of change. Many millions of movers relocate within their homelands, never to leave their familiar domicile. Mobals take the greater chance, often tempting fate. Some pay with their lives.

The desperate migrants who leave their homes in time of war and cross international boundaries to seek refuge are not, by this definition, mobals. The overwhelming majority of the millions of Pushtuns who escaped war-torn Afghanistan during the Soviet intervention and subsequent Taliban regime found sanctuary in cross-border Pakistan and Iran, where they awaited the opportunity to return, an opportunity most took when the Taliban regime had been ousted. The two million Iraqi refugees who fled into neighboring Syria and Jordan during the chaos following the American-led military invasion hope to return home as well. Transnational refugees are driven out by conflict. Transnational mobals are drawn by perceptions of opportunity and realities of need.

The Earth is in a race against time. Mobals challenge the power of place, carrying with them the assets and liabilities of locality and competing in new and unfamiliar environs for livelihood and security. Their world is rapidly urbanizing; gone will be the days when local meant rural and global meant urban. The great majority of the still-to-be-born will arrive in poor-country conurbations numbering 50 million or more, vast urban regions signaling a fundamental transformation of human society. They will be the migrants, the great internationalizers of the twenty-first century. A sufficient number of them must see their hopes translated into reality, their local values accommodated, their efforts rewarded, to yield individual commitment to the order and stability that are the aims of the globals who will continue to exercise control. In a world suffused with weapons of all kinds, there is no other option.

A NATION ASUNDER

The future of our planet, thus, will depend on the ways relationships between globals and locals evolve. Globals, whether in government, industry, business, or other decision-making capacities, flatten playing fields for each other as they traverse the world from Davos to Doha. Conferences like the G-8 legitimize or countenance actions that may be inimical to locals, whose voices are not sufficiently strong to be heard. It is the globals who build security and migration barriers, not the locals. It is the globals who mobilize armies to intervene in other states, not the locals. It is the globals who move factories from low-wage to even lower-wage environs, wreaking havoc among workers. It is the globals who control the fates of locals as well as mobals, often ruthlessly.

This, of course, is nothing new. What has changed is the scale. When states were less interconnected than they are today, and colonial powers as well as ruling minorities were able to act with far less international scrutiny, the global-mobal-local model could function with considerable autonomy. While living in South Africa during the 1950s, I witnessed the imposition of the system for which the country was to become infamous, *apartheid*, the formalization of a set of practices that had long prevailed in the country but had never been codified as national policy. When my family arrived there (from the recently liberated Netherlands) toward the end of 1948, it soon became clear to me that the de facto rules of racial segregation applied more stringently in certain parts of the country than in others. While there was discrimination everywhere, gray areas could be recognized in what was then the Cape Province, notably in Cape Town, and also in Natal, especially in its major city, Durban. Although discriminatory rules prevailed as a matter of course, there was clearly a variable geography of racial segregation. Things were tougher in the landlocked provinces of the interior than they were in the cities on the coast. Rules were stricter in small rural towns than in larger urban areas, and more often broken in the latter (Nelson Mandela had a modest office in an otherwise all-white law firm in Johannesburg). In suburbs and towns where Afrikaners were in the majority, often marked by names signifying their cultural heritage, such as Krugersdorp and Louis Trichardt, apartheid was already in full force long before it became government policy. This geographic modulation, arising from a combination of factors, seemed to function as a safety valve in a slowly integrating society (Mandela, 1994).

In the still-colonial era of the 1940s, South Africa in some ways was a microcosm of the world. A white minority had established the political, economic, and social frameworks that constituted the state. Black workers toiled in gold and diamond mines, on farms, and on public projects; whites had appropriated the means of production as well as most of the good farmland. The architects of apartheid and their collaborators, who included not just Afrikaners but many English-speaking South Africans as well, were the country's globals, guiding the economy from paneled boardrooms, driving along good highways linking all-white city centers and upscale suburbs, and controlling internal African migration in accordance with labor requirements.

South Africa's locals were the African peoples who found themselves circumscribed by the political boundaries the Europeans laid out. Several of them were veritable nations more numerous than their white rulers: the Zulu of Natal, the Xhosa (Mandela's people) of the eastern Cape, the Sotho of the highlands, the Tswana of the interior. All of them had historic homelands; all had distinctive cultures and traditions. The mines and farms and cities had drawn hundreds of thousands from their ancestral homelands into the new economy, but the majority remained where they were born. These were the most local of locals, isolated in their rural abodes and remote from the modern South Africa being forged far over the horizon.

Soon after the Afrikaner-dominated government imposed its apartheid rules on South Africa, this indigenous cultural geography became the foundation for an extension of the system. Under a grand design called *separate development*, the African homelands were cartographically defined and politically designated as national entities actually referred to as "republics." Also called *Bantustans*, they were given the trappings of statehood, complete with enhanced capitals, assembly buildings, schools, and local industries; but when all was said and done, they covered less than 15 percent of South Africa's territory. They were, in effect, domestic colonies, never capable of self-sufficiency. Of necessity, they would provide much of the labor South Africa could require. But here is how they facilitated the dominance by the globals over the locals: every black South African was forced to register as a "citizen" of his or her ancestral "republic." This meant that every African who happened to be living and working somewhere in the more than 80 percent of the country designated for whites was henceforth a foreigner in his own land, a temporary migrant worker destined sooner or later to have to "return"—even if born in, say, Johannesburg—to one of the remote "republics." By extension, no black African could expect to vote in "white" South Africa; a Zulu voter would register in the Zulu "republic," not anywhere else.

But all this was still in the future when, shortly after my arrival in Johannesburg, I had an opportunity to see the South Africa that was about to disappear. My father, a violinist, was scheduled to perform in a concert with the Durban Symphony Orchestra, and to travel from the rather barren plateau environs of mile-high Johannesburg to the palm-lined streets of this port city with its graceful waterfront esplanade was to trade one world for another. Multicultural Durban was roughly one-third Asian (mostly from India), one-third African (mostly Zulu), and one-third white. Among the whites, people with British ancestries far outnumbered Afrikaners. I stood in the back of the balcony of Durban City Hall waiting for an open seat when I noticed something I would not see again: several dozen Asian and African listeners sat in the back rows, some with tickets in hand, proving that the whites-only rule, clearly posted downstairs, was being violated by (white) box-office personnel, ushers, and others. In the days that followed, I noted that buses were not strictly segregated (as they were in Johannesburg) and that other trappings of "petty" apartheid were being routinely ignored.

In Cape Town, where my father's next appearance was scheduled, a friend of his took me to see the great university, further proof that apartheid had yet to reach its nadir. Cape Town, like Durban, was a multicultural community, but here the significant sector of the population was referred to as "Coloured," meaning of mixed ancestry. In the absence of identity cards specifying race (that, too, was in the future), many citizens of Coloured ancestry moved freely in the city, making use of public amenities mostly without hindrance. At the University of Cape Town, I saw Coloured, some African, and a few Asian students in hallways and classes. When we visited the government buildings, I learned that Coloured citizens of the Cape even had special representation in the South African parliament.

In the government's offices, however, the machinery of apartheid was being assembled. For three hundred years, South Africa had been the scene of interracial and intercultural contact, conflict, and accommodation. Its natural riches had attracted a variegated mix of ancestries and traditions. Its economic growth had engendered a great internal migration of workers. Its diverse natural and social environments had produced different solutions to the inevitable problems of multiracial living. In the half century following the end of the Boer War, South Africa had been governed by a British-dominated political party whose administration was not noted for its efficiency or vision. When the Afrikaner "Nationalist" Party contested the 1948 (whites-only) election, its platform centered on the "threat" that South Africa was drifting toward irreversible integration. Even before their victory, the designers of apartheid were planning their strategy. No longer would existing rules of segregation be locally ignored. No longer would universities in designated white areas be permitted to register students other than those of "European" ancestry. No longer would a blind eye be cast over the long-evolving residential integration of inner cities. Apartheid operated at all levels of scale: micro (personal facilities such as toilets and park benches), meso (urban-residential), and macro (regional-territorial) (Domingo, 2004). The *separate development* scheme was the logical culmination of a plan to *re*segregate South Africa and then to carry the project to its ultimate geographic conclusion. South Africa would become a "nation of nations." In the process, definitions of "nation," "republic," "development," and "government" were subverted to ideology. The globals of South Africa, microcosm of the world, would prove that separation of races and cultures was the way toward postcolonial stability and sustained hegemony, a system that would keep locals in their place and mobals under strict control.

One key lesson from South Africa in the 1950s was (and remains) that some regimes, unconstrained by international scrutiny and undeterred by multilateral sanctions or other direct costs, are able to subjugate entire populations to serve their economic, cultural, and strategic purposes. In an era when colonial powers did little to oversee each other and European dictatorships ruled harshly over African dependencies, South Africa's white-nationalist regime could implement apartheid without risk to its membership in the United Nations. From international economic organizations to sporting events, South African delegations and teams traveled the world, South Africa's globals capitalizing on the tenor of the times. In the postcolonial era, when the evils of the system led to worldwide revulsion and global condemnation, many analysts asserted that only white-minority regimes could create such perfidy. But the imperatives that engendered apartheid were human, not racial. They can be seen today, albeit in different forms, from Myanmar to Sudan and from North Korea to Zimbabwe. Might they be discernible as well in the globalizing, flattening world at large?

Even in pre-apartheid but already segregated South Africa, some locals had managed to break through the prevailing social, educational, and economic barriers and had found precarious niches on the other side. What I saw that concert night in Durban City Hall was a glimpse of the South African Paradox, as I called it in my diary at the time. Why would people rebuffed at every turn want to dress in Western attire, hear the music of European composers, observe the rules of the global concert hall? Why would they want to attend Christian churches (Afrikaners often invoked biblical interpretations to justify apartheid)? Why would they want to study at universities that educated the very elites that oppressed them? Nevertheless, by the time the Afrikaner regime implemented apartheid as official policy, tens of thousands of Africans, Coloureds, and Asians had formed a growing middle class, mobals of remarkable tenacity whose commitment to the modern order was evinced by their lifestyles.

The planners of apartheid viewed this as a threat, not the cultural achievement it constituted. The systematic rejection by the Afrikaner administration of those who had succeeded in crossing the barriers of de facto racial segregation was a distressing episode, foreshadowing their reemergence in opposition movements that would eventually play a powerful role in ending the apartheid era. The long-imprisoned

Nelson Mandela was the key figure in South Africa's essentially peaceful transition to majority government, but others who might have been bent on revolutionary change and violent retribution were once again persuaded to commit themselves to sustaining a social order not of their making—and one that would bear the imprints of apartheid for decades to come. A new, multiracial cadre of globals has taken the reins in South Africa, but as in much of the rest of the world, the problems of old persist. South Africa's new challenge is the revolution of rising expectations, for jobs, land reform, housing, education. After decades of containment, an army of millions of mobals is transforming cities and towns, generating a huge informal economy that funnels far too few hopefuls into the formal one. South Africa still is a mirror to the world. It has not yet crossed the Rubicon.

A WORLD APART

Formal apartheid may no longer disfigure the South African state, but in the world at large the incentives that gave rise to the system increasingly mark the cultural landscape, from gated communities in affluent suburbs to fenced boundaries between rich and poor countries. In South Africa, wealth was concentrated in a necklace of cities that anchored the interior and dominated the coast; poverty prevailed in the horseshoe of "Bantustans" that encircled the urban core and provided raw materials and labor for the globally linked economy. In the world today, wealth is concentrated in a highly urbanized and strongly globalized region extending from Europe through North America to East Asia and Australia, a region often referred to by economic geographers as the *global core*. The worst global poverty persists in the periphery—in Africa and Asia (figure 1.1). As the map shows, virtually all the cities in the world with the highest quality-of-life indexes lie in this demographically slow-growing core, whereas the burgeoning, chaotic megacities lie in the faster-growing periphery. Certainly the world is "flattest" in the wealthy core, roughest in the periphery.

Figure 1.1 cannot tell the whole story, of course. The global periphery contains the world's poorest countries and societies, but it has its own geographic variations. As a geographic realm, South America is economically far ahead of Subsaharan Africa. In East

Asia, national statistics for China do not reflect enormous contrasts between the rural interior, where conditions in certain areas are so bad that foreigners are not allowed to see them, and the coastal zone, where authoritarian rule coupled with market economics has created a "flattening" that is moving this area toward the conditions of the core, at least in material terms. Southeast Asia may not be part of the global core, but Singapore ranks as one of the world's most successful economies and has a very high quality-of-life index, an oft-cited symbol of globalization.

The map represents the outcome of millennia of postglacial environmental change, of centuries of colonialism and imperialism, of agricultural, industrial, technological, and political revolutions and their global dissemination, and of the enduring advantage of the head start in a globalizing world. There may have been a time when the sun never set on the British Empire, but Britain lost it all—and yet the United Kingdom still is a force in global affairs and London remains one of the world's financial capitals. The wealth and continuing influence of countries such as the Netherlands and France were assured when their empires extended from Middle America to Southeast Asia. The global core of which these countries are parts is also the region where indigenous populations were overwhelmed and very nearly extirpated by the European invasion.

Nothing underscores the contrast between core and periphery as powerfully as do demographic and economic data. As defined in figure 1.1, the global core contains approximately 15 percent of the global population but records nearly 75 percent of the world's annual income (in terms of gross national income, based on World Bank data). The periphery represents 85 percent of the planet's population, accruing just 25 percent of total income.

As such, the core attracts millions of mobals ranging from legal immigrants to asylum seekers and from illegal workers to revolutionaries. Not only are the states of the core the richest on the planet; their power also continues to permeate the countries of the periphery, spawning anger as well as hope. The great majority of migrants seeking to enter the core are drawn by the promise of work and wages, pull factors that can induce them to take terrible risks. The remittances sent home by just one successful mobal can sustain an entire extended family in Mexico, India, China, the Philippines, or a host of other countries. But a small minority have other objectives,

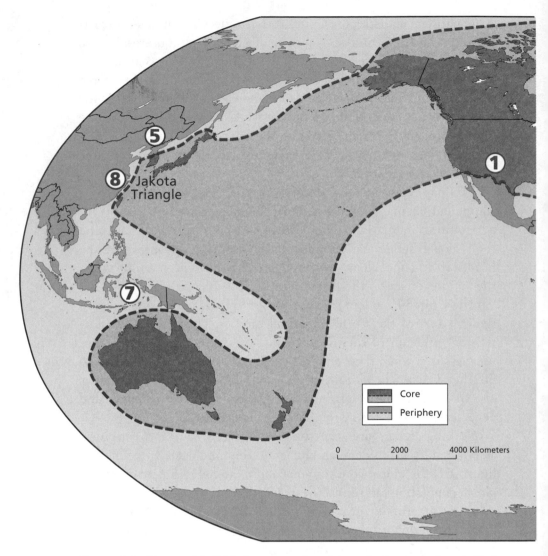

Figure 1.1. The world divided: core and periphery in the early twenty-first century. The numbers refer to places where governments try to stem the tide of undocumented migrants moving from periphery to core.

ranging from organized crime to terrorism. The control and regulation of immigration are therefore joint objectives of the states of the core.

To be sure, the management of migration should involve both source and destination—the countries of origin as well as the recipient states. But such coordination has proven difficult to achieve. When

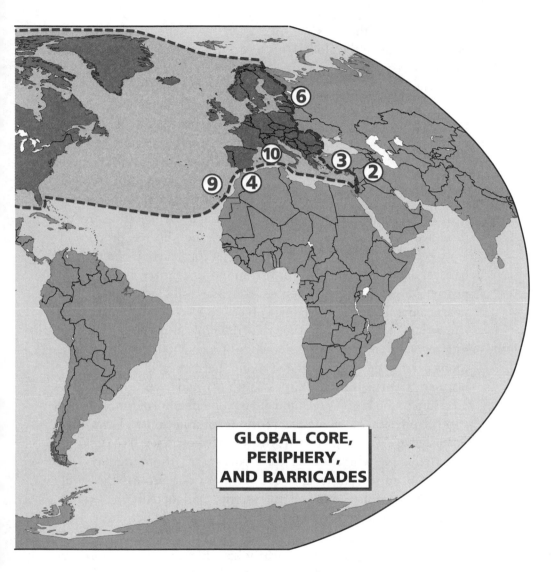

**GLOBAL CORE,
PERIPHERY,
AND BARRICADES**

U.S. President George W. Bush took office in 2001, he proclaimed his intention to reach an agreement with then-President Vicente Fox of Mexico to coordinate and regulate cross-border migration and to find a joint solution to the problem of the millions of illegal Mexican migrants already in the United States. That initiative fell victim to 9/11 and its aftermath, and by the time it was revived, public opinion had hardened, public confidence in the U.S. president and his administration had weakened, and a comprehensive solution was beyond reach. In truth, the Mexican–American case underscores what has been the norm: in the global core, piecemeal control takes precedence over comprehensive negotiation.

As the map shows, this control takes various forms, but in combination it has the effect of walling off core from periphery. Undoubtedly the most portentous manifestation of this effort is the demarcation of the border between Mexico and the United States (1) in accordance with the terms of the Secure Fence Act, an 1100-kilometer expansion and reinforcement of the barriers between joint members of NAFTA, the North American Free Trade Association that was to raise living standards in Mexico and, among other objectives, reduce incentives for cross-border migrants to risk their lives. A proportionately even larger project (2) is the ongoing construction of a physical barrier that will essentially enclose an entire country, Israel, within nearly 700 kilometers of fences, concrete walls, and intervening no-go zones. Here the proclaimed objective is security against terrorism rather than labor migration, but the project has been impugned as a revival of apartheid methodology (Carter, 2007). Another infamous barrier, the so-called Green Line, hermetically sealed Turkish northern Cyprus from the Greek south (3), and even Cyprus's 2004 accession to the European Union did not end its control function. Still another physical barricade marks the territorial limits of two small Spanish exclaves on the North African (Mediterranean) coast, Ceuta and Melilla (4), where barbed-wire fences ward off immigrants who, once on Spanish soil, would have rights to due process that could overwhelm Spanish and EU legal systems. Undoubtedly the longest-existing and best-known rampart between core and periphery is the Demilitarized Zone (DMZ) between South and North Korea (5) across their joint peninsula, a nearly 250-kilometer fenced fortification, four kilometers wide and so heavily guarded from both sides that virtually no transit occurs. Built in 1953 as a result of the armistice ending the Korean War, the DMZ came to symbolize the world's core–periphery partition only after South Korea's economic transformation and political democratization. The remaining land-based barrier, marking the eastern limit of the European Union (6), is not as effectively demarcated as the others for several reasons, including the continuing EU expansion, the transitional character of the EU–Russian frontier, and the still-ongoing ratification of the Schengen Accord, which will enhance coordination of European border, security, and information systems and thus inhibit illegal cross-EU border migration from Finland to Greece.

As the map suggests, the alternate routes for would-be mobals seeking entry into the global core are via the sea. Australia (7) has no land neighbors, but it has long experience with illegal immigrants arriving across the waters separating the north from Indonesia and New Guinea. These immigrants do not originate exclusively, or even primarily, in Australia's maritime neighbors; they also come from as far away as Afghanistan and Iraq. In response, the Australian Defense Forces have mounted a continuous surveillance and interception operation along a 3,000-kilometer stretch of the Timor and Arafura Seas, involving marine patrols and air reconnaissance. Further, in response to problems arising in detention centers in Australia, the Australian government is considering legislation that will deport intercepted asylum-seekers to island-based holding facilities where the legitimacy of their claim to asylum will be adjudicated. A different situation marks the waters between Taiwan and China (8). Taiwan, along with South Korea and Japan, is part of the so-called Jakota Triangle, the western outpost of the global core. United States aircraft carriers have patrolled the Taiwan Strait during times of tension between Beijing and Taipei, but since the rise of China's Pacific Rim, the strait is no longer an avenue for migrants. Off West Africa, EU vessels patrol the waters between the mainland and the Canary Islands (9) to intercept and return African mobals risking their lives to reach Spanish territory. And in as well as above the Mediterranean Sea (10), Spanish, French, and Italian surveillance operates to limit illegal crossings from the North African coast, on the Cuba–Florida model (11).

Many millions of legal immigrants have entered the global core and continue to do so. Even as national economies in the global core are thriving, dwindling populations and changing labor needs will require immigration to offset demographic losses. The "Western Wall" around the global core reflects a regional desire to control the influx, though growing inequalities between core and periphery are likely to determine otherwise. But that is the future. At present, in the broadest sense, the economic, cultural, and political geographies of core and periphery evince contrasts that far outweigh similarities. On average, being born in the core confers certainties and opportunities unattainable in the periphery. The exceptions are too few; the disparities grow wider. Geography and destiny are tightly intertwined.

PLACE AND DESTINY

It is not difficult to discern similarities between the geography of apartheid South Africa and the fractured world displayed in figure 1.1. South Africa's physical and cultural geography presented opportunities for the ruling white minority to exploit: a combination of natural barriers and historic black homelands, discrete urban mixtures (Asian–British in Durban, Coloured–Afrikaner in Cape Town), and concentrated resources. After creating a thriving economy with some limited opportunities for mobal professionals, the segregationists shut the doors and erected the walls of apartheid.

There is, of course, nothing unique about Afrikaners seeking to protect their privileges and advantages, their way of life and culture. It has been done by majorities as well as minorities for millennia, from Han-ruled China to Sunni-dominated Iraq. What was unique was apartheid's grand design, its essentially geographic framework. An entire state with tens of millions of citizens was reconstituted in accordance with a rigid ideology based on race and space. Even Saddam Hussein had his Shi'ite (and Christian) acolytes and collaborators in pre-intervention Iraq. The Afrikaner regime included not a single African, Asian, or Coloured participant. Exclusion is a human trait that has marked the map for as long as communities have existed. Unchecked, it can create aberrations at any scale, even the national.

In this respect, the modern core–periphery map of the world is, to be sure, different. The core region shown in figure 1.1 already is multiracial beyond anything even pre-apartheid South Africa displayed. Australia is fast becoming a plural society (Japan as yet is not); America was one from its inception; and Europe is in a difficult process of ethnic and cultural transformation. But throughout the region, the crucial decisions, including the exclusionary ones reflected by the map, continue to be made by governments very much like those of two or three generations ago. When former U.S. President Jimmy Carter invoked the term apartheid in his critique of Israeli policies toward the Palestinians, he could have enlarged the scope of his analysis (Carter, 2007). There is more than a hint of apartheid in the regional geography of the world today. Keeping locals in their place and restricting mobals to the greatest degree possible perpetuate the global dichotomy represented by the map.

The implications are far-reaching. Place and identity are closely linked. Some scholars, most recently the philosopher Amartya Sen, argue that choice and reasoning can essentially negate the power of place, although "there can be little doubt that the community or culture to which a person belongs can have a major influence on the way he or she sees a situation or views a decision...in any explanatory exercise, note has to be taken of local knowledge, *regional norms,* and particular perceptions and values that are common in a specific community (Sen, 2006; emphasis added). While all concede that talent and education are indispensable in "choice and reasoning about identity," as Sen puts it, few acknowledge that such choice and reasoning are luxuries unattainable for many, even those with some formal education. Indeed, the power of place is such that choice and reasoning are more likely to flourish when "regional norms" are left behind.

Toward the end of the twentieth century, when the Soviet Union disintegrated and Yugoslavia collapsed, many observers foresaw the demise of the state as the key player in international affairs. Replacing it would be a continuum of entities ranging from supranational blocs such as the European Union at one end and subnational units such as Catalonia at the other. Little more than a decade later, the state remains the cornerstone of international structures and systems, projecting power, protecting culture, proscribing movement. In many ways, the state remains the most obvious manifestation of the power of place, the organization of society in the pursuit of "national" goals. Today the focus is on success and debacle. In his magisterial work *Collapse,* Jared Diamond marshals a wide range of such topics to analyze how, as his subtitle states, "societies choose to fail or succeed" (Diamond, 2005). The rise and fall of empires, states, and societies have been topics of study in geography, history, and other disciplines for centuries, and the causes continue to be debated. Obviously, the oft-sudden fall (as opposed to the longer-term rise) is of the most immediate concern: we are all worried about the decline of countries and societies that matter to us. In recent years, the notion of the "failed state" and the opportunities this presents to terrorist organizations has concentrated attention on countries from Afghanistan to Somalia in new ways. In *The Closing of the American Mind,* Allan Bloom sees the disintegration of the fabric of American culture as key to the weakening of U.S. power and influence in the world (Bloom, 1987). But smaller, far less influential states have suffered breakdowns much more dramatic than the perceived decline of America. The United States may be beyond the zenith of its global stature, but it remains the planet's sole superpower: it is not collapsing. Other countries and societies, however, have indeed imploded, some with remarkable, even frightening suddenness. Diamond cites five factors that, usually in some combination, contribute to such breakdowns: environmental damage done by the population, the natural forces of climate change, the behavior of hostile neighbors, the weakening of trading partners and allies near (in history) and far (more recently), and the varying responses of different societies to similar problems. All these are fundamentally geographic, and the last one is crucial, because these variations relate directly to the comprehensive environments, natural and social, that have operated on these societies for a very long time. Can such long-term circumstances produce a "culture of failure," as has been proposed by scholars from the Hoover Institution's Thomas Sowell (1994) to the Harvard historian David Landes (1998)? It is a proposition that has aroused much critical response, but it is clearly linked to the obstacles, physical and social, that still bar millions from the planet's mainstreams of advancement.

AN ENDURING HUMAN GEOGRAPHY

The emergence and diffusion of modern humanity is a drama whose scenes are still being reconstructed and whose backdrops are still being painted. That the ascent of modern humans in Africa occurred very recently is no longer in question; the routes of dispersal of our ancestors from Africa into Eurasia and beyond are fast becoming known. Modern humans challenged their predecessor Neanderthals in Europe about the same time they reached Australia, or perhaps slightly later, around 40,000 years ago. When plant and animal domestication began and fertile, watered river basins attracted growing numbers of people, a settlement pattern emerged, roughly 10,000 years ago, that is still visible on the map today. Thus, a map of world population (figure 1.2) represents a durable demographic layout, much of it forged early and then sustained by local expansion far more than by regional relocation. China had the world's largest population a thousand years ago; it still does today. The peoples living between the Himalayas and Sri Lanka and between the Indus and Brahmaputra Rivers constituted a quantitatively matching cluster of humanity even before British

GLOBAL POPULATION DISTRIBUTION

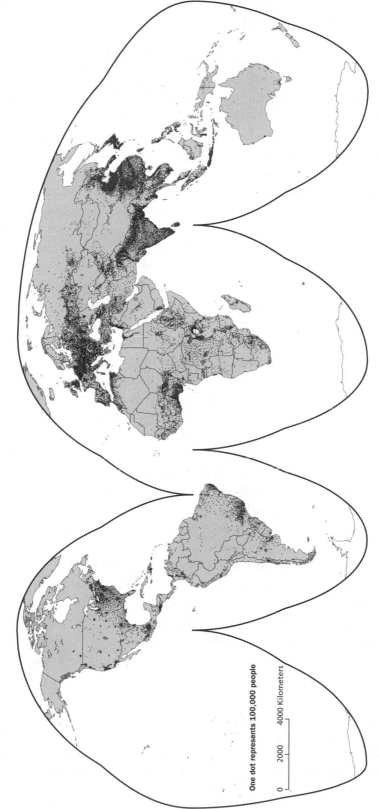

One dot represents 100,000 people

0   2000   4000 Kilometers

Figure 1.2. By this method of displaying the world's population distribution, one dot represents 100,000 people. The map emphasizes the persistence of ancient, agriculture-based patterns in the World Island (Eurasia and Africa); the two largest clusters of population lie in the global periphery.

colonialism girdled them with modern boundaries. The greatest distributional changes over the past millennium occurred *not* on what Halford Mackinder so aptly called the "World Island" consisting of Eurasia and Africa (Mackinder, 1904), but in the human outposts of the Americas and Australia, where Europeans overpowered and decimated earlier arrivals (even today, the World Island's human population exceeds the rest of the world by 5.4 to 1.3 billion). Peoples in Eurasia and Africa, as well as Amerindians and Aboriginal Australians, have lived under their current environmental circumstances—whether river basins or savannas, *altiplanos* or tropical deserts—for millennia. Except, of course, those who catastrophically damaged their natural environment or confronted significant climate change. Climate change, which we tend to view in global context, can have surprisingly local dimensions.

Aside from where ocean water already bounded living space, as in Japan, Iceland, New Zealand, and numerous Pacific islands, the irregular grid of "national" boundaries familiar to us today was superimposed on the inhabited world comparatively recently. In effect, it is the product of the last five centuries, although the notion of boundary making is much older than that. Roman and Chinese wall builders tried to demarcate and fortify imperial borders and limit human movements, but the world was not parceled out among competing powers until the colonial era. (Interestingly, among the many thousands of islands, including hundreds of large and consequential ones, fewer than a dozen were divided by "national" boundaries.) But when that boundary framework was installed, subject to modifications that are still going on, societies were compartmentalized and faced their environmental and economic challenges with new constraints. No longer could peoples who had severely damaged their natural environments move elsewhere and leave the consequences behind. No longer did open frontiers beckon those who chafed under the yoke of oppressors. Millions have perished at walls, fences, moats, and riverbanks in our newly compartmentalized world.

Figure 1.2, therefore, reflects three phases of modern humanity's geographic dispersal: first, the ancient emigration from Africa and occupation of productive Old-World environments, followed by later migrations into the Americas; second, the recent penetration of the New World by European emigrants whose technological superiority and deadly diseases decimated their predecessors, confined them to remote environs, and consigned them to isolation; and third, the recent explosion of global population, which in little more than one century has taken human numbers from one to nearly seven billion. What the map does not show is of comparable consequence: the urbanization of more than half of this population, and the accelerating rate of this momentous process. It is a process that is changing the geography of Cruiseship Earth and the destiny of its passengers.

MODELS, MOBALS, AND MIGRATION

During my years in graduate school at Northwestern University and in my first appointment in the Geography Department at Michigan State University, I heard some of the world's leading scholars express their views on the future of the planet. The geologist Arthur Howland described continental drift as "mysticism" and predicted that notions of moving landmasses would fade before what he called the "visible evidence." The political scientist David Apter predicted a "breathtaking" future for Africa, with political liberties and economic opportunities that would give Europe a run for its money. The British scientist Nigel Calder forecast a fast-cooling planet on which peoples would be driven toward the tropics as higher latitudes were engulfed by snow and ice. The biologist Paul Ehrlich warned that the population explosion would create vast famines afflicting billions, causing global dislocation and disaster before the end of the twentieth century.

All this is to emphasize how hazardous even short-range predictions can be, but the virtue of such prognostications is that they tend to engender vigorous and often productive debate. An example is the transmogrification of the so-called demographic transition model over the past half century (figure 1.3). This model purports to reflect and predict the stages of natural growth through which national and regional populations have gone and will go. A half century ago, the cycle showed three stages and assumed that all populations would go through a high-growth period (the "population explosion") followed by a continuing, significant expansion. A couple of decades ago it became clear that certain populations (the most highly urbanized ones among them) were experiencing a low-growth fourth stage. Now it is evident that, for various reasons, a growing number of societies (that is, countries) are exhibiting a fifth stage of "negative growth," in demographic parlance, meaning that their populations are shrinking. In combination, these factors are

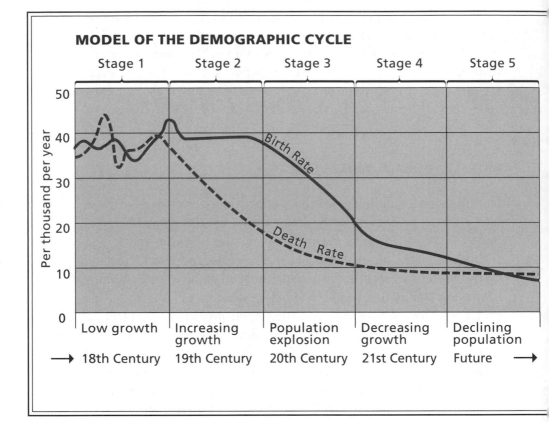

Figure 1.3. Fast-declining death rates and still-high birth rates created the population explosion of the twentieth century; some countries still are in the third stage of the cycle, but others are in stage five, their populations stable or declining. The global rate of natural increase today is in stage four.

leading to the conclusion that the global population, during the present century, will in fact cease growing altogether and may begin to decline. Predictions of the level at which this will take place tend to range from 9 to 10 billion, but we know how risky long-range prognostications are.

What is beyond doubt is that declining national populations need infusions of immigrants to compensate for the shrinkage. Policymakers in Japan, one of the states whose populations are in accelerating decline, seem to believe that the process can be managed without significant substitution, and Japan remains by far the most ethnically and culturally homogeneous among larger societies today. But immigration is transforming other countries and regions. For all its barriers against asylum-seekers, Australia is becoming a multicultural society through legal immigration. Fifty years ago, when Australia had less than half the population it has today, 95 percent were of European ancestry and three-quarters came from the British Isles. Eugenic (race-specific) immigration policies kept things this way into the 1970s, when Australia celebrated its bicentennial. Then those policies changed, and the criteria for legal immigration shifted to money and skills rather than ancestry. By the early 1990s, Australia was admitting nearly 150,000 immigrants annually, mostly from Hong Kong, Vietnam, China, the Philippines, India, and Sri Lanka (a proportional number in the United States would be more than two million *per year*). The influx created social problems that required a reduction in legal immigration, but about 80,000 continue to arrive annually, some of them well-heeled globals but many others mobals in search of opportunities and better lives—and still others seeking asylum for legitimate reasons. Sydney, already home to nearly one-quarter of Australia's population, is the main recipient of the Asian influx and has become a mosaic of ethnic districts. With this have come increased crime, gang violence, drug use, disturbances, and other conditions not usually associated with life in the "lucky country." But for every incident of this kind, there are thousands of mobals who arrived in Australia with few resources, played by the rules, and thrived in this free, open, and acceptant society.

The migration issue ranks high among American and European concerns, and immigration has transformed North American and Western European societies in significant ways. In the United States, as noted above, the presence of an estimated 12 million illegal immigrants—the most mobile of mobals—became a political issue during the G. W. Bush administration, when proposals to confer some legitimacy on these mobals were combined with plans to reinforce the barriers to cross-border migration from Mexico. The United States, by far the largest affluent state in the world, adjoins a country that is representative of the periphery, and Mexico forms a conduit for mobals beyond its own borders in Central America. But the 2006 UN *Report on Migration* underscores how comparatively limited the global migration flow remains. From 1990 to 2005, the number of migrants in the world rose from 155 million to 191 million, well below 3 percent of the planet's population. Even where migration is facilitated rather than obstructed, notably within the expanding European Union, the percentage of workers crossing international borders remains remarkably low. Again, the overwhelming majority of our planet's inhabitants still live out their lives within the countries and communities in which they were born. These locals far outnumber the mobals—even when the richer countries of the global core need the latter in growing numbers.

MIGRANTS AND MOTIVES

The United Nations and other agencies grapple with problems of definition when it comes to identifying migrants. The figures just cited relate to transnational (international) migrants, mobals who have crossed one or more international borders to reach their intended destination and who have lived outside their original homeland for one year or more. It is a reflection of the powerful constraints on long-distance migration that the number of these mobals is as small as it is, and the number of *intercultural* migrants is even smaller. Mexican immigrants to the United States are international as well as intercultural migrants, as are Indians and Pakistanis moving to Western Europe and Nigerians immigrating to the United Kingdom. But the millions of Pushtuns who moved from war-torn Afghanistan to Pakistan during the Soviet intervention and stayed there for years as the conflict raged were international, but not intercultural, migrants. Today the war in Iraq is generating a massive international emigration from Iraq to its immediate neighbors (Syria and Jordan), of which only a small fraction is becoming intercultural in the form of the small minority reaching Europe, America, or other parts of the non-Muslim world. The great majority of these refugees will probably return to Iraq.

International migration involves far smaller numbers, of course, than does internal migration. Many hundreds of millions of migrants are on the move without crossing international boundaries. One of the great migrations of the past generation continues within China, where the economic rise of the Pacific Rim draws millions of villagers from rural west to urbanizing east. Rural-to-urban migration is a global phenomenon involving far more internal than international migrants, and truly international cities (such as New York and London) are far outnumbered by burgeoning megacities growing mainly through domestic aggregation (Tokyo, São Paulo, Mexico City, Lagos).

While models of future migration flows predict that international migration will expand, all suggest that the rate of increase will not match the needs of either destination or source. Looking at the process geographically, it is clear that the poorest of the poor countries of the world are contributing the smallest share of international migration. A veritable trafficking and smuggling industry has sprung up to exploit those hoping to reach the global core, and only a comparative few can raise enough money to take the risk. Another key indicator shows that when the standards of living of source and destination converge, the flow of migrants declines. This might appear to be a favorable development, and it is often cited as one objective in addressing the Mexican–American dilemma: raise living standards in Mexico, and cross-border migration will dwindle.

But the domestic population of the United States is not (yet) experiencing the rapid aging and shrinking that marks populations elsewhere in the global core, creating an additional dilemma for this country. In Mexico and elsewhere in Middle America, income and wealth disparities are great and abject poverty is still a massive problem, generating reservoirs of mobals seeking to cross the border. In the United States, income inequalities are growing, workers' wages are stagnant, and jobs are being lost. It is a recipe for trouble in an already-plural society that has taken in immigrants by the millions, and the illegal-immigration issue at times assumed an ugly tone during the 2007/08 election campaign following the defeat in Congress of President Bush's "amnesty" proposal.

Who benefits? While America's flexible labor markets can absorb many of the millions of workers crossing the border, Mexico and its citizens are the major beneficiaries of the process (Mexico annually receives from its mobals some $25 billion, accounting for 3.4 percent of the country's gross domestic product). In the European Union, things are different. One immediate consequence of the aging of populations affects the number of available young entrants into the labor force. In the global core, about 140 jobseekers still are available per 100 workers retiring annually, but toward 2020, the ratio will be below 90. Thus the need for immigrants will grow exponentially, despite negative perceptions of migrants at their destinations. For example, although it is often argued that migrants reduce the wages of low-skilled workers, studies show that, over time, low-paid migrants cause locals to seek and secure higher-paying employment. And what about the situation at the source? In the poorer world, the UN report states, there are more than 340 candidates for every 100 jobs that become available annually. Joblessness and poverty create markets for political, religious, and other forms of extremism. Internationally coordinated migration could be the planet's safety valve, but its conduit remains mostly blocked. Meanwhile, intercultural conflict between mobals and locals, occasionally punctuated by acts of terrorism, strengthens the determination of those seeking to limit the flow even further.

A BARRICADED WORLD

With a population approaching seven billion and international migrant numbers hovering (in 2008) around 200 million, our planet thus is not as amenable to movement as its purported flatness implies. While major historic migrations involving tens of millions of migrants altered the distribution produced by prehistoric human dispersal, outlines of the latter still remain imprinted on the modern map. As populations grew numerically, societies variegated vertically, and cultures diversified ideologically, political power made its appearance on the ground in the form of walls, fences, fortified riverbanks, and buttressed mountain ridges. European imperialism completed a process begun during the earliest phase of state formation by superimposing on the world a boundary framework that, from Serbia to Somalia, is still evolving. That boundary framework, drawn in ignorance of much of the world's natural-resource base and with often deliberate disregard for cultural geographies, encumbered the world and its modern states with inequalities and obstacles unforeseen by its designers. A good atlas map—or better yet, a globe—reveals some of these disparities, ranging from sheer size and relative location (more than 10 percent of the world's countries are landlocked) to distance from, or proximity to, the mainstreams of international interaction. More specialized maps indicate how the roulette of partition favored some states and disadvantaged others in terms of raw materials, natural environments, and opportunities.

Today's world is not just boundary-barricaded but also regionally fractured. The core–periphery dichotomy described above is just one manifestation of this; Samuel Huntington described another in his "Clash of Civilizations" (Huntington, 1996). A more geographic framework, based less on power and conflict than on the spatial realities of culture and ethnicity, assembles the world's approximately 200 countries into a dozen "realms" (figure 1.4). But no matter how you

WORLD GEOGRAPHIC REALMS

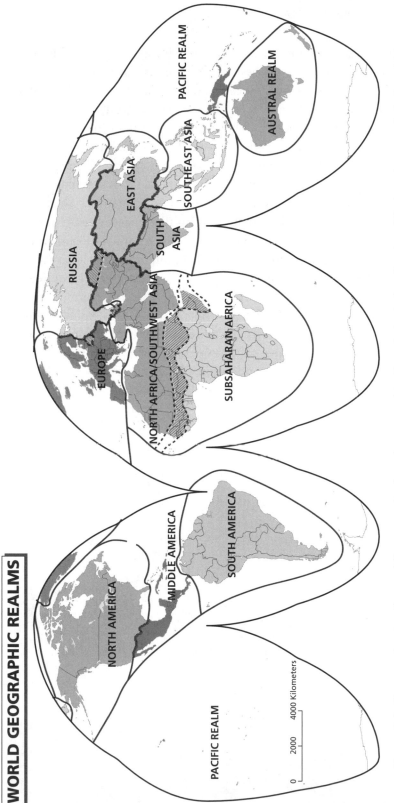

Figure 1.4. One way to view the world's geography, based on a combination of physical, cultural, political, and economic factors. Not many regional borders are sharply defined, but at this scale only a few major transition zones can be shown, as in Africa, Central Asia, and Eastern Europe.

look at it, ours remains a divided world whose obstacles and barriers constrain countless would-be mobals who, as poverty-stricken and powerless locals, have no chance of escape and who cannot influence those who determine their fate. Others, seemingly less constrained, better educated, and more capable, find contentment in containment, or perhaps resignation, weighing the risks and uncertainties of relocation against the certitudes of tradition and custom. Whatever the circumstances, the great majority of our planet's human passengers live their lives in the natural and cultural environs into which they were born, many eager but unable to join the modest stream of intercultural mobals and still remote from the corridors of globalization.

This partitioning—global, regional, national, local—slows the leveling of the social platform of the planet, the "flattening" implied by globalization. From mother tongue to medical access, from pervasive religion to political ideology, from endemic conflict to environmental peril, from lifeways to lifestyles, place and destiny are inextricably linked. Such is this variable geography of opportunity and constraint that globe-trotting globals and localized locals live in very different and very unequal worlds.

2

THE IMPERIAL LEGACY OF LANGUAGE

Language is the essence of culture, and culture is the epoxy of society. Individually and collectively, people tend to feel passionately about their mother tongue, especially when they have reason to believe that it is threatened in some way. Ever since the use of language evolved in early human communities, some confined in isolated abodes and others on the march into Eurasia, Australia, and the Americas, languages have arisen, flourished, and failed with the fortunes of their speakers. Linguists estimate that tens of thousands of such languages may have been born and lost, leaving no trace. Some major ones, including Sumerian and Etruscan, survive fragmentarily in their written record. A few, such as Sanskrit and Latin, live on in their modern successors. But the historical geography of language is the story of a loss of linguistic diversity that continues unabated. At present, about 7,000 languages remain, half of them classified by linguists as endangered. In the year from the day you read this, about 25 more languages will go extinct. By the end of this century, the Earth may be left with just a few hundred languages, so billions of its inhabitants will no longer be speaking their ancestral mother tongues (Diamond, 2001).

If this projection turns out to be accurate, the language loss will not be confined to those spoken by comparatively few people in remote locales. One dimension of the "flattening" of the world in the age of globalization is the cultural convergence of which linguistic homogenization is a key component. Some of my colleagues view this as an inevitable and not altogether undesirable process of integration, but if I may be candid, most of those colleagues speak one language only: English. Having spoken six languages during my lifetime (I can still manage in four), I tend to share the linguists' concern over the trend. English has the great merit of comparative simplicity and adaptable modernity, but as it reflects historic natural and social environments it is sparse indeed and no match for the riches of French or even

Dutch. If such contrasts can arise and persist among closely related languages in Europe, imagine the legacies of major languages such as Yoruba, Urdu, Thai, and others potentially endangered as language convergence proceeds.

Linguists today are much concerned over the loss of indigenous languages, as endangered tongues pass quietly from the scene when the few village elders still speaking them die. Already, youngsters in the community will be using a tongue with wider circulation, and no passionate campaign to save the fading language is mounted by locals. If such an effort *is* made, it is likely to come from outsiders aware of the particular significance or value of the syntax, grammar, or vocabulary as these relate to the ecological setting of a language, or the way the language reflects the "world" views of its speakers. The great majority of the languages being lost have never been written or recorded, but among them some are likely to contain crucial pieces of evidence concerning such matters as environmental change, early migration, ecology, and belief systems. A growing movement is under way to document as many such languages as research funds will allow, but the accelerating rate of loss will render it inevitably incomplete.

This salvage effort is all the more difficult because of one particular aspect of the geography of language. In a very general way, the biological principle of the species-richness gradient seems to hold true for the distribution of discrete languages as well. In biological context, it has long been clear that the number of animal and plant species per unit area decreases with latitude: the higher the latitude, the fewer the species. Thus a single square kilometer of tropical rainforest contains thousands of plant and animal species; a square kilometer of tundra may contain only a few dozen. Associated with this gradient is the tenet of species dominance. In tropical rainforest environments, where the number and diversity of species are very large, it is often the case that no single, or group of, species is clearly dominant. But in higher latitude environments, a few species, such as an evergreen tree or a large herbivore, tend to predominate.

So it is, in an interesting way, with languages. Warm, moist, low-latitude environs harbor numerous languages often spoken by small groups of people; on the island of New Guinea, for example, more than 900 languages remain in use, none with regional dominance. In Sub-saharan Africa, more than 2,000. But higher latitude Europe is home to only about 200 languages—and among these, a few are strongly dominant. This means that the great majority of the threatened languages are embedded deeply in remote, densely forested, tropical areas, where recording them is especially difficult. In 2008, about 400 of these languages were identified as immediately endangered.

Such dwindling of cultural variegation might be seen not only as a consequence, but also as a benefit of globalization. With fewer mutually unintelligible tongues, wouldn't the world's peoples understand each other better? The evidence for this proposition is weak. Conflicts certainly break out between peoples speaking different languages, but speaking the same (or a mutually comprehensible) language does not seem to avert or even ameliorate hostilities. Protestants and Catholics in Northern Ireland have spoken the same language for centuries, as did communists and nationalists in post-Qing China, and Sunni and Shia in post-Saddam Iraq. Humans have a way of finding reasons to engage in violent conflict, and a universal language probably would not alter that predisposition. A linguistically "flat" world would not be likely to be a more peaceable or a fairer one.

On the other hand, converging language use would undoubtedly have a positive effect on economic interaction. In the arena of economic globalization, contractual and other legal misunderstandings often arise from linguistic confusion, placing a high price on bilingual (and multilingual) skills. Some observers argue that enhanced economic interaction will serve to mitigate tensions that could lead to conflict, putting a positive twist on the loss of linguistic diversity.

On the inhabitants of the global core as well as the periphery, language confers advantage and imposes liability. Being born into a family whose mother tongue is regionally dominant and globally dispersed (English, Spanish, French) endows a child with a lifetime of opportunity that begins in preschool and continues beyond retirement, a cultural legacy of imperial times. Being born into a family whose home language is that of a minority, or in a society whose linguistic mosaic is variegated, confronts a youngster with far greater challenges. The former is the good fortune of hundreds of millions of globals. The latter is the fate of billions of locals. Take a look at the commercial literature of globalization, and you see that advertisements for professionals at all levels tend to stipulate language ability in English and at least one other world language, and that business schools from Sweden to Singapore conduct all or most of their courses in English. If the power of place is substantially defined by language, a key to leveling the playing field lies in competence in the current *lingua franca*.

EARLY DIFFUSION, LATER DISPUTES

The world today is a Babel of languages, a patchwork of tongues so intricate that it would seem to defy orderly interpretation. Some properties of languages are obvious enough; it is not difficult, for example, to identify languages that are different but distinctly related to each other. Such are the similarities between these related languages that their common origin and comparatively recent divergence are beyond doubt. As noted earlier, the Latin of Roman times lives on in the Romance languages of today. In just a few centuries, the language of the architects of the Roman Empire, imposed from Britain to the Bosporus, was superseded by a quintet of derivatives (Italian, French, Spanish, Portuguese, Romanian) combining the implanted with the local. The Romans were the globals of their time, but they could not prevent the regionalization and differentiation of their language. Might English go the same way?

How languages evolved and devolved are questions that have challenged linguists for centuries, and geographic factors are key to solving the puzzle. It is likely that discrete languages emerged (and died) quickly and in large numbers while humans moved into open frontiers and lived in small communities subsisting on hunting and gathering. But when plant and animal domestication enabled larger groups to settle more or less permanently, the number of languages began to decline and the number of speakers of surviving languages grew. When modern states emerged and "national" languages became part of the identity of nations, minority languages not only withered but became targets for suppression. More recently, some endangered languages have been rescued through the concerted action of speaker-activists and their nonindigenous supporters. Welsh is enjoying a revival, and the decline of Maori and Hawaiian has also been reversed. Still, the overall trend is toward fewer languages.

This makes reconstructing the evolutionary tree of language ever more difficult. If it is true that our species originated from the "Real Eve," as Stephen Oppenheimer calls the African woman who hypothetically gave birth to the first humans (Oppenheimer, 2003), might there have been a language ancestral to all others? As languages multiplied and diversified, which among them retain affinities and which do not? This detective work is so interesting and challenging that it and its prickly personalities are becoming a riveting saga of science and strife. The giant name in this arena is that of Joseph Greenberg of Stanford University, whose lifetime of research yielded much of the framework that continues to form the basis for this ongoing debate. He gave spatial expression to the concept of language families, clusters of languages with close relationships, proposing that most of the world's 7,000 languages can be grouped into about 17 such families, including, prominently, the so-called Indo-European language family that incorporates nearly 150 languages ranging from Hindi and Urdu in the east to Iranian and Kurdish in the center and German and English in the west (figure 2.1). He grouped the approximately 2,000 African languages into four families, and the numerous indigenous languages of the Americas into three (Greenberg, 1963, 1987). As time went on, and especially after his death in 2001, Greenberg's work engendered much criticism, and his map was revised almost continuously. Some linguists now argue that there are as many as 150 language families in the Americas alone, and that his vaunted African scheme is similarly a gross oversimplification. But in other areas his conclusions remain unchallenged, and the map is a useful first impression of the layout of the legacy of language.

LANGUAGES GLOBAL AND LOCAL

Mention "loss of linguistic diversity," and what comes to mind is not only the extinction of endangered tongues but also the triumph of the "world languages," the Indo-European languages, led by English, the Latin of the latter day. True, versions of Chinese are spoken as the mother tongue (or first language) by about 1.2 billion people, about three times as many as English, but it is English, not Chinese, that is spoken around the world, a lasting legacy of the waves of globalization propelled by the British Empire and sustained by America's global impact. There was, as the saying goes, a time when the Sun never set on the British Empire. Today the Sun never sets on the English-speaking world.

WORLD LANGUAGE FAMILIES

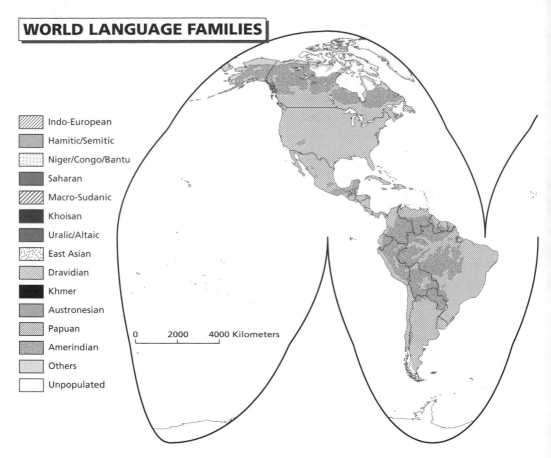

Indo-European
Hamitic/Semitic
Niger/Congo/Bantu
Saharan
Macro-Sudanic
Khoisan
Uralic/Altaic
East Asian
Dravidian
Khmer
Austronesian
Papuan
Amerindian
Others
Unpopulated

0   2000   4000 Kilometers

Figure 2.1. On the question of world language families, no scholarly agreement exists. This map shows the most uncomplicated version, with 15 language families among which the Indo-European family (which includes English) is most widely dispersed. Modified from M. Ruhlen, *A Guide to the World's Languages* (Stanford University Press, 1987) and J. Greenberg (1963 and 1987).

In any case, the listing of Chinese as the world's leading language, as is routine in gazetteers and textbooks, is misleading. Chinese characters can be read by hundreds of millions of Chinese citizens who cannot understand their neighbors' speech, so written Chinese rather than the spoken word has the greater claim to universality. Although no reliable data exist, *Putonghua*, as the locals call Mandarin Chinese, may be spoken by no more than half of all citizens, and those fluent in it are heavily concentrated in China's historic northern core area and in the economically burgeoning east. Chinese call

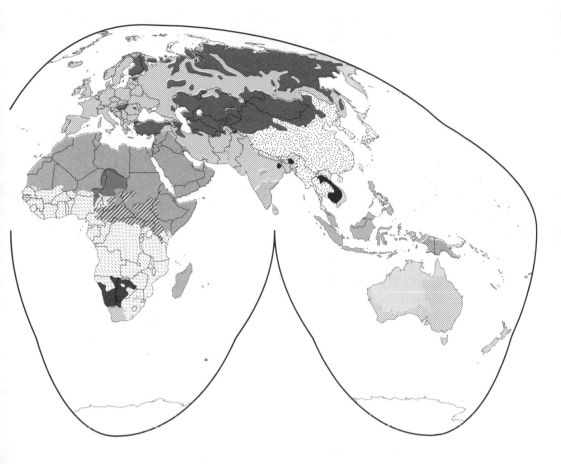

themselves the "people of Han," but their ethnic unity is countered by a linguistic map revealing more than 1400 dialects, most of them mutually incomprehensible. The number of dialects is far greater in the south than in the north, but official maps delimiting a "Northern Mandarin" and a "Southern Mandarin" do not begin to reflect reality. Chinese cultural geographers describe the linguistic mosaic in China as more complex than that of Europe, suggesting that official maps showing "dialects" of a national language have more to do with politics than with reality. Not just China's ethnic minorities, therefore, find themselves at a linguistic disadvantage when they migrate to the workplaces of China's Pacific Rim; China's own Han locals, more often than not, cannot converse in Mandarin, China's language of the powerful.

How can a language not be universal and yet be readable by almost all? Watch Chinese television in local areas, and you will see news reports subtitled by Chinese characters, part of the government effort to promote Mandarin nationwide. Indo-European languages also use characters, but only for numbers. Take the number 5, understood by all Europeans when printed. But consider its various pronunciations: five, cinq (French), fünf (German), vijf (Dutch), cinque (Italian). It quickly gets more complicated when characters are strung together—as in 571. Still, Europeans who absolutely do not understand each other instantly share the meaning of 571. So the virtue of characters is that they overcome a mutual unintelligibility of spoken language, giving some veracity to those maps claiming Mandarin as China's "national" tongue.

Even if only half of China's Han can speak and understand Mandarin, this represents some 600 million speakers. Thus Chinese, the dominant member of the Sino-Tibetan language family, still is in the numerical lead, but Chinese is hardly on track to become a world language to compete with English: it remains geographically confined and would require an unlikely conversion of communication technologies. While no single Indo-European language outranks Chinese in terms of users, the major languages of the Indo-European language family in combination far outnumber Chinese. English (400 million), Spanish (310), Hindi (305), Portuguese (165), Russian (150), Bengali (130), German (100), French (80), and Italian (60) are among Indo-European languages of global consequence, several of them national languages diffused widely beyond state borders during the colonial era.

As such, these national languages formed the vehicles of cultural dominance in the colonial periphery. French colonial policy could be (and was) encapsulated by one word: *assimilation*. Bringing the virtues of French and the values of France to the colonial empire was the ultimate goal in a Francophone world whose elite—and later the masses—would embrace this, the supreme European culture. Always, the French were (and are) fiercely, even aggressively protective of their language; to this day the French government assembles representatives of present and former Francophone dependencies and territories, from Martinique to Vietnam and from Senegal to Quebec, at an annual international conference convened to sustain and promote it. A former French President, Georges Pompidou, liked to say that "it is through our language that we exist in the world other than as just another country."

ASCENT OF ENGLISH

But it was English, not French, that became the language of globalization. In its colonial, postcolonial, and neocolonial and globalizing forms, English became the language of nations from the United States to New Zealand and the language of social elites from Nigeria to Malaysia. In plural societies thrown together by imperial boundaries, English became the *lingua franca*, the medium of administration, civil service, commerce, and higher education. By the beginning of the Second World War, before the population explosion in the global periphery changed the picture, English was the home language for nearly 10 percent of the world's population. Following the Allied victory, it appeared that English would accelerate its ascent and become the first truly global tongue. Then the population explosion altered the picture.

In the traditional cultures of the former colonial periphery, multilingualism was (and remains) nothing new. In Subsaharan Africa and New Guinea, locals often speak more than one language, because markets attract sellers from villages where other tongues prevail. In some areas, languages of regional commerce, such as KiSwahili in East Africa and Hausa in West Africa, have accrued tens of millions of speakers. Hausa is spoken across interior West Africa by as many as 45 million people in several countries; Swahili is now the national language of Tanzania and, with English, has the same status in Kenya. But the colonial conquest changed the situation for billions of locals and mobals. In traditional society, multilingualism of the indigenous kind conferred certain small but important advantages on those more skilled than others. The colonists' language, however, was the language of power, and achieving literacy and fluency in it opened new windows of opportunity. Multilingualism took on a totally novel cast. In Francophone Africa and Asia, those who were most accomplished were rewarded with status and influence at home and often with further "assimilation" through funded study in France. In the British Empire, colonial subjects whose English was good rose in political as well as administrative ranks, serving their rulers as representatives of the Crown as they kept control over indigenous domains. From tax collectors to school principals, money lenders to post office clerks, the advantage was with the Anglophones. A new and crucial layer had been added to the linguistic hierarchy.

While linguists struggled to recreate the theoretical map of indigenous language families, the harsh reality of the real world showed a different pattern. English, French, and Spanish had compressed the native languages of North America into small remnant reserves; only in Andean and Amazonian South America and in smaller domains of Middle America did substantial Native American ethnolinguistic areas survive (figure 2.2). In Australia and New Zealand, Aboriginal and Maori languages had been overwhelmed by English speakers. South Africa had become a "bilingual" country, the "bi-" standing not for the languages spoken by the largest numbers in the country, but for the two languages of power: Afrikaans and English. When decolonization gathered momentum, first in Asia and then in Africa, newly independent states proclaimed English, French, Spanish, or Portuguese as their "official" language, sometimes in conjunction with a local one. India, for example, recognizes English and Hindi; Brunei, English and Malay; Djibouti, French and Arabic; the Central African Republic, French and Sango. But Angola to this day recognizes only Portuguese; Senegal, French; Nigeria, English; and Equatorial Guinea, Spanish.

Where does this leave the locals, the people who are born into an ethnolinguistic area untouched by a connective regional language and remote from the official one? In countries where the official language is ex-colonial, capability in that language is the *sine qua non* for membership in the governing, administrative, or commercial elite. Starting life in a remote village and being taught in a local, indigenous language without early exposure to the language of this political and social elite puts locals at an immediate and usually lasting disadvantage. In countries where modernization has brought job opportunities requiring facility in English, for example, the high-tech

Figure 2.2. Two views of the indigenous language pattern of the Americas. Joseph Greenberg identified three overarching families (A); others discern sixteen or more (B). Obviously the matter is not settled. The larger map is modified from several sources, including J. Diamond and P. Bellwood, "Farmers and Their Languages: The First Expansions," *Science* 300 (2003), p. 600.

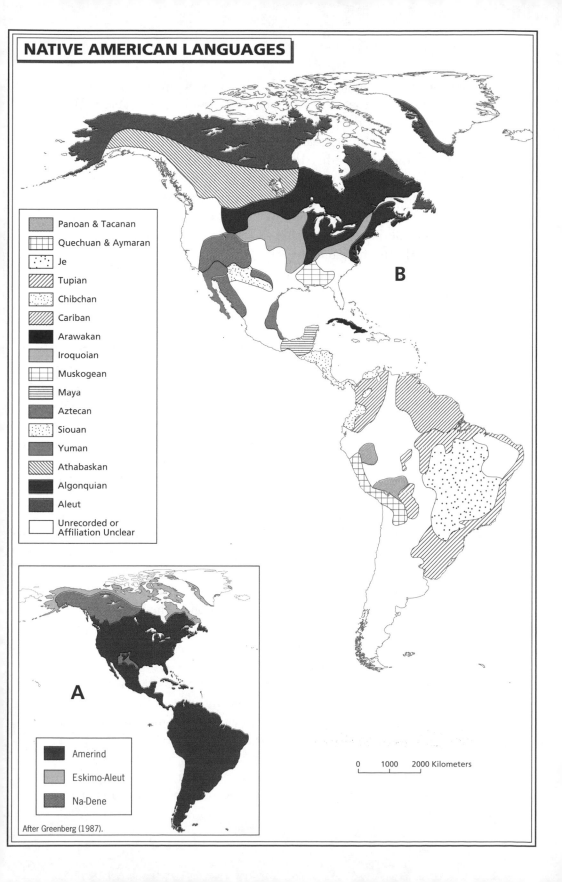

NATIVE AMERICAN LANGUAGES

Panoan & Tacanan
Quechuan & Aymaran
Je
Tupian
Chibchan
Cariban
Arawakan
Iroquoian
Muskogean
Maya
Aztecan
Siouan
Yuman
Athabaskan
Algonquian
Aleut
Unrecorded or
Affiliation Unclear

B

A

Amerind
Eskimo-Aleut
Na-Dene

After Greenberg (1987).

0   1000   2000 Kilometers

and outsourced industries of India, mobals who find employment are those who have the "language advantage" and are thus able to climb the first rung on the globalizing ladder. Most of those who have that advantage grew up in urban learning environments where bilingualism was the norm rather than the exception. Even in multilingual India, however, they remain a small minority. Their world may be flatter than that confronting the locals, but in 2008 they numbered just over one million workers in a labor force of 400 million. India, like much of the global periphery, remains a society whose locals find their world anything but flat.

THE CHANGING TEMPLATE

If hundreds of millions of locals find themselves disadvantaged because they do not speak the Indo-European languages of globalization, might they forge their own Esperantos, creating alternatives to "standard" languages, and in effect, usher in a new era of language formation even as old indigenous languages continue to die? Such innovation has occurred before, of course, in the rise of informal languages of commerce like Wes Kos along the shores of West Africa and various forms of Creole in the islands of the Caribbean. But today the prospects are different. As noted in chapter 1, the great majority of the approximately three billion still-to-come additions to the global population will reside in the global periphery. And the accelerating rate of urbanization implies that a fast-growing segment of this population will cluster in the enormous megacities of the future, where they will speak the language of their parents—and invent ways to interact with their peers. In so doing, they will hybridize the vocabularies of television, entertainment, advertising, shopping, employment, and other sources to devise composite derivatives that become the idioms of their urban habitat.

This global development, which is in the process of spawning hundreds of new forms of English in urban environs around the world, is thus generating new languages even as old ones die out, a by-product of globalization whose ultimate consequences are not yet clear (Crystal, 2003). It stands in sharp contrast to long-term efforts of nation-states to preserve and codify their national or "standard" languages and to distinguish among those who spoke the language of the social elite and those who revealed themselves as being of lower status by opening their mouths. The standard language was more than a matter of personal identity: it was a way of protecting the privileges of the upper classes. The "King's English" was the English spoken by well-educated people in and around London, and no BBC news anchor would speak anything less. Watch the BBC News today, and it is clear that things have changed.

But the notion that there is merit (and advantage) in preserving and sustaining the standard language is not defunct. In Britain, English for several centuries has been protected by the National Language Project, and the British Received Pronunciation (BRP) remains the standard to which speakers aspire. It is not surprising that "standard" English is the English of the capital; so it is in France, where the French spoken in and around Paris was made the standard and official language in the sixteenth century. Four centuries later, the French found themselves compelled to mount a major campaign, complete with civil penalties, to combat the use of "foreign" (mostly English) terms in commerce, advertising, and other public displays. As figure 2.1 indicates, Chinese is spoken across China from northeast to southwest, but, as noted earlier, Chinese has numerous dialects, many of them mutually unintelligible. Until the great transformation brought about by the Pacific Rim economic boom of the past three decades, which has produced an unprecedented cultural mix in China as millions of mobals moved eastward, most Chinese citizens could be readily identified locationally by their dialect, the baggage of place. When China's communist rulers decided to proclaim a "standard" spoken Chinese, they opted for the version heard in the capital, Beijing. Only a minority of Chinese speak this purest Northern Mandarin (its Chinese name means "civil servant language"), and doing so identifies the speaker as a resident of the country's heartland. But the *Putonghua* that will eventually emerge from the maelstrom of China's economic and social transformation is likely to differ significantly from the Mandarin promoted by the communist leaders in Beijing.

Until the late twentieth century, the Chinese language remained essentially confined within the borders of the state. Chinese speakers in Taiwan and in the diaspora communities of Southeast Asia were among numerically small exceptions; Chinese was the language of a billion, but a world language it was not. Today, that is changing. China's economic transformation at home entails massive involvement abroad ranging from commodity procurement to infra-structure investment and from cultural diplomacy to educational exchanges. China's leaders encourage important trading partners to enhance or initiate Chinese studies at schools and universities, funding classroom teaching as well as university education wherever such offers find acceptance (one enthusiastic recipient in recent years has been Zimbabwe, where schools are teaching Chinese and the University of Harare has a Beijing-supported Chinese Studies Center). China's ascent to superpower status will undoubtedly propel Chinese into the global linguistic mix.

It is nevertheless unlikely that Chinese in its Northern Mandarin form will challenge European languages in the world abroad. Chinese will become a part of a linguistic reformation some aspects of which can already be observed in cities where Chinese and English have long coexisted. It may come as a surprise to first-time visitors to long-British-ruled Hong Kong that Standard English is not more widely known to cab drivers or shop owners, but Hong Kong's more than seven million people use many more tongues than just English and Chinese. They are in the process of devising their own hybrid language some call Chinglish, creating a medium for local interaction the basics of which can be quickly grasped. In Chinese-dominated but also multilingual Singapore, where English, Chinese, Malay, and Tamil have official status, you can hear a similar urban Esperanto referred to as "Singlish." It is a process going on (with components varying according to the regional geography) from Amsterdam to Auckland.

Even as entire languages are lost at the local bottom of the pyramid and standard languages are eroded by hybridization at the global top, historic attributes of the culture of language are also endangered. Perhaps the most consequential among these is a property of many Asian and most African languages: tone. Chinese, for example, is not just spoken: it is also intoned. The same word may have several different meanings according to the way it is "sung," a refinement also found in Yoruba but not in English, in Bemba but not in German. In the case of Chinese, Mandarin uses four tones: level, rising, falling, and high-and-rising. These tones distinguish words that have the same series of consonants and vowels but mean different things (in African "terrace-tone" languages, this gets even more complicated). Take, for instance, the Mandarin word "mi." In various intonations, this can mean the noun rice or the verbs to squint or to befuddle. This obviously makes standard Chinese a difficult language to learn for people brought up in a non-variable-tone language environment, but when tonal and nontonal languages meet and hybridize, tone is soon a casualty.

That is a greater loss than might be imagined. Research has shown that people in the Western world who have musical training (and are thus familiar with changes in pitch) have an easier time learning Chinese and other tone languages than those who do not. The neuroscientist Patrick C. M. Wong, in a study carried out at Northwestern University, suggests that this might work both ways: native speakers of tonal languages may do better at learning to play instruments (Nagourney, 2007). Even before we know what evolutionary asset we may be losing, the homogenization of language may end a significant chapter in our cultural history.

Meanwhile, the internationalization of language through new technologies (the Internet principally), lack of quality control (the Wikipedia phenomenon, for example), urbanization (much of it internal to large countries such as China and Brazil), and changing public attitudes toward linguistic correctness (such as the quick incorporation of slang and newly minted terms in media and dictionaries) reflect a new era in the history and geography of language. For mobals, this new era may signal new opportunities, but it also requires new forms of multilingualism: it will not be enough to achieve fluency in one "standard" language when norms are rapidly changing. For globals, the changing cultural geography of language will pose unanticipated challenges as "world" languages start taking on local characteristics, losing their international status. David Graddol cites the example of Swedish, "now positioned more as a local language of solidarity than one for science, university education, or European communication" (Graddol, 2004). In this perspective, even the long-term supremacy of Standard English in the wider world is by no means secure.

Nevertheless, English currently is still ascending, especially in the global core (figure 2.3). The expansion of the European Union is accelerating this process, in part because of recent political history. German still has the disadvantage of being linked to the war in the West, and Russian remains associated with the repressive communist era in the East. Although the European Union recognizes 20 official languages, creating a costly muddle of translations, EU committees

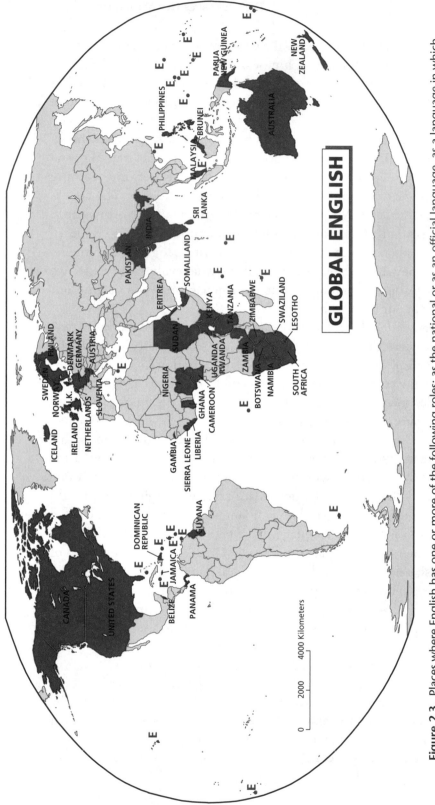

Figure 2.3. Places where English has one or more of the following roles: as the national or as an official language, as a language in which more than 50 percent of the general population has fluency, as the *lingua franca* of government, higher education, and commerce in plural societies, and as an outpost dating from colonial times. Data from several sources, including R. G. Gordon, Jr. (ed.), *Ethnologue: Languages of the World* (Dallas: SIL International, 2007), *Book of the Year 2007* (Chicago: Encyclopaedia Britannica 2007), and Graddol (2004).

and civil servants work in three: English, German, and French. Among these, English is increasingly dominant, and English is the lingua franca during EU discussions in Brussels, although familiarity with English still varies widely in the realm (figure 2.4). English is also spreading through the school systems of Eastern Europe in the wake of the momentous 2004 expansion of the European Union. "In Central Europe...knowledge of English has become a basic skill of modern life comparable with the ability to drive a car or use a personal computer" (*Economist*, 2004).

In the global periphery, English is spreading in the nodes and along the corridors of globalization, but like Latin before it, English is also diverging into various forms that are likely to presage the language map of the future. English is now taught to hundreds of millions of schoolchildren throughout the periphery, but even as they learn the standard version, they are blending what they learn in class with what they see and hear in the media, mixing and adapting "their" English in ways that reflect local environs. Chinglish, Singlish, Yinglish, and other such versions will evolve locally, but they will have enough in common to form the basis for mutual comprehension in the globalizing age.

THE FUTURE PLAYING FIELD

The standard version of English (or something close to it) may be on the way to becoming the *lingua franca* of Europe, but even the global core has corners in which globalization proceeds essentially without the global language. Take the train from Narita International Airport to the heart of Tokyo, and you are greeted by what seems to be a familiar, somehow American scene, except that the traffic keeps left and the crowds are more formally dressed and, in general, more orderly. The people on the Ginza's wide sidewalks are also more homogeneous ethnically than, perhaps, in any other major city in the world. Even at the height of the tourist season, Japanese overwhelmingly outnumber visitors. Glass-and-chrome high-rises flank Tokyo's major avenues, international hotel chains stake their claims to prime locations, and the big names of international commerce, from Sony to Chanel, crowd the city center. Have lunch in one of Tokyo's many top-floor restaurants, and you overlook one of the world's signature landscapes of globalization.

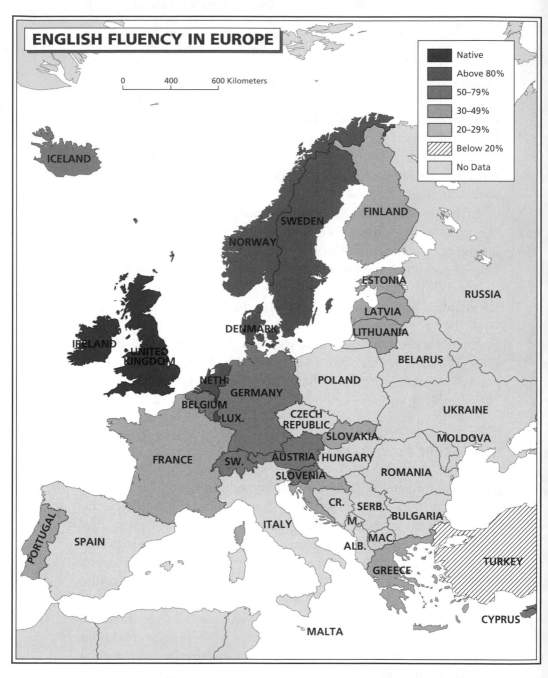

Figure 2.4. English proficiency in countries of Europe. English is spoken by large majorities of the population in the Netherlands, Denmark, and Sweden, and by more than half the people in several other countries. Data from the European Commission's *Special Eurobarometer 243*: "Europeans and Their Languages" (Brussels, 2006) and Wikipedia; information for Switzerland, Norway, and Iceland are estimates. Data for several Eastern European countries are unavailable.

But the linguistic landscape displays only the thinnest veneer of English. To globals, the Tokyo skyline might suggest that the leading language of globalization is ubiquitous here, but mobals and locals know better. Japan guards and nurtures its language as carefully as does France, perhaps even more so. Written Japanese is not nearly as susceptible to Anglicization as is French, and unlike France, Japan has strongly resisted the influx of intercultural migrants despite its declining and aging population. Again unlike French, Japanese did not become a world language; Japan's imperial conquests came late, remained geographically restricted, and did not last long enough. During modern periods of adaptation and invention, the Japanese borrowed and adopted knowledge and skills from the British and the Americans (driving on the left is a legacy of the former), but English usage made only the slightest inroads. Japanese remained the language of technology and modernization, even after the American military conquest and Japan's subsequent resurrection. What the Japanese proved is that you can have globalization without Anglicization. Although Japan's governing and technological elites are bilingual, and English is a school subject, Japan's universities, research institutions, and global corporations conduct their discourse mainly in Japanese. Currently, less than one percent of Japanese claim fluency in English (according to an estimate in *Ethnologue*, 2007), far fewer than in any of the original EU countries (figure 2.3). If this is the case, not many more than 100,000 Japanese, in a population of 127 million, are bilingual in English. Yet Japan is one of the most powerful forces of globalization, its economy among the largest in the world.

If this is possible in Japan, what does it say about the primacy of English in the globalizing world of the future? One of the implications of the planet's demographic prospect discussed in chapter 1 is that the percentage of people speaking Standard English as their first language will decline throughout the twenty-first century, because the bulk of the coming growth will be in countries where English does not have a strong presence. Three generations ago, nearly 10 percent of the planet's population spoke English at home, but various estimates suggest that this number is now down to 6 percent and will decline to 5 percent by mid-century (Graddol, 1997). The notion that Standard English will become the universal language in the wake of the current wave of globalization still has currency, but the evidence points in other directions. A combination of factors, ranging from the protectionism of Japan and France to nationalism as displayed by Arabic-speaking countries and expansionism now carrying Spanish into new frontiers, will affect its prospects. And English itself, like Latin 2000 years ago, is undergoing modifications that suggest that it will become the common base for numerous new versions (McArthur, 1998). Thus, the role of English appears to be changing from its heavily protected standard version to an adaptable undercarriage for communication ranging from the flexibly informal to the necessarily rigidly precise (for example, in scientific contexts). In this latter form, it may indeed continue to provide the dominant medium for international communication, perhaps for generations to come, but even so it will by no means constitute the only one. As a result, there will not only be various "Englishes" horizontally, but also vertically. Just as Hong Kong "Chinglish" has limited similarity to Lagos "Yorlish" (Yoruba-English), so scientific English will differ strongly from business English, one of the powerful catalysts of the still-continuing ascent of English in such regions as the European Union and the Pacific Rim (*Economist*, 2007a). And while some societies will resist English penetration as a matter of national policy, this only serves to enhance the value of fluency in more than on major language of which English is one.

To locals and prospective mobals, this means that bilingualism and multilingualism are the key to a better future. It is well established that people speaking English as their first language are among the world's least multilingually capable, whether in Britain, America, or Australia. The imperial legacy of English has left a residue of indifference as well as incompetence, revealed most recently in the Iraq War by the statistic that out of approximately 1000 employees in the U.S. Embassy in Baghdad, only six were completely fluent in Arabic. While many Americans loudly proclaim that immigrant Hispanics should be subject to "English only" regulations, comparatively few English-speaking Americans have responded to the latest immigration by becoming bilingual themselves. But in an increasingly multilingual world, English-only speakers may find themselves at a growing disadvantage, and locals able to achieve bilingual competence are more likely to succeed when they become mobals. Even as growing numbers of children are learning English as a second language in Indonesia and China, some national governments, including Chile and Mongolia, have set the goal of bilingual competence for all students as a matter of educational policy. David Graddol is quoted as predicting that "within a decade nearly a third of the world's population will all be trying to learn English" (*Economist*, 2006). As a result, bilingualism and multilingualism, with various versions of English in the mix, are likely to be the norm of the future, with English-only notions (and speakers) relegated to the dustbin of history.

To millions of villagers born this decade in the global periphery, local language still pervades personal identity, its constraints impeding the road uphill. But the pattern of language is undergoing revolutionary change even as the demographic map heralds a new era. Urban locals will increasingly outnumber their rural contemporaries, and in the ethnic neighborhoods of future multicultural megacities their social identities will be less leavened by language. They will learn other tongues and they will forge their own. For them, multilingualism will be key to surmounting the power of place.

3
THE FATEFUL GEOGRAPHY
OF RELIGION

If language is the mucilage of culture, religion is its manifesto. Any revelation of identity through language happens only when the speaker begins talking, and even then that identity remains in doubt except perhaps to the most experienced ear. Is that skilled KiSwahili speaker a Mijikenda from the Kenya coast or a Kamba from the interior? Is that cultivated French speaker a citizen of Senegal or a resident of Paris? Did those fellows at the bar in São Paulo mix some Brazilian terms with their Japanese, and are they mobals rather than visitors?

Religious affiliation is another matter. Hundreds of millions of people routinely proclaim their religion through modes of dress, hairstyles, symbols, gestures, and other visible means. To those who share a faith, such customs create a sense of confidence and solidarity. To those who do not profess that faith, they can amount to provocation. For the faithful, religion is the key to identity. And such identity is part of the impress of place. Religion and place are strongly coupled, not only through the visible and prominent architecture of places of worship but also because certain orthodox believers still proclaim that their god "gave" them pieces of real estate whose ownership cannot therefore be a matter of Earthly political debate. To some, the Holy Land is a place where Jesus walked. To others, it is a gift from God. To the latter, it is worth dying for.

Countless millions have perished for their faith, but comparatively few for their language. Dutch schoolchildren of a former generation used to learn the story of a captured boatload of medieval mercenaries plying the Zuider Zee. To a man, the captives claimed to be Dutch. The captain of the boarding party had a simple solution: any real Dutchman would be able to pronounce the word *Scheveningen*, a fishing port on the North Sea coast. Those who got it right were given amnesty. Those who failed were thrown overboard and drowned. It is an unusual tale. Language, dialect, accent, and syntax can confer advantage, open (or close) doors to opportunity, and engender social judgments. But they are not historically linked to mass annihilation.

There is nothing in the religious dimension of culture to match or mirror the phenomenon of multilingualism. The Baha'i movement, based on a religion founded in the mid-nineteenth century by a Persian prophet, asserts the ultimate and inevitable convergence of all of humanity's belief systems, but despite its intellectual appeal and worldwide dissemination, its global impact is negligible. Other "universalist" religious movements have had even less unifying influence. Whereas children learn their parents' language and then, depending on their circumstances, are taught to, seek, or are compelled to widen their linguistic horizons, religious indoctrination has the opposite goal and effect. By the time they are able to read and write, children of religious households are enmeshed in the ritual and dogma of their parental faith, and only a tiny minority later convert to another religion. To watch seven- and eight-year-old boys bloody themselves in imitation of their Shi'ite elders as they march in the annual Ashura pilgrimage to commemorate the death in A.D. 680 of the prophet Muhammad's grandson is to realize the depth of this inculcation.

It is, however, just one (albeit extreme) manifestation of a global phenomenon whose effects are ultimately similar. The precepts of the faith may be implanted through rote learning of the entire Quran, as happens in Islamic schools called *madrassas*, by evangelical education in Christian "Sunday Schools," or by teachings based on notions of reincarnation in Buddhist seminaries, but the results tend to be the same: an often unquestioning belief in received religious dogma and an inability (for reasons discussed later) to tolerate, or even consider, alternative convictions. This intolerance is a key factor in the perpetuation of any religion and the sustenance of its domain, but its intensity varies, not only between but also within the faiths. Religion can constitute a dominant ingredient in the power of place, and that power varies geographically.

Again unlike language, religious belief and sectarian adherence entail sensitivities easily injured. Criticism of one's language or dialect tends to be internalized, and ethnic slurs can arouse wider resentment. But nothing matches the passion incited by religious insult or humiliation. What is seen as a minor instance of freedom of expression in secular context may be regarded as a capital offense by those who view themselves as defenders of their faith. The interpenetration of religions—through migration, proselytism, commerce, military action—not only complicates the global religious landscape, but increases the probability of insult, intended or otherwise.

Religion's global geographic variation, like that of language, is changing. Even as Christian evangelicals challenge major denominations in their historic redoubts and Sunni and Shia Muslims compete in the Islamic domain, religious conservatism, also referred to as fundamentalism or revivalism, is rising worldwide. In this form, religious priorities are invading political arenas in many countries. As a result, religion is turning into a countervailing force, roughening rather than flattening the landscape of globalization.

RELIGION AND ECOLOGY

As is the case with human languages (yes, there are others), the global mosaic of religion is dense and varied. Taking into account all local belief systems as well as world religions, the total number runs into the thousands; and here, too, the species-richness gradient makes its appearance, but with a twist. Given the large number of small human communities in low-latitude tropical forests in South America, Africa, Southeast Asia, and New Guinea, it is not surprising that these ecological environs have engendered numerous belief systems. Higher latitude zones, including deserts such as the Kalahari and Gobi, have fewer communities living in larger, often emptier spaces (nomadism, obviously, is not a rainforest pursuit). In the moister tropical zones, moreover, a substantial majority of local and stable communities have developed polytheistic belief systems, worshipping numerous deities and spirits and attaching religious connotations to ancestors, animals, and plants. Peoples of the desert and steppe, on the other hand, tend to be monotheistic, believing in the existence of one deity only, although some also acknowledge lesser gods and adversaries such as devils and dragons. As in the case of languages, the religions that dominate the world map today are those originating in the drier higher latitudes, not those of the rainforest. You are not likely to find a missionary from Papua trying to convert Belgians to his faith. But it is no surprise to find Mormon missionaries from (desert) Utah among the forest dwellers of Africa or South America.

Cultural geographers and anthropologists noted such regional contrasts a long time ago, and initially drew conclusions about relationships between climate and "civilization" that reflected the unconstrained racism of their times. Anthropologists talked of mid-latitude (European) ecosystems producing superior cultures; geographers hypothesized about "environmental determinism" that ensured intellectual excellence, religious and moral superiority, family values, and personal virtues. One of the leading geographers of his time, Ellsworth Huntington, summed it up in a textbook this way: "The people of the cyclonic regions rank so far above those of other parts of the world that they are the natural leaders.... [T]he contrast between the energetic people of the most progressive parts of the temperate zone and inert inhabitants of the tropics...is largely due to climate" (Huntington, 1940). Nazi Germans seized eagerly upon such scholarly confirmation of Aryan supremacy, and colonial powers saw in it a justification for their "civilizing" and Christianizing missions. The horrors of the Second World War and, in its aftermath, growing doubts about the colonial venture contributed to the virtual demise of cross-cultural research based on (or even remotely related to) ecological factors. For about a half century, most anthropologists focused on the customs and rituals of particular peoples and eschewed comparisons; cultural geographers distanced themselves in every possible way from the legacy of environmental determinism.

Not until the past decade did serious research again begin to address the question that had led Huntington and others astray: in what ways are cultural traditions and ecological circumstances interrelated? Among the key catalysts in this reconsideration was the appearance of a neo-determinist work by a highly respected scholar whose scientific accomplishments ensured its credibility (Diamond, 1997). Another came when a prominent and admired economist, less encumbered than geographers by disciplinary sensitivities, focused on climate as the key factor in the perpetuation of poverty and the continuation of conflict in poverty-stricken areas of the world (Sachs, 2006). A third factor was the growing realization that the wholesale rejection of environmental determinism had virtually halted research in an arena that, when appropriately investigated, would yield important insights into the fates and fortunes of human societies, ancient and modern.

Some of this research related directly to the question of religious traditions and their spatial variation. Anthropologist Melvin Ember concluded that the gods of monotheistic societies in rainforest environments (of which there are some) tend to be far less controlling or threatening than those invented by desert dwellers, whose deities and dogmas often represent punishment and retribution (Ember, 1982). He reported that desert societies are more likely to be centralized, hierarchical, and militant, and that their omnipotent gods impose their judgments through promises of heavenly or hellish afterlives. The status and role of women, too, differ markedly. Among traditional rainforest peoples, women commonly ensure the stability and continuity of communities because several generations live in the same or nearby village; they may play important roles in local trade and other communal activities and are far less likely to be regarded as inferior. In many traditional desert cultures, women not only do most of the heavy work but are dominated by men who control their lives, conceal their persons, and isolate their activities. It follows that attitudes toward sex and marriage are more relaxed among forest dwellers than among those in the desert.

On what Mackinder called the World Island, where the great monotheistic religions were to arise, the link between dry environs and monotheism probably emerged with the earliest herding economy, when livestock, and especially cattle, became the first substantial property of value owned by humans, and men were the owners and defenders. Patrilineal descent systems led to monotheism: resources in the form of livestock, pastures, and water could only be expanded at the expense of others, for which God provided the vindication. Polytheistic farmers, male and female, must be overpowered, and controls put on women, in effect making them property of men as well. In the Americas, indigenous cultures living in arid environments never developed herding economies; most combined some farming with hunting and gathering and remained matrilineal, including the Iroquois.

What are the wider implications? Robert Sapolsky writes that ours is a planet "dominated by the cultural descendants of denizens of the drier world. At various points [they] have poured out of the Middle East, defining large parts of Eurasia... subjugating the native populations of the Americas, Africa, and Australia. As a result, ours is a Judeo-Christian/Muslim world, not an Mbuti-Carib-Trobriand one.... The desert mind-set, and the cultural baggage it carries, has proven extraordinarily resilient in its export and diffusion throughout the planet." He adds that rainforest traditions are not only less likely to spread, but also less resilient when uprooted. Not just languages, but also belief systems are being lost as "rainforest cultures, with their fragile pluralism born of a lush world of plenty, deliquesce into the raw sewage of the slums of Rio and Lagos and Jakarta" (Sapolsky, 2005).

If this seems to overstate the case, notably in terms of the "lush and plenty" of rainforest environments whose ecological fluctuations can pose severe existential challenges to communities inhabiting them, there can be no doubt that the power of place is substantially defined by belief systems, and that the most powerful of these arose beyond the forested tropics. The resulting process of dissemination continues today. Just what the future of religion is in megacities such as Lagos and Jakarta remains an open question, but it is clear that the faiths of the forest will play no role in these urban cauldrons.

RELIGION ON THE MAP

Although the map of world religions, like that of world languages, is of necessity a generalization, it does accurately portray the dominance of comparatively few belief systems over much of the inhabited planet and the crowding of many others into smaller and shrinking domains (figure 3.1). It is further possible to carry the language-family analogy into the religious context, because the dominant religions (Christianity and Islam, but also Hinduism and Buddhism) can be viewed as discrete families, even though their members (sects, denominations, orders) may not always be on good terms.

Cultural geographers and others studying the spatial and functional properties of religions are confronted by fast-changing patterns, even at the level of scale represented by figure 3.1. The map shows that the two dominant religions prevail over approximately 70 percent of the planet's inhabited territory. Christianity, a family of faiths that had its origins in the Middle East, is today the leading religion in the global core and in contiguous lands in the Americas and Eurasia. Islam, born six centuries later on the Arabian Peninsula, is the prevailing religion in the global periphery. Christianity spread into Europe, became the state religion of the Roman Empire, and dispersed worldwide on the wings of colonialism and migration even as

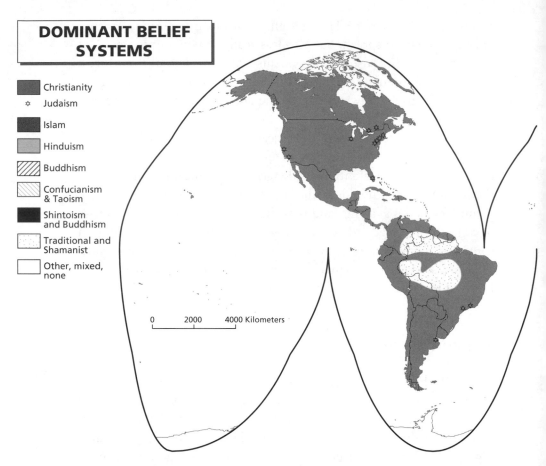

DOMINANT BELIEF SYSTEMS

- Christianity
- ☼ Judaism
- Islam
- Hinduism
- Buddhism
- Confucianism & Taoism
- Shintoism and Buddhism
- Traditional and Shamanist
- Other, mixed, none

0   2000   4000 Kilometers

Figure 3.1. The domains of the major religions. At this scale, the map cannot display sectarian divisions or even significant religious minorities (such as the large Muslim presence in Hindu-dominated India). In tropical Africa, Christianity is the leading non-indigenous faith. Confucianism and Taoism are belief systems rather than religions in the traditional sense.

it split along sectarian lines. Islam brought to the heart of the World Island a burst of creative energy that forged a domain extending from Iberia to India and from Eastern Europe to Western Africa. To this day, the geographies of the two global religions are starkly different: Christianity disseminant and scattered, Islam contiguous and concentrated. Only Islamic Malaysia and Indonesia reflect a time when Islam, too, rode the waves.

What the map does not show are the numbers. Christianity still lays claim to the largest number of adherents, some 1.6 billion by

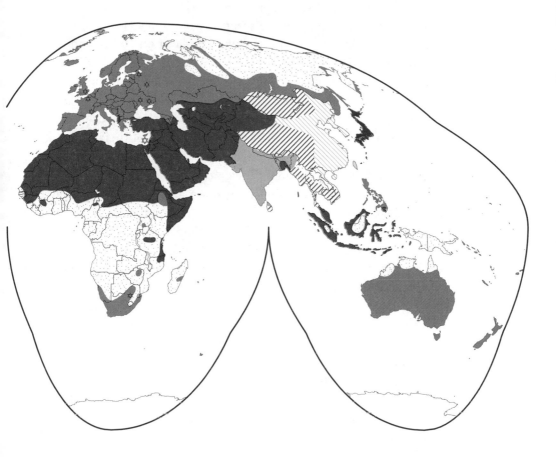

latest reports, but many of Christianity's churches stand in countries that are losing population as well as interest in the teachings of the faith. Islam's followers are variously reported to number somewhere between 1.2 and 1.3 billion, and Islam is gaining rapidly because the populations in its part of the periphery are still increasing faster than the global average, and because Islam's appeal among disadvantaged and disaffected locals continues to grow. Today, the largest Muslim state lies not in the Islamic heartland of Southwest Asia, but on the islands of Southeast Asia.

Neither Islam nor Christianity, however, prevails in the two largest population clusters on the planet. Islam has a significant foothold in India, where Muslims constitute 14 percent of the population, and Christian religions are making inroads in China, where data are unreliable but estimates suggest that eight percent of the population may have been converted. But between them, India's Hinduism and China's domestic belief systems account for about one billion adherents, although (and here the map makes an important point) their spatial extent, in global terms, is comparatively limited. From the map it appears that western China is mainly Muslim or Buddhist, but compare figure 3.1 to figure 1.2, and one is reminded that the overwhelming majority of Chinese live in the eastern one-third of their country. The entire combined Islamic-Buddhist area in western China (including Tibet and Xinjiang) contains fewer than 30 million of China's 1.3 billion people, and the Chinese presence among the indigenous inhabitants is approaching half the total population there.

By what it can—and cannot—show, the map identifies three kinds of belief systems. The genuine global (and globalizing) religions, of which Christianity and Islam are the two giants, have the widest distribution across the planet. Buddhism, also a global religion in historic terms, has far fewer adherents (under 400 million currently) but, as the map reveals, is also widely disseminated, its major presence dominating several states in Southeast Asia. Judaism, with fewer than 20 million members, was present at, and infused, the birth of both Christianity and Islam, but at the scale of figure 3.1 its presence is barely discernible despite its global diffusion. The regional (sometimes called ethnic) religions include Hinduism, more than twice as numerous as Buddhism but much more confined spatially; the Chinese belief systems; and other local faiths such as Jainism, which arose in South Asia in the sixth century B.C. in reaction to the cruel and ritualistic practices of early Hinduism; Sikhism, which emerged about five centuries ago, also in India, as a movement to combine the best features (and negate the worst) of Hinduism and Islam; and Shintoism, a blend of Buddhism and local beliefs that became the state religion of Japan in the nineteenth century. And for want of a more satisfactory rubric, the numerous smaller, often shamanist religions of the equatorial forests and other remote locales are referred to as traditional religions, mapped as such on figure 3.1 but, at a larger scale, shown to be surviving in areas far beyond the tropics.

Although figure 3.1 unavoidably delimits religious realms and sectarian regions by sharp lines, such discreteness is rare on the ground. The Muslim minority in dominantly Hindu India may be the largest cultural minority in the world, but it is only one of hundreds of such minorities living on the other side of religious divides marked on the map by lines. Albania is nominally Christian Europe's only Muslim-majority country today, but significant Muslim minorities inhabit other European countries, and should Kosovo's independence drive succeed, Muslim majority will be proportionately larger even than Albania's. When it comes to sectarian divisions, the mosaic becomes even more intricate. On the by-county map of the United States, the Southeast is predominantly Baptist, the Northeast significantly Roman Catholic, the upper Midwest Lutheran, the interior West Mormon. The complexities of the sectarian map of Iraq have only recently come to Americans' attention; these involve far more than a Sunni–Shi'ite split belabored by politicians. Numerous smaller sects complicate the cultural mosaic of Iraq, voiding any notions of a three-way split of the country.

And the map, as noted, is changing rapidly. The revival of the Russian Orthodox Church in the post-Soviet era is only one manifestation of this ongoing process; the expansion of Islam in Europe is another. In Africa, the traditional religions are losing not only to Christian missionary activity, but also to the advance of Islam along what has been called Africa's "Islamic Front" (de Blij, 2005). It has been suggested that today's map of world religions will someday represent but a transitional stage in the evolution of philosophy and science, but for the present it represents the outlines of a formidable challenge to those born in the shadows of its minarets, pagodas, steeples, and shrines.

Figure 3.1 is a legacy of millennia of religious maturation, and the scholarly quest for the origins of religious belief is as riveting as the search for the "original" language ancestral to all. That geolinguistic search, as noted in chapter 2, may be fruitless as well as pointless; languages probably arose independently in numerous locales, and several gave rise to enduring families. In the case of religion, the issue has recently become a matter of public as well as academic interest as scholars have come to view its relatively recent birth (in context of humanity's emergence some 170,000 years ago) in evolutionary and neurological as well as philosophical and moral terms (Dennett, 2006). This research has shifted focus from the quest for evidence of ancient religions and their influence on later ones—was Zoroastrianism the first monotheistic belief system and was it the source of that principle implanted in Judaism and Christianity?—to other arenas, including genetics and neuroscience. In any case, it is no more probable that there was a single ancestral religion than that there was an original matriarchal tongue. Belief systems emerged in response to competition and challenge, provided advantage and explanation, and guided behavior and convention. They did so under widely varying environmental and social circumstances and evolved into numerous forms, among which a half dozen gained primacy.

ON EURASIA'S EASTERN FLANK

After three millennia of interaction and competition, one might expect that the planet would be showing evidence of a religious convergence, a softening of the dictates of place. But consider the two wings of Eurasia and the opposite seems to be the case. The major Chinese belief systems, prominently including Confucianism and its approximate contemporary, Taoism, arose about the same time as Zoroastrianism in Southwest Asia and Buddhism in South Asia, a time of extraordinary philosophical creativity in the mid-period of the first millennium B.C. Yet the Chinese belief systems were and are not theistic; Kongfuzi, as Chinese *pinyin* spells Confucius, was not a prophet who dealt in promises of heaven or threats of hell. Rather, he disavowed the divine ancestry of China's rulers, disdained supernatural mysticism, and focused his teachings and work on the downtrodden, the weak, and the landless. Kongfuzi tutored the poor, thus ending the aristocracy's exclusive access to knowledge (and hence power), and taught that human virtues, not godly connections, should determine a person's place in society. Although revered as a spiritual leader after his death in 479 B.C., it was his practical guidance, encompassed in a mass of philosophical writing, that became the roadmap for the People of Han and for China over the centuries that followed.

In truth, a substantial part of the work attributed to Kongfuzi did not come from his pen, although he did author what has become known as the Confucian Classics, 13 texts that formed the basis for education and demeanor in China for two millennia. A blend of Confucian, Taoist, and Buddhist thinking (Buddhism reached China during the Han Dynasty, long after Kongfuzi's death) became China's state ethic if not a circumscribed faith. In turn, local belief systems, of which there were many, merged with the national creed to create, as figure 3.1 suggests, a region of Chinese religions.

Some maps drawn in the West show China as atheist or nonreligious, which reflects the viewpoint of their cartographers. True, Chinese belief systems do not involve an omnipotent deity or assurances of an afterlife of the kind guaranteed by Christianity or Islam. But elements of Taoist philosophy survive in Chinese religious thinking in the form of *Feng Shui*, the art and science of organizing living spaces and structures in such a way as to channel favorably the life forces that are presumed to exist in nature. To accomplish this, those affecting the land, from builders to gravediggers, consult *geomancers*, who know the desires of the powerful spirits of ancestors and dragons as well as tigers and pandas. When a new building is planned in Hong Kong or Shanghai, the architects and engineers will know how to place it, where to put the entrance, and what the best approach route is. Fail to consult the geomancers, and one risks misfortune or worse.

China's rulers have always had a difficult relationship with Han subjects who strayed from the national ethic to embrace an alternate faith, and with minorities who adhere to other religions as a matter of tradition. Mao Zedong not only wanted to expunge the imprint of Confucianism from China's cultural landscape; he also declared communist China to be an atheist state on the model of the Soviet Union. The Communist Party's minions tirelessly pursued any citizens suspected of covert religious activity, and among Han Chinese the Cultural Revolution effectively wiped it out. But China, as was the Soviet Union before it, remains a multicultural empire, and the vast country includes minorities not only speaking non-Chinese languages but also practicing non-Chinese religions. As figure 3.1 shows, Lamaist Buddhism prevails in the "autonomous regions" of Tibet (Xizang) and the adjacent province of Qinghai, and the forced exile of the Dalai Lama remains a dark shadow over Beijing's administration. And China has 10 Islamic minorities numbering about 25 million Muslims, among them the restive Uyghur of Xinjiang in the far west whose demonstrations and occasional acts of violence have been met by repression and executions. Muslim schools there are tightly monitored and their student numbers severely limited. Things have gone better in the more restrained Hui community of 10 million centered on the city of Linxia, where more than 80 mosques serve the faithful who have learned to balance their Islamic beliefs with their Chinese citizenship (Yardley, 2006). On the other hand, the sensitivity and insecurity of China's communist rulers has been on revealing display in their near-hysterical suppression of the Falun Gong, a quasi-Buddhist self-improvement movement whose organized activities, ranging from mass calisthenics to educational gatherings, were deemed a threat to the state.

Allegiance to Christian faiths among Han Chinese is what troubles the Beijing regime more. Roman Catholicism had some surviving underground adherents when the market reforms began three decades ago, when they were encouraged to come out into the open. Ever since, though, Catholics have been carefully monitored, and Roman Catholic priests must be approved by the government, which has led to disputes with the papacy. The still-potent power of the Vatican, on vigorous display in countries of the global core, is anathema to Beijing.

The Pacific Rim economic boom that transformed the eastern littoral of Han China in one generation could, in all likelihood, not have happened the way it did had China been in the grip of a strong religious hierarchy. In this sense East Asia was indeed "flat"—internal mobals and external globals could meet in the common quest for economic advantage, facilitated by political decree, without having to deal with monks, mullahs, or ministers. None of the major players on this field had religious baggage heavy enough to slow the reforms. China's geomancers had a field day in the burgeoning cities on and near the Pacific coast, but renascent Confucianism had no impact on the economic boom. American companies and Japanese investors knew better than to add religious issues to the commercial stew. None of the many minority locals who took jobs in the mushrooming cities was impelled by religious fervor to demand social change. What happened on the western Pacific Rim is often referred to as a miracle, but the miracle was more than just economic.

THE WEST: COLLISION OF CULTURES

At the opposite end of Eurasia, migration is also playing a major role, but in an economic and political transformation of a different kind. As figure 3.1 shows, Europe's Christian history, involving bitter medieval sectarian conflicts, yielded a dominantly Roman Catholic south, a mainly Protestant north, and a largely Orthodox east. No longer visible on the contemporary map, except in small remnants in the east, are the centuries of Islamic rule over much of Iberia early in Islam's ascent and over Eastern Europe in its later heyday. Over more than a hundred years, including most of the twelfth century, European religious and political leaders organized a series of Crusades to confront Islamic rule in the so-called Holy Land, wresting control of Jerusalem from the Muslims, losing it again, but establishing footholds in the Levant that would open the door to later European penetration.

The sectarian fragmentation of Christianity began early and continues to this day; the three major divisions of the faith are only the broadest outlines of this fracture. Christianity had become the state religion of the Roman Empire, but the empire soon broke apart, and the church centered on Constantinople (now Istanbul) went its own way as the Orthodox (Eastern) Church. In the west, Rome became the center of the Roman Catholic Church and the papacy, and much of Western Europe fell under its increasingly authoritarian rule. The inevitable reaction came during the fifteenth and sixteenth centuries with the teachings of Luther, Calvin, and other "protestant" reformers. Civil wars among Christians, involving the most terrible cruelties recorded in painful detail by artists of the time, cost hundreds of thousands of lives as the Protestant movement grew steadily stronger.

Europe's resultant north–south split carried over into the colonial Americas, where southern lands were colonized by southern (Catholic) Europeans and northern areas afforded refuge to Protestants seeking an escape from war and oppression (figure 3.1). In Europe itself, the scientific revolution beginning in the sixteenth century created the basis for the Enlightenment, the emergence of rationalism in philosophical and political thought. Now the basic tenets of Christianity, not just the dogma of one sect or another, came under intellectual scrutiny, and concepts of God and nature were freely discussed. Among the results of this discourse was the spreading realization that without sectarian coexistence, all else Christian, and indeed European, would be at risk.

The Enlightenment set in motion the gradual secularization of European cultures, earlier in the more Protestant north but also in the south, where the Roman Catholic Church today continues to lose its influence over national policies covering marriage, birth control, abortion, and other personal practices. Whether in the mainly Protestant north or in the dominantly Catholic south (though hitherto less so in the east), Europeans are abandoning their churches and living secular lives, responding to surveys by stating their disdain for irrelevant Biblical narrative and medieval ritual. In Britain in 2007, only 6 percent of the nominally Christian population identified itself as regular churchgoers. Disillusionment arising from the Second World War undoubtedly accelerated this trend, but more practical issues—later marriages, weaker families, costlier living, urban pressures, uncertain futures—also mattered. Europe in the aftermath of the war was not only shattered but also disheartened, its economies ruined and its prospects shadowed by the Soviet-communist partition. Rather than religious rededication, it was economic revival, spurred by the Marshall Plan and ensured by the Treaty of Rome, that became Europe's preeminent goal.

Into this postwar disarray entered an element not confronted in Europe since the collapse of the Ottoman Empire: Islam. While the People's Republic of China was closed and shuttered to outsiders (except for a few Soviet "advisers"), Europe lay open to the world and needed labor. Again unlike China a generation later, Europe's workers came from external sources, including colonies and former colonies near and far. China's internal labor movements created logistical but few cultural problems. Europe attracted a Muslim influx at a time when Islam was in vigorous doctrinal evolution. Even as Christian churches stood virtually empty, Islamic mosques rose above traditional townscapes. Robes and burqas made their appearance on city streets; arguments erupted over headscarves for women and prayer rooms in the workplace. Countries that had incorporated and accommodated other immigrants (for example, from the Malukus and Suriname in the Netherlands, from West Africa and the West Indies in the United Kingdom) found themselves facing a different challenge with the arrival of more self-segregating, religiously more proactive mobals from Morocco and Algeria, Pakistan and Afghanistan.

It is revealing to view this influx in the context of the geography of Islam's sectarian evolution in the postcolonial period. Just as Europeans had laid their own sectarian differences essentially to rest, and the European Union could peacefully engage in a debate over whether its Christian heritage should even receive mention in the draft constitution, Europe found itself enmeshed not only in Christian–Islamic disputes, but also in the sectarian conflicts roiling

Islam itself. There is a medieval echo in the intensifying Sunni–Shi'ite split in Islam, exacerbated by the American intervention in Iraq and the end of the Sunni dictatorship there. While the issue of the succession to the Prophet Muhammad lies at the source of it and is therefore ancient Arab history, its geography was altered fatefully when, early in the sixteenth century, the ruling Persian (non-Arab) dynasty was persuaded to designate Shia Islam as the state religion of an empire that extended from present-day Iraq and Azerbaijan across Iran to parts of Afghanistan and Pakistan. In the absence of this decision, Shi'ites probably would have continued to constitute small, scattered minorities in a Sunni-dominated religious realm. But today, some 15 percent of all Muslims are Shias, Shi'ite Iran lies at the core of a large, contiguous sectarian domain, and growing Shi'ite minorities exist in neighboring (as well as more distant) countries from Saudi Arabia to Syria and from Lebanon to Yemen.

Meanwhile, technologically capable, energy-rich Iran's assertive leadership in pursuit of nuclear power and in opposition to Israel dismays Sunni governments near and far. In the decade before it invaded Kuwait, Sunni-ruled Iraq fought a bitter war against Iran costing an estimated one million lives in which the Iranians sacrificed countless child-soldiers; had Iran possessed nuclear weapons, the toll would undoubtedly have been many times higher. In the first decade of the twenty-first century, Iran not only pursued nuclear capability but, through its belligerent president and with the blessing of the religious establishment, preempted the Sunni position on Israel. Furthermore, Iran sponsors and funds the terrorist organization Hizbullah, which, in Lebanon, has carved out a veritable state-within-a-state that proved capable of prolonged combat with Israel in 2006.

These frictions and conflicts became part of the European scene as the Muslim influx accelerated. Decades before the aftermath of 9/11 enmeshed European governments in the campaign in Afghanistan, and long before the American invasion of Iraq provided justification to Islamic terrorists for their violent acts, Europe had become part of the battleground of Islam. The Turkish immigration to Germany, creating a minority now approaching four million, came without historic colonial entanglements, but about one-fifth of the total were Kurdish, transplanting long-standing Turkish–Kurdish animosities onto German soil. The majority of France's five million Muslim immigrants came from formerly colonial Algeria in the wake of a bitter war for independence, and among them were significant numbers of Berbers as well as Arabs. Spain's colonial involvement with Morocco as well as its proximity to North Africa contributed to the legal as well as illegal immigration of more than a million Moroccans, although many more moved north to France, Belgium, and the Netherlands. The United Kingdom's Muslim population originates from numerous Muslim countries (or countries with Muslim minorities) once part of the British Empire, including Pakistan, India, Nigeria, Bangladesh, and Sri Lanka.

Western (and southern) Europe received immigrants from other source areas as well, but those from countries or areas where Islam is the exclusive religion brought with them especially heavy doctrinal baggage. The early indoctrination of children is not unique to Islam among religions, but no other major religion imposes its dogmas and divisions on the young as stiflingly as does Islam, and none segregates and relegates women to the same degree. Certainly there are comparable instances of extremism in other religions (Dawkins, 2006). But Islam's fervid recruitment and its demand of intense commitment put pressures on children, and especially boys, that are unmatched. These young locals find themselves in a social web in which unquestioning submission to authority, faith-based education, limited horizons, and frustrated aspirations become daunting obstacles when they seek new opportunities as migrant mobals.

These problems are worsened by the circumstances in which these immigrants find themselves in Europe. European governments have tried various systems to accommodate their mobals, and with some success; in Britain, for example, Hindu and Sikh communities have exhibited striking upward mobility. Not only did these South Asian groups leave their historic rivalries mostly behind, but their members tend to support each other in their aspirations in the United Kingdom. On the other hand, British "mosque committees are often dominated by factions pursuing sectarian rivalries that have South Asian origins.... [C]lans try to preserve a rural tribal outlook and prevent talented younger people from obtaining positions of responsibility. Not surprisingly, radical voices that insist that loyalty to a global Islamic faith take precedence over allegiance to the British state enjoy growing appeal" (Gallagher, 2007). Not only do Europe's Islamic mobals find themselves repelled by what they see as a decadent, irreligious society, but many are additionally thwarted by their own imams and their conservative allies, sustained by the global Wahhabist network and its vast fiscal resources. To them, notions of a flat world are simply irrelevant, and thousands have returned, radicalized by clerics advocating a global *jihad*, to fight the decadent West in Iraq and Afghanistan.

Although Europe's Muslim influx has created opportunities for Islamic extremists to plan and execute terrorist acts, and while such acts, including the 2004 Madrid train bombings and the 2005 London subway murders, undoubtedly contribute to Europeans' misgivings about the future, a far more important struggle is under way whose outcome will have a vital impact on Europe's social, political, and economic future. About 70 percent of Britain's 1.6 million Muslims are less than 40 years old, and the percentage for Western and Southern Europe as a whole is not much lower. A growing number of resident Muslims are no longer mobals, having attained citizenship and had children born in Europe. The fact that the young perpetrators of the London attacks included several British-born Muslims who had gone to public schools, played local sports, and showed few signs of unusual maladjustment shocked the nation, especially when their connections (and terrorism-related travels) to their ancestral homelands were revealed.

European governments are reconsidering the merits of multiculturalism and appear to be realizing that exceptional group rights for ethnoreligious (read Islamic) communities may produce leaders in those communities who gain and retain power by obstructing internal diversity and by isolating their followers from European society. By converting potentially integrationist mobals back into subservient locals, these leaders are transferring the most inflexible and retrograde properties of their faith from their conservative homelands to a Europe that still carries the scars of its own sectarian wars half a millennium ago. It is a battle of divergent principles in a realm whose indigenous population is shrinking and many of whose inhabitants have reflectively lost faith in faith—only to be confronted by the vigor, demographic as well as religious, of an unending stream of immigrants with an unshakable belief in belief. Those who ask "A Muslim Europe?" as did the *Atlantic Monthly* in 2005 are not guilty of hyperbole (Savage, 2004). Europe's economic, political, and social future is now inextricably enmeshed in Southwest Asia's past.

A GLOBAL ENDARKENMENT?

The contest between Islam and other faiths takes many forms in various regions of the world, and Europe is only one part of what is in effect a global stage for it. Even as Islam's sectarian divisions generate intra-Islamic conflicts ranging from political quarrels to deathly violence, and states, tribes, and clans in the Islamic world have long and continuing histories of internecine strife, Islamist movements confront Roman Catholics in the Philippines, Chinese secularists in Xinjiang, Buddhists in Thailand, Russian rule in the Transcaucasus, Indian control over Kashmir, Ethiopian power in the Horn of Africa, and other adversaries from Sudan to Sulawesi. Muslim mobals are arriving in countries far from the Muslim world—in Chile, Brazil, South Africa, Australia—and minarets rise in Lima, Buffalo, Vienna, Seoul, Saigon. There was a time when Islam diffused chiefly by contiguous expansion. Now it is spreading by relocation as well.

Islam's progressive contact with the rest of the world is subjecting the faith to scrutiny and analysis unprecedented in its history. The Quran and the Hadith are being read and examined as never before. The religion's (and its scriptures') designation and treatment of women have become topics of intense debate. How does a host country respond when an imam declares in a sermon before a males-only assembly that the beating of women is not only allowed but encouraged by the Quran (2:234) when such violence is against the law of the land (Bouazza, 2002)? Why does Islam, alone among the major religions, mark conversion to another faith as apostasy, punishable by death? Why is there no outcry among Sufi (moderate) Muslims when an Indian author of Muslim descent is subjected by an Iranian *ayatollah* to a *fatwa* authorizing his murder, as happened in 1989? Why cannot Muslims tolerate discourtesy, however outrageous, as represented by the cartoons depicting the Prophet Muhammad published by a Danish cultural magazine in 2006, and respond without violence and threats? How can significant minorities (and a few majorities) of surveyed Muslims express approval or "understanding" of terrorist acts on the basis of historic misdeeds going back as far as the Crusades?

To be sure, the mountainous intellectual topography of Islam has some high as well as many low points, and the questions just raised can be answered in part by citing the "demonstration effect"—the need to be seen to express solidarity with one's cohorts and ensure approval from religious leaders as a matter of self-preservation in community or clan. But the aggregate effect is to focus global opinion on Islam's low points. It is not true that having exceptional talent, productivity, ambition, or judgment is universally perilous in Islamic society; but it does entail risks measurably greater than in other religious contexts. In 2002, an Iranian court sentenced a university professor to death for publishing a proposal advocating an Islamic Enlightenment, but he was saved (for a jail term) when thousands of students took to the streets in protest. That such a sentence could be handed down at all is indicative of the steep incline between the vast depths of religious dogma and the few heights of rationalism in this historic and civilized society. Here is one reason why the number of books published per capita in the contiguous Islamic realm is about one-ninth of that of Europe. And here is a reason why hundreds of thousands of talented Iranians have made a success of their lives in non-Islamic societies.

The impractical notion of an Islamic Enlightenment (or Reformation) has been the topic of many a treatise in the post-9/11 period, but before adherents of other faiths take it upon themselves to issue such a prescription, they should perhaps consider developments in their own religious domains. In recent years the exposure of endemic pedophilia has revealed what is surely one of the darkest chapters in the annals of the Roman Catholic Church, not only in America but also in Europe: in Ireland "it is now estimated that the *un*molested children in religious schools were very probably in the minority" (Hitchens, 2007). Christian critics who are quick to castigate their Muslim cohorts in Saudi Arabia for the treatment of the Islamic kingdom's women might refocus their attention on the misdeeds perpetrated in the cathedrals and churches of their own faith.

From the resurgence of Christian fundamentalism in America to the rise of Hindu "nationalism" in India, and including Judaic and even Buddhist orthodoxy, religions over the past generation have taken on a reactionary tinge, a back-to-basics posture that in some ways resembles the very dogmatism for which Islam supposedly needs an Enlightenment. Christian fundamentalism continues to burgeon as a powerful political as well as religious force in America, where the same activists who promote literal interpretations of Biblical texts and who indoctrinate children at the earliest opportunity also demand that these same children, in their schoolrooms, have a "choice" between evolutionary theory and so-called intelligent design.

Such fundamentalist revivalism is not confined to the geography of America's new "Bible Belt"; it may have a southern and southeastern core, but it has adherents nationwide. Some education leaders in the State of Kansas wanted to introduce intelligent design in the classroom; a major courtroom battle was needed in Pennsylvania to stave off a similar initiative. Nor is it limited to America, where Christianity faces none of the erosion it confronts in Europe. In 2005, the Minister of Science and Education in, of all countries, the Netherlands proposed an "academic debate" to consider how intelligent design "might [even] be applied to schools and lessons" (Enserink, 2005).

A significant consequence of the unlamented demise of Soviet communism is the revival of the Russian Orthodox Church in a society with constitutional but brittle separation between church and state. Church leaders are engaged in a vigorous campaign to insert religious dogma into public-school curricula, arguing that children should be exposed at a very early age to Orthodox tradition and liturgy. They have succeeded in implanting Russian Orthodox chaplains in the military and cast other faiths, including other Christian denominations, in unfavorable light. The leader of the church, Patriarch Alexy II of Moscow, often asserts that Orthodox beliefs and "the Slavic soul" are one and the same, and that the former is the spiritual and cultural foundation of the latter. Therefore, he argues, all Russian children must know about Russian Orthodoxy in order to understand the nation's history and heritage.

The Russian Orthodox Church has become a powerful player in the politics of a culturally plural and residually secular society, and surveys indicate that the church is gaining ground even as followers of Islam and Buddhism, two other faiths of historic presence in the country, are relegated to lower status. Impressively robed clergy are prominent at official government functions, and many people in the streets can be seen to wear crosses. Nevertheless, school administrators in Russia's nearly 90 regions have some leeway in yielding to church pressure, so place still makes a difference: in a very general way, the greater the distance from Moscow, the less pervasive the power of the religious bureaucracy.

Some observers suggest that the resurgence of Christian fundamentalism, which accelerated in America after 9/11 and has impelled electoral candidates to court radical preachers and their legions of followers, is in large part a reaction to the global ascent of militant

Islam and its terrorist threat. But Christian conservatism also is a response to the rise of modern popular culture, much of which borders on the obscene. As a vehicle of cultural globalization, "concerts" involving onstage nudity, sexual innuendo, foul language, and other displays of decadence are deemed a threat to social standards and "family values" not only in conservative societies in the global periphery but also in religious circles in the global core. China's secular regime tries to control (to some extent) the content of such displays; the religious reaction in parts of the Western world is to go back to basics, whatever these may be perceived to be. Concepts of morality vary across cultures, but threats to it tend to elicit similar responses.

And religious horizons are being darkened in other areas of the world as well. In India, Hinduism has for millennia been faith as well as way of life, its fundamental doctrine that of karma, involving the transferability of the soul. All beings, animals as well as people, have souls and are arranged in a hierarchy determined by their behavior in past and present lives; good behavior leads to promotion, bad behavior to demotion. Thus the principle of reincarnation is a cornerstone of Hinduism: mistreat an animal in this life, and chances are that you will *be* that animal in a future life. The ideal is to keep moving up the ladder and then to escape from the eternal cycle through union with Lord Brahma, the creator. Although Hinduism is often referred to as a polytheistic faith and there seem to be countless gods in its pantheon, the other prominent ones—Lord Vishnu the preserver, Lord Shiva the destroyer, Lord Ganesh the elephant god—their wives, and the many lower ones, are all manifestations of the creator, Lord Brahma. And while it is often said that Hinduism has nothing equivalent to a Bible or Quran, it does have a holy book, the Bhagavad-Gita, a guide to the faithful and a chronicle of the gods.

Hinduism's incarnation-based reward system may encourage good behavior, but it also places a massive burden on those who are lowest on the ladder of life, because it implies that the lowest castes have themselves (in an earlier life) to blame for their condition. These people, once called "untouchables" but now referred to as *dalits* ("oppressed" or "broken"), are among the world's most disadvantaged locals and comprise as much as 15 percent of India's population. About 40 percent of the population are designated as backward castes, one important step above the lowest, and perhaps 20 percent are upper castes, at the top of which are the Brahmans, men in the priesthood (non-Hindu minorities constitute the remainder). Successive Indian governments have tried to help the lowest castes, with greater effect in urban than in rural areas. In the thousands of isolated villages in the countryside, dalits are often made to sit on the floor of their classroom (if they go to school at all); they are not allowed to draw water from the village well because they might pollute it; and they must take off any footwear when they walk past higher caste houses. But in the cities, the lowest castes have reserved places in schools, a fixed percentage of State and federal government jobs if they qualify, and a quota of seats in State and national legislatures.*

India has a history of clashes between its Hindu majority and large (15 percent) Muslim minority, but Hinduism's image has long been pacific and nonconfrontational. Centuries ago, India was under Muslim domination, but colonialism and partition created a dominantly Muslim Pakistan and Bangladesh and a Hindu-dominated India. While Hinduism had diffused into Southeast Asia before the colonial intervention, Buddhism and Islam overwhelmed it there and left isolated Hindu outposts, of which the Indonesian island of Bali is in many ways the most significant. But when the British colonists transported Indian workers to far-flung places such as South and East Africa, Malaysia, Fiji, and Guyana, Hindu holy men made no effort to proselytize or convert locals to Hindu beliefs. To this day, Hinduism remains an ethnic religion; religious conversion is not an issue when Hindu mobals arrive as intercultural migrants.

It is all the more troubling, therefore, that this placid religion has been infused with a vigorous nationalism that is altering the social landscape of India (and, not incidentally, the map of India itself). India is a multicultural country in every sense of that term, but a concept called *Hindutva*—Hinduness—has become the rallying cry of religious conservatives who want to remake India into a society in which Hindu principles will be standard. Hindutva enthusiasts want to impose a Hindu curriculum on the schools, change the currently flexible family law in ways that would make it unacceptable to Muslims, control and inhibit the activities of missionaries of other faiths,

---

* When the term "state" appears in this book, it refers to a country, for example the state of India. When it is capitalized, as in the State of Michigan, it refers to a constituent part of a country. Thus the State of Queensland is part of the federal state of Australia.

and forge an India in which non-Hindus are essentially outsiders. A powerful political party adopted these ideas and had notable electoral successes, although the good news is that its appeal has recently waned. Nevertheless, Hindutva retains a large core constituency and has taken on the trappings of a Hindu version of religious fundamentalism (Fernandes, 2006).

Certainly the ever-present tension between Hindus and Muslims plays a role in this development, a tension heightened regularly by disputes with Pakistan over Kashmir and periodically by terrorist attacks that Indians blame on Pakistani Muslims, such as the terrible train bombings in Mumbai (pre-Hindutva name: Bombay) in 1993 and 2006. One of the worst incidents of domestic strife, in Gujarat State in 2002 where more than 1000 Muslims were killed by rampaging Hindu mobs, came at the height of the first wave of Hindu-nationalist fervor and was not followed by appropriate prosecution of the perpetrators. Some observers refer to India as "one of the three largest Muslim countries in the world," but of course it is nothing of the sort any more than Bangladesh is one of the largest Hindu countries in the world (Sen, 2006). India's enormous Muslim minority of more than 160 million has little formative influence on the politics of state. Moreover, it fares poorly in economic as well as social terms: in some of India's States, education and poverty indicators show Muslims falling behind even dalits (Sengupta, 2006). Less than 4 percent of Muslims complete secondary school. India's Muslim minority has a small number of wealthy and successful globals (including the scientist who developed India's first nuclear weapon), a huge mass of poor locals, and almost no middle class. But India is a democracy, and so the country's poor Muslims vote overwhelmingly against the upper caste party that espouses Hindutva. The implementation of the Hindu fundamentalists' program would spell trouble for a society whose tolerance for diversity is *sine qua non*, but India is not immune to the radicalism of the Endarkenment.

Proponents of Hindutva, however, may meet their match in India's chaotic and corrupt democracy. Reverting a multicultural country as vast as this to rules as rigid as Hindutva's is likely to prove impractical and may produce a backlash not just among non-Hindus but among Hindu globals and mobals as well. Indeed, globalization seems to be having a reverse impact on one of Hinduism's key tenets, vegetarianism. In 2006, India's National Sample Survey reported that the country's per-capita consumption of poultry meat had doubled in five years and that the consumption of other meats was also rising. The trend was attributed to dropping prices, ready availability, and the growing stream of Indian globals and mobals traveling overseas where they could more easily ignore the religious strictures of home. While the conservative Bharatiya Janata political party (BJP) railed against such violations of Hindutva's code, growing economic interaction with the rest of the world was even eroding Hinduism's taboo against the consumption of beef and water buffalo meat, production of which was rapidly rising.

For India's locals as well as mobals, the country's current economic rise spells hope. Jobs for which Indians used to leave the country are now arriving in the automobile factories of Chennai and the supermarkets of Delhi (Luce, 2006). So strong is the need for Indian engineers that salary gaps between local and overseas jobs are shrinking. The burgeoning telecommunications industries may not pay anything like their American or European counterparts, but mobals preferring not to emigrate have made Bangaluru (Bangalore) the high-tech capital of India. And here's evidence of the flattening world for globals: recent American college graduates are arriving in India for corporate training, having spurned U.S. jobs in favor of experience in the periphery and a future in an Indian high-tech firm. Still, before we jump to conclusions regarding India's own flattening, consider this: the internal migration stream from India's mostly poverty-stricken countryside to its job-producing cities is just one-tenth the size of China's. In India's 600,000 villages, hundreds of millions of locals begin their lives malnourished, impoverished, and without the education that would give them the chance to escape from deprivation and indoctrination. In 2008, nearly half of all of India's children under five remain underfed and an estimated 250 million citizens survive on less than one dollar per day. For them, the factories of Chennai and the office parks of Bangaluru might as well be on Mars.

If religious fundamentalism can afflict a faith as avowedly peaceable as Hinduism, what of Buddhism, whose image of tranquility and contemplation would seem worlds away from assertive Islam and Christianity? Buddhism (like its even more life-venerating cognate, Jainism) is a philosophy of life, an ethical system more like Confucianism than a religion in the Muslim or Christian sense. This is not to say that Buddhism does not have its vigorous advocates; the father of the faith, whose life spanned most of the fifth century B.C., proclaimed his distaste for Hinduism's caste system and preached that salvation could be achieved by anyone through self-knowledge, self-control, and virtuous living. Growing up as a prince in a small kingdom in what is today Nepal, he was appalled by the misery he saw around him, and as the Buddha (the enlightened one) he chose to lead by example. He taught tirelessly, traversing South Asia and gathering a relatively small but devoted following.

Buddhism had its Shi'ite moment when its philosophies, a couple of centuries later, came to the attention of a powerful South Asian emperor, Asoka. Not only did Asoka commit himself to run his kingdom in accordance with Buddhist principles; he also sent missionaries to carry the Buddha's message to distant lands and peoples. It is possible that, late during Asoka's reign, there may have been more Buddhists in South Asia than Hindus, and it is certain that Buddhism later diffused far and wide: west toward the Mediterranean, south into Sri Lanka, north into Tibet, and east as far as Korea, Vietnam, and Indonesia. But even as it spread abroad, it began to lose steam in its source area. Hinduism revived, and the arrival of Islam dealt Buddhism severe setbacks throughout its domain.

As time went on, Buddhism split into numerous branches, of which the two leading ones are meditative Mahayana Buddhism, prevailing today from Vietnam to Japan and whose followers regard the Buddha as a divine savior, and Theravada Buddhism, dominant in Southeast Asia from Myanmar to Cambodia and visible in the cultural landscape through its dramatic pagodas and the saffron robes of its monks. The Lamaism of Tibet and Zen Buddhism of Japan are other manifestations. Unlike other sect-fractured religions, however, Buddhism has no history of sectarian strife. And over the past two centuries or so, Buddhism has proved its global appeal, gaining adherents in the Western world even as it was under pressure from communist and other autocratic regimes in its latter-day East and Southeast Asian strongholds.

Religious radicalism has not inflamed Buddhism as it has other global religions, and in that sense Buddhism has evaded the Endarkenment plaguing other major faiths. But Buddhist-dominated societies have been (and are) in conflict with followers of other belief systems, and it is clear that Buddhists, too, can abandon their principles in the face of threats and provocations. Still, such conflicts do not take on the religious intensity historically associated with the two largest religions. In Sri Lanka, whose population is 75 percent Buddhist, the majority confronts a mainly Hindu (Tamil) minority fighting for an independent state and a smaller Muslim minority caught in the middle. While the war is bitter and costly, it has never taken on primarily religious overtones, although Buddhist monks do engage in public demonstrations in support of the government side and play an increasingly obstructionist role in blocking government concessions to the Tamil rebels. In Thailand, where the overwhelming majority of the people adhere to Buddhism, a conflict has developed with the small Muslim minority in the southernmost provinces, on the border with (mainly Muslim) Malaysia. While the Islamic side proclaims this to be a case of religious oppression, the Thai government sees it as a matter of national security. Americans recall the self-immolation of Buddhist monks during the Indochina War; their protests were political, not religious, and their expectations were not of virgins in paradise, but of altered conduct on Earth. Their dramatic suicides were not aimed at American forces or innocent civilians. No attacks were launched against Vietnam's Christian churches in the name of Buddhism.

Nevertheless Buddhism, when it is the society's dominant faith (as it is not only in Sri Lanka but also in Myanmar, Thailand, Cambodia, Bhutan, and, of course, Tibet) or where it retains significant strength, as is the case in Laos, where about half the people adhere to it, makes a major mark on the cultural landscape through distinctive architecture as well as modes of dress. This is especially the case in the broad swath of Theravada Buddhism that extends across southern Southeast Asia, and in the monastic Lamaism of Tibet, where huge mountaintop monasteries dominate the countryside. It is less so in Vietnam, where most of the approximately 50 percent of the population that identifies itself as Buddhist adheres to Mahayana rules, which do not require service as monks or nuns and involve personal rather than demonstrative meditation and worship. In Thailand and Myanmar, the pagodas and stupas of Theravada Buddhism create striking, gold-infused vistas that confirm its dominance of the culture.

Indeed, Buddhism is recognized as the official belief system in Cambodia and as preeminent in Thailand, has special status in Sri Lanka, and in its Mahayana form is the state religion of the remote mountain kingdom of Bhutan. In Thailand, where more than 90 percent of the people are followers of the Theravada school, the national charter states that the government "must patronize and protect Buddhism and other religions." Ironically (because it is perhaps the most devoutly Buddhist society of all), it does not have such recognition in Myanmar, whose military regime has plunged the country into social malaise and economic ruin, where joining a monastery is about the only hope for job-seeking youngsters. If the streets of Myanmar's towns seem to be full of monks of all ages, it is because religion in some ways is the largest industry and monasteries provide minimal sustenance and some protection for their entrants. The Buddhist establishment had been remarkably passive in the face of the generals' excesses, even with hundreds of its order languishing in jail for nonviolently expressing their views, but in 2007 the situation changed when thousands of robed monks took to the streets in protest, flanked and cheered by tens of thousands of citizens. Ultimately it was to no avail. Citizens died in the streets, the protests faded, and the regime prevailed once again.

That even placid Buddhism is not immune from radicalization was underscored in Thailand following the outbreak of strife in its six southern (Muslim-majority) provinces, referred to earlier, where neither violent repression nor attempted conciliation could subdue an Islamic insurgency. As it happened, this issue arose during a crisis in the national government, resulting in the drafting of a new constitution. Buddhist nationalists (as they called themselves) demanded that the wording of the existing charter be strengthened in favor of Buddhism, arguing that the faith was under threat and required stronger government protection. This was accompanied by the spectacle of thousands of monks in religious garb marching behind elephants (the Thai national symbol) through the streets of Bangkok, representing a conservative clergy that is infusing Theravada Buddhism with a nationalist strain inconsistent with the precepts of the faith (*Economist*, 2007b). This crisis, too, waned, but not before a vein of radicalism was exposed in Buddhist activism.

Buddhism is often seen as the kindest of the major religions, but it shares with Hinduism the notion of demotion on the incarnation ladder as punishment for sins in a previous life. A nun caring for an abandoned, deformed child will believe that the child's disfigurement is evidence of dreadful misdeeds in a past life, tempering her sympathy. Nevertheless, Buddhism's sects are not at war with each other, Buddhist monks tend to lean to persuasion rather than conversion, and nothing comparable to Hindutva has arisen in the countries and cultures where Buddhism is the prevailing belief system. Some critics of Buddhism point to Jainism as the "enlightened" version of Buddhism, acceptable to even the fiercest critics of religion, but in truth Buddhism's essentially passive doctrines contribute little to the deadly sectarian divisions of this world (Harris, 2004).

Locals in Buddhist societies are no more programmed to proselytize their beliefs among adherents to other faiths than are Hindus or Sikhs. Although Buddhism has outliers in countries beyond its core area (for example, in Taiwan, South Korea, and Hawaii), Buddhist mobals tend to find no Buddhist communities in the world cities to which they migrate; the communities to which they move tend to be Vietnamese or Thai or Cambodian first and Buddhist (an often distant) second. Although Buddhist religious leaders naturally seek to assemble and instruct their adherents in such settings—the exiled Dalai Lama produces a steady stream of philosophical writings aimed at his own followers as well as a wider audience—they make no concerted effort to convert others to their beliefs. In general, they accommodate rather than confront behavior seen as decadent or depraved. Buddhist society in Thailand tolerates the country's notorious sex industry; its leaders leave no doubt as to their disapproval, but no Buddhist morality squads descend on Pattaya or Phuket to put robes and veils on bar women and drag off their male clients.

The twenty-first century Endarkenment, therefore, afflicts Islam and Christianity primarily and globally and Hinduism secondarily and locally. Other religions and belief systems have their revivalist (to use Islam's favored term) sectors with, as in the case of Judaism's Orthodox movement, disproportionate political power; but it is the Islamic and Christian domains into which the overwhelming majority of locals are born and from which the greatest number of mobals originate. By the time they interact, many have been radicalized by the internal conflicts of their faith and by the exhortations of fundamentalists capitalizing on interreligious strife. By seeking to implant their creeds through proselytism or compulsion in areas dominated by other beliefs, they complicate an already tense cultural mosaic and drive the world toward the cataclysm some of their own scriptures anticipate. Religion is in some ways the most powerful among the powers of place; religious convergence and interactive moderation would mitigate the cultural stresses associated with it. As it is, religious fervor intensifies, worsening social divisions and countering progress toward the flatter world of globalization.

4

THE ROUGH TOPOGRAPHY
OF HUMAN HEALTH

If we made a map of the world showing locales with prevailing good public health as mountains and areas with poor health as valleys, the resulting global topography would look rough indeed. The unequal distribution of health and well-being across the world is matched by inequities of health within individual countries, even inside regions and provinces. Whatever the index, from nutrition to life expectancy, from infectious disease to infant mortality, the geography of health displays regional variations that add a crucial criterion to the composite power of place. If it is obvious that the medical world is not flat, the question is whether the landscape of human health is flattening out.

Certainly health is a matter of natural environment, cultural tradition, genetic predisposition, and other factors, but power has a lot to do with it as well. In general, the poorest and weakest on the planet are also the sickest. The fact that, in the twenty-first century, 300 million people suffer from malaria and more than one million (mostly children) die every year has as much to do with figure 1.1 as it does with tropical environments and adapting vectors. The rich and medically capable countries of the core never sustained a coordinated campaign to defeat (or at least contain) malaria, a disease of the periphery of much lower priority than maladies of the mid-latitudes. Medical research in the United States and elsewhere did produce treatments for victims of the deadly HIV/AIDS pandemic that has taken more than 25 million lives over the past three decades, most of them in Subsaharan Africa, but those costly remedies are reaching far too few sufferers outside the global core.

The obvious link between persistent poverty and endemic disease, so evident from virtually any medical-geographic map of the global periphery, was one of the key factors that spurred all 191 members of the United Nations in 2002 to sign the UN Millennium Declaration, among whose eight Development Goals are the reduction of child mortality, the eradication of extreme poverty and associated hunger, and the defeat of major diseases, including malaria and HIV/AIDS. No scholar has done more to publicize and promote those goals than the economist Jeffrey Sachs, who, in his remarkable book *The End of Poverty*, underscores the link between geography and health, between place and wellness (Sachs, 2005).

Ancient, persistent malaria and modern, virulent HIV/AIDS bracket a host of diseases of the tropics, and the species-richness gradient referred to in earlier chapters plays its role here as well. Low elevations in low latitudes harbor a far greater number and variety of vectors, from mosquitoes to snails and from flies to worms, than higher latitudes (and higher altitudes) do. Malaria is not a threat to a child born in Mongolia or Chile, Finland or New Zealand. It constitutes a mortal danger to hundreds of millions of locals in lowland tropical Africa, South and Southeast Asia, and equatorial areas elsewhere. The mortality figures do not begin to reflect the impact of malaria on populations vulnerable to it. Where malaria is endemic, survivors develop a degree of immunity but are often debilitated. For locals seen by global visitors as listless and lazy on their jobs, malaria may be the energy-sapping cause. And malaria is only one of many infectious diseases to which tropical populations are exposed. There is progress, but it remains slow and by no means universal. For hundreds of millions, birthplace and wellness remain closely linked.

Tropical forests are among the riskier environs for human inhabitants. In much of tropical Africa and smaller areas of southern Asia and South America, wildlife and humans still live in close proximity, raising the risks of disease transmission from the former to the latter. Research indicates that HIV/AIDS in humans originated in Africa from a virus carried by chimpanzees in the area where Cameroon, Congo, and Gabon meet, and that this simian AIDS virus jumped species as long as 50 to 75 years ago (Altman, 2006). Since then, but initially undetected and confused with other diseases, HIV/AIDS has shortened life expectancies in Africa to levels not recorded for centuries, has incapacitated an entire generation and has orphaned 20 million children. It was not the first time in human history that people living amidst wildlife paid a terrible price, and it is unlikely to be the last.

And the hazard is not confined to wildlife sources. Smallpox, measles, and tuberculosis viruses made the jump from cattle to humans following livestock domestication; influenza came from pigs and ducks in what Jared Diamond calls the "lethal gift of livestock" (Diamond, 1997). We may now be in a preliminary stage of still another such transfer involving both domestic and wild birds in the diffusion of "bird flu." People born, and living, in close proximity to animals, wild or domesticated, are at higher risk.

In addition to these and many other vectored and nonvectored infectious diseases, human populations display a clustering of genetic maladies encoded on their chromosomes over time and inherited across generations. This is a tendentious arena of research, because it involves systematic biological differences between groups of people in different locations and invokes race as a factor in health. But it has long been known that the frequencies of particular alleles (alternate forms) of genes for specific blood and immune system proteins vary geographically (Cavalli-Sforza et al., 1994). Certain genetic disorders inherited over generations display strong geographic identity, including enzyme-related metabolic malfunctions such as lactose intolerance and blood cell abnormalities such as sickle cell anemia, as well as gene-influenced diseases such as type 2 diabetes mellitus and hypertension (Garfield, 2007).

In recent years, research in medicine as well as genetics has revived an argument long believed settled: whether human "races" are exclusively social constructs or whether they indeed exist, though not in the form entrenched in popular imagination (Leroi, 2005). An important study of more than 1000 people reported that "without using prior information about the origins of individuals, [the authors] identified six main genetic clusters, five of which correspond to major geographic regions, and subclusters that often correspond to individual populations" (Rosenberg et al., 2002). In other words, when computers sort DNA data from people around the world, humankind falls into six regional groups: African, European-Southwest Asian, Central-South Asian, East Asian, Amerindian, and Pacific, with subsets of local populations such as Basque, Pushtun, and Maya. This has implications for medicine as well as cultural geography, because identical treatment may not yield the same results across all populations. And it underscores the continuing vulnerability of locals in the periphery born into high-risk ecological and evolutionary environs remote from the knowledge and power concentrated in the global core.

GEOGRAPHY OF LIFE AND DEATH

Nearly a half century ago, the late British geographer L. Dudley Stamp used a series of lucid maps to illustrate geographic dimensions of global health and well-being (Stamp, 1964). His cartography not only revealed the regional endemism of vectored tropical diseases such as malaria and yellow fever, but also traced the frightening penetrations of higher latitudes by nonvectored infectious diseases with tropical origins, notably cholera. A look at this still-informative work tells us how much the medical landscape has changed since then— and how pervasive and enduring the planet's health problems are. Malaria has receded geographically but continues to afflict millions. Cholera no longer threatens cities in the global core with devastating pandemics, but deadly outbreaks continue. Dengue fever seemed to be on the way out but is making a comeback. HIV/AIDS was still in the future in 1964 but is now a major pandemic (Gould, 1993). Today the global human population is more than twice as large as it was when Stamp's book was published, and the medical gap between global core and periphery still is enormous.

The example of cholera is especially telling. Even today, with cholera's causes known, its prevention understood, and a vaccine available, cholera continues to kill, evincing the dangers still lurking, especially in crowded urban places with inadequate sanitation and in areas destabilized by armed conflict. Cholera made a reappearance in northern Iraq in mid-2007 and reached Baghdad in September of that year, an event that, amid the carnage of war, made little news. But the disease continues to plague the periphery.

The symptoms of cholera are well known. In the worst cases, intestinal blockage occurs within hours of infection, diarrhea and vomiting follow, and dehydration results. Unless treatment is quickly available, the skin shrivels, blood pressure falls, and muscular cramps and coma presage a convulsive death that may come as soon as two days or as late as a week after exposure. Not all of those infected die, but cholera's toll is always comparatively high among those infected and untreated.

To Europeans and Americans protected by environment and distance from tropical diseases, cholera had been an especially terrifying sickness, a lurking threat described by colonial settlers whose cause was uncertain and whose course was dreadful. An ancient malady long confined to its South Asian source area, cholera in the early nineteenth century quite suddenly spread to East Asia, East Africa, and Mediterranean Europe. That pandemic, beginning in 1816, abated in 1823, but by then its very name struck fear in people worldwide. No one knew what caused the disease or what measures to take when it invaded, and victims died by the thousands from Italy to Japan and from Turkey to Zanzibar. Then, in 1826 and again in 1842, cholera reached Western Europe and North America, wreaking havoc in England and the United States during two pandemics lasting 11 and 20 years respectively. The geographer G. F. Pyle elaborated Stamp's original map to chronicle the two-pronged attack that diffused cholera from its 1842 twin arrivals in New York and New Orleans into the Midwest and across the Rockies to San Francisco (figure 4.1).

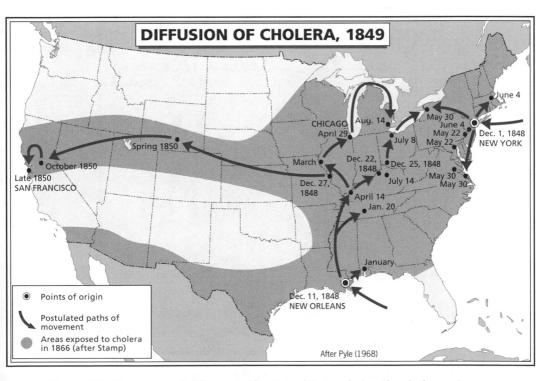

Figure 4.1. The routes of diffusion in the United States during the cholera epidemic of 1849, based on first dated reports of its appearance in specific locales. From L. D. Stamp (1964) and G. F. Pyle, "The Diffusion of Cholera in the United States in the 19th Century," *Geographical Analysis*, 1 (1969), p. 59.

It was during this third pandemic that the British physician-geographer John Snow used a still-famous map to confirm his theory that contaminated water was to blame for the transmission of cholera (figure 4.2). When the 1842 pandemic struck England, Snow mapped every new case and every death in London's densely populated Soho district, marking each victim's abode with a dot. Thousands of people fell ill in Soho, and more than 500 died. Snow's evolving map soon revealed a clustering of casualties around the intersection where Broad and Lexington Streets met. In the middle of that intersection stood a communal water pump, and Snow saw to it that the handle of that pump was removed, making it inoperable. Almost immediately, new cases in the area dropped to near zero, confirming the role of water in the spread of cholera and pointing the way toward protection against it (Johnson, 2006).

Figure 4.2. Physician-geographer John Snow marked each death and every new case of cholera in the London district of Soho with a dot on his 1854 map of the outbreak in England. Eventually the clustering of the dots pointed to the cause: contaminated water in the public well at the corner of Broad and Lexington Streets.

Boiling (and otherwise purifying) water is not, however, a luxury available to all who must use and consume it, and even after Snow's verification of the water–cholera link, still another pandemic erupted, beginning in 1865 and lasting a decade. In the United States it broke out on the East Coast in May 1866 and in New Orleans a couple of months later, spreading along the Great Lakes and up the Mississippi Valley and reaching Chicago, but sparing the West Coast. Knowledge of the deadly potential of contaminated water reduced the death toll in America and Europe, and by the end of the century it appeared that cholera was again limited to its South Asian source area and was no longer a worldwide threat.

That assessment, however, was premature, as events in the twentieth century proved. Occasional but local outbreaks in crowded urban areas of South and Southeast Asia could be contained and barely made the news, but in 1972 a deathly flare-up in Naples, Italy, reminded Europeans that cholera still posed a risk, even in the global core. Worse was to come: in the mid-1970s an outbreak of epidemic proportions struck 29 countries in Africa, its impact heightened by the violence repeatedly engulfing Rwanda and neighboring areas of the Congo. As the region's lakes and rivers were contaminated by countless corpses, cholera diffused widely, and only a massive international relief effort mounted in 1995 eventually stemmed the tide.

Nor were the Americas spared. The hemisphere had been free of cholera for more than a century when, in December 1990, the first cases of what was to become a serious epidemic were reported in a *barrio* of Lima, Peru, where the local water supply had become contaminated. Fast-spreading and virulent, this epidemic in its first year infected some 400,000 people and killed nearly 4000; five years later, every country in the hemisphere had been affected, more than one million people had been sickened, and approximately 10,000 had succumbed. Cholera struck rural as well as urban residents (in its initial diffusion through neighboring Ecuador and Chile, toxic irrigation waters and contaminated shellfish played a role); airplanes carried newly infected victims to normally cholera-free destinations, where others were exposed before diagnoses could be made.

The persistence of cholera into the twenty-first century continues to put millions at risk, even when the dangers are known, remedies are understood, and short-term vaccines exist. When areas in the global periphery are afflicted by cultural conflict, the incidence of disease always rises, as has been the case in eastern Congo and Rwanda. Again in the current decade, cholera has surged during the terrible crisis in Darfur and neighboring Chad. But cholera also continues to erupt under other circumstances, for example, in Senegal in 2005 when an outbreak occurred during and after a pilgrimage involving an estimated one million Muslims, and the resulting epidemic was worsened by heavy rains that flooded much of the capital, Dakar, with a population of three million. In 2006, economics rather than religion lay behind a major cholera epidemic in Angola, booming as a result of its rising oil production and the return of political stability. Poor sanitation in the burgeoning shantytowns encircling the capital, Luanda, coupled with a widespread shortage of drinking water, resulted in a cholera outbreak that quickly spread through the city and into the countryside. By the end of the year, the estimated toll had reached 50,000 cases and 2000 deaths. In 2007, the renewed collapse of order in Somalia led to still another outbreak in Mogadishu and Kismayu along the coast and, according to media reports, in the interior as well.

This tenacious geography of cholera forms a stark reminder that the planet's medical landscape is anything but even. Global businesspeople or tourists are no longer required to show a cholera vaccination certificate when they embark on a tropical journey, but those wanting it need only to call a clinic to be inoculated. In the unlikely event that a traveling global is infected in some tropical locale, medical intervention is available and affordable, and serious consequences are highly unlikely. But locals and mobals in the path of political violence or in the maelstrom of urbanization tend to face the risk without adequate access to remedies or preventive measures.

GLOBAL WARNING: DENGUE ON THE RISE

Cholera is only one of the risks faced by locals and mobals in the periphery. Unlike cholera, dengue fever, known as dengue hemorrhagic fever (DHF) in its most virulent form, cannot be averted by adequate sanitation practices or vaccination. Another disease originating in wildlife (in this case, monkeys in Southeast Asia), dengue fever today is resurgent. There is no known preventive treatment or antiviral cure, but there never was any doubt regarding its transmission.

The four known viruses that cause this disease are transmitted by mosquito species, among which the female *Aedes* mosquito is most efficient. The cycle is similar to that of malaria: the mosquito bites and ingests the blood of an already-infected person (a "host") and then bites someone not yet infected, thus enlarging the pool of hosts and spreading the risk as well as the malady. The symptoms at first suggest a severe flu, but as the fever rises the victim is wracked by nausea and vomiting, blinding headaches, unbearable joint pain, and fast-spreading rashes. In its most extreme form, DHF, it can cause internal and external bleeding and death. The World Health Organization (WHO) reports that between 2 and 3 percent of those infected die even when hospital treatment is available; when it is not, the toll can be as high as one in five.

Dengue fever (locals call it "breakbone fever") is an old malady, but its modern, death-dealing virulence is something comparatively new. It may have originated in Southeast Asia, spread to the Americas, and probably reached the eastern United States via the Caribbean in the late eighteenth century. In that form, it produced aches and pains and rashes, but it was not a killer (Meade and Earickson, 2005). The original vector in its source area, the *Aedes albopictus* mosquito (popularly known as the "tiger mosquito" because of its striped legs), preferred dense vegetated environs and left urban areas pretty much alone. As a result, urbanization actually reduced dengue fever's overall impact. But then the *Aedes aegypti* mosquito diffused worldwide from Africa, and this "supervector" not only invaded urban areas but also escalated dengue fever into deathly DHF.

The eradication of the *Aedes aegypti* during a massive campaign in the Americas is a story often told in conjunction with that of the construction of the Panama Canal, made possible by the defeat of yellow fever, but the mosquito never was exterminated in other parts of the tropics and continued to spread eastward. In the 1950s dengue fever made a comeback in the Philippines and Thailand, and this time urban populations were not spared. This was the start of a pandemic that took a far heavier toll, killing tens of thousands in Southeast and South Asia in its virulent DHF form. Meanwhile, the *Aedes aegypti* mosquito was recolonizing Middle and South America, a comeback with serious implications not only for dengue fever but also for diseases still closely associated with it, yellow fever and West Nile. Even dengue fever's original Asian vector, *Aedes albopictus*, made its appearance in a Texas port in boatloads of automobile tires and spread from there as far north as Virginia (Meade and Earickson, 2005). As a result, dengue fever has become endemic throughout the tropics and subtropics and now poses a health risk in city, suburb, and country-side (figure 4.3).

Again as in the case of malaria, the best defense against dengue fever involves attacks on the vector by preventing it from breeding, by spraying high-risk areas, and by sleeping under mosquito net-ting. But tropical heat and standing water are the mosquito's allies, and global warming and urban crowding are reversing a long-term decline that, just decades ago, seemed to presage the end of dengue fever as a serious threat. WHO assessments paint a bleak picture: den-gue fever is surging throughout the global periphery, and especially in Middle and South America. More than 100 low-latitude countries are affected, putting about 2.5 billion people at risk, most of them in urban areas. The WHO reports that dengue fever afflicts about 50 million people a year, a majority (as with malaria) children, of whom about 500,000 develop a form of dengue fever intense enough to require medical treatment (Budiansky, 2002). And these numbers are rising: Mexico reported nearly 30,000 cases in 2006, more than four times the number recorded five years earlier. DHF's incidence in Brazil in 2007 was about 50 percent higher than in 2006. Paraguay, by many measures the poorest of South America's major states and proportionally one of the world's worst-affected countries, in late 2007 reported a stunning tenfold increase over the previous year (*Economist*, 2007c).

Southeast Asia is another hotbed of dengue infection. Indonesian hospitals in 2007 treated nearly 100,000 cases and recorded about 1000 deaths; Malaysia and Thailand also counted infections in the tens of thousands. Even Singapore, known worldwide for its rigorous mosquito-control program, had more than 3000 cases by the autumn of 2007 (Arnold, 2007). Medical geographers leave no doubt that global warming is the key issue in a reversal that has major implica-tions for the future of populations in the periphery, but another fac-tor is the apparent adaptability of the vector. Not only is the mosquito enlarging its habitat due to climate change, but it is establishing itself in urban environs as never before. For the first time, dengue fever has made its appearance in areas of the global core, including the southern United States.

COUNTRIES AND AREAS REPORTING DENGUE FEVER, 2007

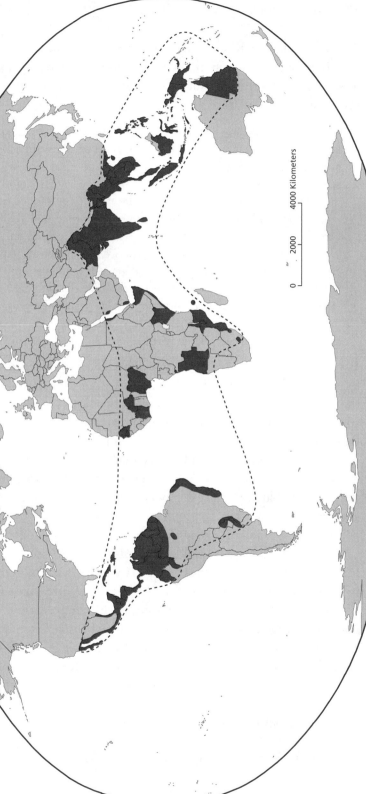

0   2000   4000 Kilometers

Figure 4.3. Dengue fever is on the rise and appears, from this map, poised to invade the southern United States, possibly on two fronts. Obviously the malady does not stop at international borders, so that the dashed line extrapolates the officially reported data to suggest its current extent.

As with cholera, though, dengue fever still is mainly a threat to the periphery, where the risk to globals is proportionally far lower than it is to locals. A recent narrative in an American newspaper describes the experience of a global visitor:

> Finishing my lunch at an open-air restaurant in downtown Bangkok, I felt slightly queasy. But by the time the taxi arrived back at my hotel, sweat was pouring out of my armpits, the folds of my stomach, even my shins, and my leg joints buckled....As I got out of the taxi, I collapsed onto the street. The taxi driver shoved me back into his cab and [drove to] Bumrungrad International...Hospital. I barely made it to the emergency room before I passed out. When I woke...my...doctor, trained in America, immediately put me at ease...."We're pretty sure you have dengue fever." My temperature had topped 104, but the doctor quickly determined that I did not have DHF....While I rested in a spotless room, he designed a program for my recovery, recommended a week of convalescence, and prescribed an array of medication for the searing joint pain. (Kurlantzick, 2007)

The global traveler then reflects on his good fortune, having seen local clinics in neighboring Myanmar, where patients had to bring their own bedding, bandages, and even needles. And when his fever spiked during his recovery, he walked to a nearby local hospital in Bangkok: "I sat on a hard bench in the middle of a waiting room littered with cigarette butts and empty plastic bottles. For over an hour, no one called me. When a nurse finally approached me, she warned that there would not be any doctors around for hours, and then turned and walked away." He had an experience common to locals in the periphery, for whom the road to better health has potholes aplenty.

A story told by entomologist Paul Reiter of the U.S. Centers for Disease Control and Prevention (CDC) in Atlanta and reported in 2002 by Stephen Budiansky in *Science* summarizes the core–periphery contrast in the geography of life and death: when dengue fever surged as its supervector multiplied in Central America, Mexico, and southern United States, the incidence of dengue fever reported along the Rio Grande showed an astonishing contrast. In Texas during the last two decades of the twentieth century, there were 64 reported cases. On the other side of the river, the Mexican States of Tamaulipas, Coahuila, and Chihuahua that border Texas reported 62,514 cases over the same period. This nearly 1000-to-1 ratio prevailed even though the population of the *Aedes aegypti* vector was known to be greater on the U.S. side of the river than on the Mexican side (Budiansky, 2002). The cause, Reiter points out, lies in economic conditions: in the Mexican cities and towns, window screens were relatively rare, and air conditioning still was the privilege of a small minority, so people—whether inside or out—were far more exposed to the disease carriers on the Mexican than on the American side. Extrapolate these circumstances to the availability of medical services on the two sides, and it is clear that even on the doorstep of the global core, the medical landscape is anything but flat.

WATER AND WELLNESS

The two foregoing examples describe maladies transmitted by water and mosquitoes respectively, but water plays the key role in both: the mosquito vector that transmits dengue fever (among other diseases) could not have its impact without being able to breed in hospitable pools and puddles of standing water. Water being the essence of life, it is no surprise that disease vectors thrive in it, and the clean, treated water that is the norm in the global core is far less ubiquitous in the periphery. Diarrheal diseases kill even more children annually than malaria, most of them (two million annually) in tropical Africa and Asia. The WHO reports that more than one-third of the world's population does not have access to improved sanitation. This still is a marked improvement over the proportional situation two generations ago, when more than half the planet's population was deprived of it, but the absolute numbers are not as encouraging: the population explosion exacerbated the sanitation problem exponentially.

Paradoxically, economic development in the form of dams, artificial lakes, irrigation schemes, and other water-control projects can actually worsen public health in the areas affected. Slow down or stop the rushing water in a creek or canyon, and you may expose local inhabitants and workers to diseases even as houses and jobs transform the economic landscape. Help shantytown residents who need taps and pumps store rainwater in cisterns and barrels, and you may multiply the mosquito population.

Reports of such unintended consequences abound, from the colonial-era Jezira irrigation scheme in Sudan, where the White and Blue Niles meet, to the High Dam on the Nile at Aswan (artificial Lake

Nasser) and the Volta Dam in Ghana. All caused increases in a disease called schistosomiasis by medical specialists and bilharzia by victims, a debilitating malady transmitted by freshwater snails. This vector sends infected larva into still or slow-moving water, which enter the body through the skin or body openings when people bathe or work in it. Once inside the body, they develop into mature worms whose eggs wreak havoc on the liver, kidneys, bladder, and other organs, eventually causing internal bleeding and severe skin rashes. In children, it stunts growth; in adults, it causes malnourishment. Schistosomiasis weakens the body against malaria, HIV, and other infectious diseases. You can live with bilharzia for 20 years or more, but its impact eventually spreads throughout the body and wears it down.

By some estimates, schistosomiasis is second only to malaria as humanity's most serious infectious disease, even though it is relatively confined to Africa (where it is most severe in two forms), South America, and East Asia, sparing India (figure 4.4). In tropical Africa, where schistosomiasis has been spreading markedly in recent years, some 700 million—virtually the entire population—may be at risk and almost 200 million are infected (Fenwick, 2006). Other estimates are lower, but all agree that more than 200 million persons in the global periphery suffer from it. All it takes is a drink from contaminated water or a swim, a bath, or a day's work in waters where the vector thrives to become a victim who may not be aware of her or his infection until much damage has been done. But dams continue to be built, and the latest of these often spectacular projects—China's Three Gorges Dam—may produce still another public health emergency because the Chang-Yangzi catchment area has long been affected by the *S. japonicum* form of schistosomiasis (figure 4.4).

Despite these troubling circumstances, there has been some progress against bilharzia in Middle and South America, parts of China, areas of Egypt, and all of Japan as a result of coordinated medical intervention, notably in Japan, and improved sanitation conditions elsewhere. In Africa, a drug (praziquantel) has been available for about two decades, but its cost has only recently put it within the reach of millions, and there may be hope for a reversal in what is still a worsening picture. Optimists point to the near defeat of another African water-related infectious disease, guinea worm, as a case in point. The guinea worm is a parasite that has caused immeasurable suffering to millions; its disease, dracunculiasis, is one of the most dreadful afflictions imaginable.

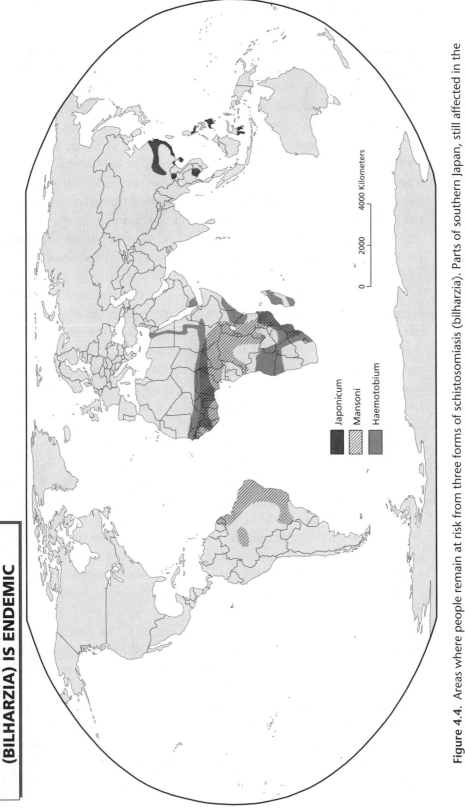

AREAS WHERE SCHISTOSOMIASIS (BILHARZIA) IS ENDEMIC

Japonicum

Mansoni

Haemotobium

Figure 4.4. Areas where people remain at risk from three forms of schistosomiasis (bilharzia). Parts of southern Japan, still affected in the 1980s, are now clear of the disease. Modified from G. Pyle, *Applied Medical Geography* (Silver Spring: Winston-Halsted, 1979), p. 47.

The vector is a water flea that hosts the larva of the worm, ingested by drinking water from canals or wells. The guinea worm then grows into an adult under the skin, reaching as much as 50 to 120 centimeters (20 to 50 inches) in length; a blister develops through which the worm protrudes to release millions of larva. Treatment involves pulling the worm out of the body, traditionally by winding it around a stick, often resulting in further infection. Although there is no vaccine or cure against dracunculiasis, prevention is possible through the use of larvicides and water filters. A coordinated campaign involving the WHO and several other agencies and concentrated in the worst-afflicted areas (notably southern Sudan and western Africa) has had remarkable results, so that in 2005 the WHO reported fewer than 13,000 cases—just 10 percent of the total a decade earlier.

But the continuing prevalence of other water-related diseases, especially in Africa, underscores the numerous risks faced by billions in the global periphery. In this first decade of the twenty-first century, there have been 198 million cases of hookworm in Africa alone, 173 million of ascariasis (roundworm), 162 million of trichuriasis (whipworm), and, worldwide, 120 million incidences of lymphatic filariasis (known as elephantiasis because of the grotesque swelling of lower limbs in its extreme form). Among the last, some 40 million people are effectively incapacitated (Budiansky, 2002). And while progress was being made against it, onchocerciasis (river blindness), vectored by flies, still affects approximately 18 million people in Africa. Yellow fever, once in retreat, is now surging again as a result of the continuing spread of its mosquito vector, *Aedes aegypti*, and claims about 30,000 lives annually. Water plays a role in all of them, either containing the vector, as in the case of schistosomiasis, or sustaining it, as it does the mosquitoes and flies that transmit other maladies.

The impact of water-borne disease on rural as well as urban populations in the periphery may be most severe in tropical Africa, but polluted waters endanger billions elsewhere, too. The tragic story of Bangladesh, where a nationwide project designed to bring clean water from underground sources to all villages resulted in widespread arsenic poisoning and cancer, is not unique (Chowdhury, 2004). In India, cultural as well as economic circumstances create a public health crisis that endangers the country's future. Hinduism's tenets make the Ganges (Ganga) River sacred, its ceaseless flow and spiritual healing power manifestations of the Almighty. Religious tradition has it that the river's water is immaculate and that no amount of human or other waste can pollute it. On the contrary: just touching the water can wash away a believer's sins. How much better to bathe in it and drink it! And this is what countless millions do in the temple-lined riverfront towns, entering and immersing themselves in one of the world's most severely polluted streams even as industrial waste, sewage, and animal and even human corpses float by. Countless thousands become ill, and many die, but tradition endures, and the river takes its toll even as it heals the spirit.

If the Ganges and its religious connotations make for a unique combination of circumstances, it remains true that the world's core–periphery division is also a clean-water partition. Safe water is ubiquitous in the global core; the estimated one billion people without access to it constitute about one-fifth of those in the periphery. Even where religion does not impel the consumption of polluted water, unclean surface streams may form the sole source of the ultimate essence of life, and thus the source of sickness as well. Many scientists warn of a global water crisis during the present century, and planetary warming may indeed cause it, but today the problem remains one of cost and priorities, of place and primacy.

THE MENACE OF MALARIA

About thirty years ago, an American tourist in Kenya fell ill while on safari in a national park. He had spells of high fever and chills and periods of intense perspiration, complained of nausea and severe headaches, and vomited repeatedly. He was rushed to a Nairobi hospital, where foreign visitors suffering from malaria were occasionally treated before being sent home. This case was unusual: he lapsed into a coma, suffered shock and renal failure, and died shortly thereafter, but not before his plight had come to the attention of the American media. More space was devoted in the press to this dramatic and unusual incident than worldwide malaria usually got in a year. Television commentary centered on the risk of international travel and the preventives available to globals before leaving the country. Comparatively little was said about the billions of locals in the periphery who, if they survive childhood, live with the risk of malaria, or with the debilitating aftermath of infection, every day.

On the day you read this, about 3000 people will die of malaria worldwide, most of them, again, in tropical Africa. Every 30 seconds, a child dies from malaria in Africa alone (Fenwick, 2006). More than one million locals—the overwhelming majority of malaria victims are locals—will die of it this year. The WHO estimates that about 300 million people suffer from the symptoms of malaria, but other approximations are significantly higher. Malaria totally incapacitates tens of millions and causes hundreds of millions to struggle in exhaustion with chronically severe anemia (Meade and Earickson, 2005). Living with the enervations of malaria is the lot of literally countless people in the poorer areas of the world, countless because many of them never go to a clinic, never see a doctor, and never become part of official statistics.

Everyone knows that mosquitoes transmit malaria, but the geographic question is why malaria causes so many more deaths in tropical Africa than in all other regions of the world combined. As it happens, the cause lies in the nature of the vector. The *Anopheles* mosquito comes in about 60 species, all of which transmit various forms of malaria, but the one prevailing in tropical Africa—where it has co-evolved with humanity—is by far the most efficient. This, *Anopheles gambiae*, carries the deadliest among the malaria parasites, *Plasmodium falciparum*. Furthermore, unlike many other species, this mosquito prefers to bite humans rather than animals, greatly increasing the rate of transmission. After taking blood from an already-infected host, the mosquito needs to live between ten days and two weeks for the parasite, which multiplies in its body, to reach its salivary glands. Once there, it enters the victim's body (commonly a child's) during the next bite.

If it were not for *Anopheles gambiae*'s preference for humans, this cycle would be far less efficient than it is in tropical Africa. In South Asia, where malaria is also endemic but much less deadly, the mosquito species responsible for most transmissions also feeds on cattle, greatly reducing the chance that two consecutive bites will involve people. Researchers calculate that, as a result, the likelihood of transmission in tropical Africa is between eight and nine times as high as it is in India (Dunavan, 2005).

Nor are all variants of the disease equally deadly. The type spread by *Plasmodium falciparum* is most lethal, causing the great majority of deaths annually. But there are three additional forms of malaria transmitted by other mosquito species in South and Middle America, Asia, New Guinea, and neighboring Pacific islands that are less fatal (New Guinea has the worst of it outside of Africa). And in any case, all forms of malaria can be prevented or treated, the occasional fatality—such as that Kenya tourist—excepted. For a time, chloroquine looked to be the answer to malaria worldwide, producing "one of the greatest public health advances ever achieved by a drug against an infectious disease" (Wellems, 2002). Highly effective, cheap, easily taken, and with few side effects, chloroquine vastly reduced the death toll from malaria during the 1950s and 1960s, when additional attacks on the vectors—notably through the use of the pesticide DDT—suggested that malaria's days were numbered. But then the parasites began to develop resistance to chloroquine, and alternative drugs proved to be unsatisfactory substitutes. Soon, malaria was resurgent, its toll rising dramatically, especially in Africa. The first coordinated attack on the disease had failed. Since then, other drugs have yielded the same results: early success, later weakening as a result of parasite resistance. The latest hopes are the artemisinin-based "wonder" drugs derived from the woody wormwood plant *Artemisia annua*, long used in Chinese traditional medicine, that cure 90 percent of patients within days—but the first signs of resistance-related mutations were recently found in several parasites (Vogel, 2005). Experience with drugs has led many activists to recommend alternate (or combined) strategies, including the dissemination of pesticide-treated mosquito nets and the renewed spraying of pesticides banned during the 1960s for their toxic effects.

The earlier campaign's failures notwithstanding, a map showing the prevalence of malaria over a period of half a century reveals that the malady was essentially driven out of the global core and then left to fester in the periphery (figure 4.5). That is one reason why malaria was the only vectored infectious disease mentioned by name in the headings of the UN Millennium Development Goals; calls soon arose for the resurrection of the worldwide campaign against malaria (Sachs, 2002). Although malaria is probably perceived in the global core as a tropical-climate disease (and heat certainly energizes its vectors), mosquitoes capable of transmitting it range from equatorial to polar latitudes, their only prerequisite being the availability of water, even for just a few weeks in high latitudes. Indeed, malaria plagued Western Europe even during the Little Ice Age four centuries ago,

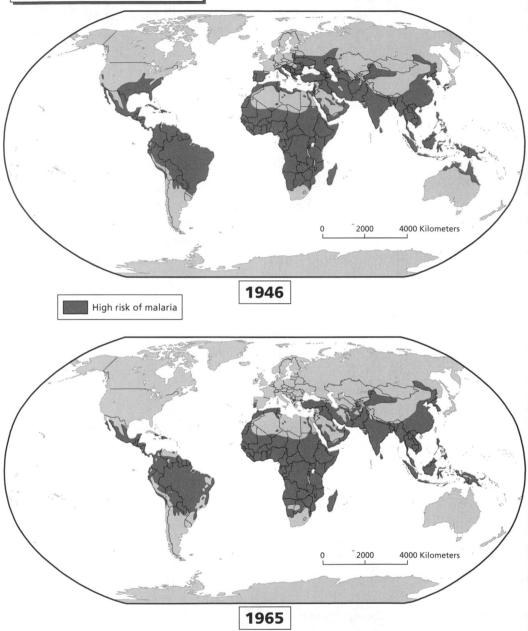

MALARIA: AREAS OF HIGH RISK, 1946–2005

High risk of malaria

1946

0   2000   4000 Kilometers

1965

0   2000   4000 Kilometers

Figure 4.5. Although malaria continues to take a huge toll every year, these maps indicate that the areas of high risk have shrunk significantly over the past six decades, the result of worldwide efforts to control its vectors and to reduce exposure, especially among children. The decade of the 1990s saw major progress in India, and by 2005 the largest remaining area of high risk lay in Africa. In recent

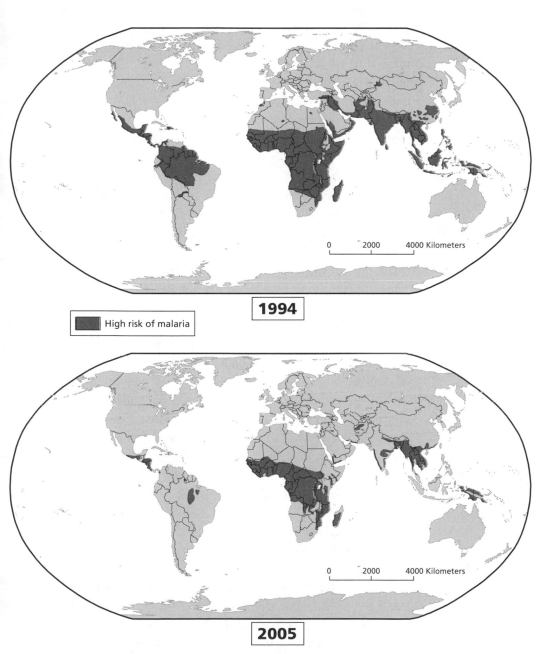

1994

High risk of malaria

2005

years anecdotal reports of a resurgence of the malaria mosquito and the return of malaria to recently vacated areas have been causing concern, and some scientists attribute such developments to global warming. From United Nations World Health Organization and J. D. Sachs and J. L. Gallup, "The Economic Burden of Malaria," *American Journal of Tropical Medicine and Hygiene* 61 (2001), p. 85.

and outbreaks occurred in Scandinavia as recently as the nineteenth century. Spain, Portugal, and Italy suffered from malaria until the late 1960s. The Netherlands declared itself malaria-free in 1970; Canada had outbreaks in the 1800s and the United States did not declare victory over malaria until 1954. Malaria's ouster from the global core is a relatively recent accomplishment.

What figure 4.5 reflects is a combination of antimalaria tactics available and affordable in economically richer countries and less obtainable in poorer ones. In the United States, malaria still was endemic in much of the South as recently as the 1940s, but the invention of the window screen was fast diffusing through the country, and air conditioning in homes and automobiles would soon change the habits of millions. Local, State, and national programs of mosquito control reduced the vector's overall numbers as well as the percentage of parasite carriers. In the late 1990s, Mexico still had large areas of high risk, but the American South had been malaria-free for nearly a half century.

In Africa, however, the situation had deteriorated, improving only in a small number of locales where experimental remedies were being tried. A combination of Africa's especially virulent parasites and efficient, adaptable vectors, its persistent and in many areas worsening poverty, the collapse of public health facilities, the population explosion, the continuing prevalence of other vectored infectious diseases, and the impact of the HIV/AIDS epidemic made tropical Africa the world's most malaria-vulnerable realm. In 2007, malaria still was endemic in all or part of more than 100 of the world's countries, more than 40 of them in tropical Africa. Of the world's population approaching seven billion, 40 percent live in areas where malaria is endemic. Of tropical Africa's more than 700 million inhabitants, more than 90 percent live with the effects or threat of malaria—if they survive childhood.

As figure 4.5 shows, the retreat of malaria between the 1940s and the 1990s never touched Africa, except in the far south where the realm extends southward beyond the Tropic of Capricorn. South Africa reported malaria cases into the mid-twentieth century in what was then its northern (Transvaal) and eastern (Natal) provinces, and Botswana and Namibia later than that. By the mid-1990s, these three countries and historically malaria-free Lesotho (because of its mountainous elevations) were the only four malaria-free states in the realm. Malaria lingered in southern Moçambique and in the adjacent *lowveld* of Swaziland, but in effect South Africa's *highveld* and adjacent areas, Africa's wealthiest region, also comprised its least malaria-afflicted zone. A combination of economic and environmental conditions—the latter including high elevations in the east and desertlike aridity in the interior and west—gave southern Africa advantages against malaria that other parts of the realm did not have. In the north, some progress was made in the area of the elbow of the Niger River and along the Atlantic coast, but none in the forest and savanna zones of West Africa.

In any case, notions of the eventual eradication of malaria have been abandoned in favor of various means of control. Even as the UN Millennium Development Goals identified "combating" malaria as a priority, it had become clear that malaria would not be subject to the rising optimism involving predictions of victory over waterborne infectious diseases (Fenwick, 2006). The malaria map of 2015, when it is drawn, will not continue the sequence shown in figure 4.5: "More than 1.7 billion people live in once-endemic areas in which transmission had been greatly reduced but is now reinstated, and in which the ecology is unstable and the situation is deteriorating. The mosquito vectors are resistant to all the major insecticides, the agent is resistant to all the major drugs, and the ancient scourge is upon us again" (Meade and Earickson, 2005). This means that behavioral interventions are the key, especially the dissemination of insecticide-treated mosquito netting, free or affordably; hundreds of millions of children in the periphery sleep in housing without windows or screens and thus totally exposed to malaria's vectors. If infants and children can be protected until they have had a chance to learn preventive behaviors such as recognizing the time of day when mosquitoes are especially aggressive (which varies by vector and locale), and when they are sufficiently mature to benefit from the partial immunity acquired from their mothers, the terrible infant and child mortality from malaria will decline. This does not mean that the debilitation of malaria will disappear, but it will strike fewer, take effect later in life for more victims, and reduce the menace of this malady overall. Bring technology to bear on the attack on the vectors' breeding places (helicopter spraying has long been part of the arsenal in the global core), and use pesticides as a matter of choice between evils. And continue research on new preventive drugs as old ones are defeated as part of a war on malaria that will save more lives than any "war on terror." But "victory" will be equally elusive.

On what grounds are medical geographers pessimistic over the observed resurgence of malaria? Global warming is sometimes cited as a cause, but no concrete evidence exists as yet, and as noted above, malaria is not strictly a tropical disease (Botkin, 2007). Nevertheless, anecdotal reports suggest that malaria is again moving upslope in East Africa, where the phenomenon is indeed attributed to warmer temperatures.

The recent recolonization of the tropical Americas by *Aedes aegypti* may have more to do with global trade and human modification of the biotic environment than with any planetary warming. This vector probably first reached the Americas from Africa in water containers carried aboard the slave ships of the seventeenth century, spreading the yellow fever that delayed the construction of the Panama Canal three centuries later. The massive campaign against it, however, did not eradicate it completely, but left it in niches remote from human habitation. One of these is the upper canopy of equatorial rainforests. Biologists report that you can walk across the forest floor without ever being bitten by the mosquito—until you reach an area where tree-cutting, settlement, and farming are in progress. With the ground covered by downed canopy, mosquito vector and human victim are again in close proximity, and an old cycle of infection restarts. Yellow fever is on the rise again, hitherto mostly in rural areas of poor countries, but the WHO warns that urban outbreaks could begin again at any time. And the vector also is implicated in the recent diffusion of West Nile fever. Such scenarios give rise to concerns about the future of malaria, which, vectored by *Anopheles darlingi*, is already spreading in South America through the same deadly parasite that kills so many people in Africa and, in lesser but still substantial numbers, in India. What if *Aedes gambiae*, Africa's supervector, colonizes tropical Asia or the Americas?

Another worry centers on a hallmark of globalization: migration. As noted in preceding chapters, the number of mobals as a fraction of the Earth's human population still remains small, but it has long been clear that labor migrations play a role in the diffusion of infectious diseases (Prothero, 1963). The danger actually works two ways: migrating mobals expand the host population for infectious diseases they carry from their source areas, potentially contributing to their further diffusion; but the mobals themselves also fall victim to endemic diseases against which locals may have some acquired passive immunity but migrants do not.

Malaria, perhaps more than any other malady, symbolizes the contrasts between global core and periphery when it comes to health. It is still endemic in vast areas of the world; it kills disastrously, it puts billions at risk, and its debilitations afflict countless millions who survived infancy and childhood but have the misfortune to suffer its degenerative exhaustions for life.

MULTIPLE BURDENS FOR MANY

While no one would claim that the Earth is medically "flat," it is troubling to note that conditions in large areas of the periphery are in some ways worse than they were a half century ago. Many locals in the global periphery carry the burden of multiple diseases, not all of which can be detailed here, ranging from tuberculosis to trypanosomiasis (sleeping sickness) and from trachoma, a disease of the eye persisting in poorer areas of the world, to measles (still a serious local threat). In many countries of Subsaharan Africa, the source of the current HIV/AIDS pandemic, the "slim disease" has lowered life expectancies to levels not seen since medieval times and is in the process of orphaning some 20 million children.

The relationships between HIV/AIDS, tuberculosis, and malaria illustrate one aspect of this complicated picture. It is well known that HIV/AIDS weakens the immune system, so that many victims stricken by HIV/AIDS die from other causes, notably tuberculosis. Now it is also clear that those carrying HIV are likely to be more vulnerable to malaria, because the damage inflicted on the immune system by the virus allows the malaria parasite to multiply more easily and faster. This makes the carrier of both HIV/AIDS and malaria a more efficient host for transmission than someone infected by malaria alone.

In truth, hundreds of millions of locals in areas where endemic diseases overlap carry the debilitations of two, three, even as many as six maladies. The slow-moving or standing waters where the parasites of schistosomiasis thrive are also favorite breeding grounds for mosquitoes that spread malaria. The same muddy ground that risks hookworm penetration of the human foot can transmit diarrheal diseases via the mouth; twice as many African children die annually from diarrheal diseases than from malaria. The same poor sanitation that risks cholera can pass on the bacteria that cause trachoma. The same mosquito that spreads yellow fever also transmits dengue fever. Even if the statistics show that infant and child mortality in the global periphery are declining and life expectancies (tropical Africa excepted) are rising, such data do not tell the whole story. It is the geographically variable *quality* of life that renders the global medical landscape anything but flat.

PARADOX OF GLOBALIZATION

For some globals, though, the world has indeed become medically flatter—the same globals who travel the world on business or as tourists along those corridors of comfort provided by wide-bodied aircraft, air-conditioned automobiles, and "international" hotels. They can count on the best medical care available should they fall ill in places far from home because they have the funds, the knowledge, and the support system to secure it. That combination of advantages is one of the products of globalization: the wealthy elites in many poor-country cities of the periphery, combined with often-substantial numbers of expatriates, require modern medical care usually provided by both private and some public hospitals.

The experiences of globals in such faraway facilities are almost universally favorable, notably their low cost. This has led to what is in effect a new industry: medical tourism. Globals now compare the expense of treatment ranging from a facelift to knee replacement and find that they can travel halfway around the world, have their surgery, and convalesce on a tropical beach or at a superior spa for less than they would have paid for the operation in America or Europe—sometimes as much as 75 percent less (Woodman, 2007). A global network of insurers, hospitals, doctors, and support services is drawing a fast-growing clientele from the global core; in 2007, an estimated 150,000 Americans, some of them uninsured and looking for low-cost treatment, traveled abroad for health care. Some governments, India, Thailand, Brazil, and the Philippines among them, are getting involved, helping the industry and promoting the concept.

The government of Singapore has announced that it expects to attract as many as one million "medical visitors" annually within five years.

Does this development confirm that the Earth is getting flatter? On the contrary: several of the countries pursuing globals with medical needs do not have adequate public medical services for their own people, and they are already losing locally trained medical personnel to higher salaries paid in the core (American hospitals are actively recruiting South African nurses; Indian physicians emigrate to the United Kingdom and America by the hundreds). Domestically, the higher salaries paid by the medical-tourist industry are drawing doctors away from local hospitals and clinics. The contrasts between resortlike hospitals for foreigners and overcrowded facilities for locals are causing angry commentary in the media. But the globals have the advantage, and not just Americans and Europeans. The fastest-growing clientele in recent years has come from oil-rich countries in Southwest Asia, where wealth cannot always buy the highest standard of medical care.

To globals who travel the planet at will, good health can be pursued to the ends of the Earth. To locals who live with endemic diseases and genetic vulnerabilities, place continues to wield a menacing power over destiny.

5

GEOGRAPHY OF JEOPARDY

Everyone lives with risk, every day. In the United States, more than 100,000 persons die from accidents every year, nearly half of them on the country's roads. Worldwide, an average of more than 5000 coal miners perish underground annually, a toll often forgotten by those who oppose nuclear power generation on grounds of safety. From insect bites to poisoned foods and from smoking to travel, risk is unavoidable. Certain risks can be mitigated through behavior (not smoking, wearing seatbelts), but others are routinely accepted as inescapable. A half century ago, long before hijackings and airport security programs, the number of airline travelers continued to increase robustly even as airplanes crashed with considerable frequency. Today, few drivers or passengers are deterred by the carnage on the world's roads, aware of it though they may be. Risk is part of life.

Risk, however, also is a matter of abode, of location. Who, after experiencing or witnessing on television the impact of a hurricane, a tornado, an earthquake, a volcanic eruption, a flood, a blizzard, or some other extreme natural event, has not asked the question: "Where in the world might be a relatively safe place to live?" Geographers, some of whom have made the study of natural hazards and their uneven distribution a research priority, don't have a simple answer. But on one point they leave no doubt: people, whether individually or in aggregate, subject themselves to known environmental dangers even if they have the wherewithal to avoid them. Many Americans build their retirement or second homes on flood-prone barrier islands along coastlines vulnerable to hurricanes. The Dutch, who have for many years been emigrating from the Netherlands in substantial numbers, are leaving for reasons other than the fact that two-thirds of their country lies below sea level. From Indonesia to Mexico, farmers living on the fertile slopes of active volcanoes not only stay where they are, but often resist even temporary relocation when volcanic activity resumes. From Tokyo to Tehran, people continue to cluster in cities with histories of devastating earthquakes and known to be situated in perilous fault zones. Fatalism is a cross-cultural human trait.

In some ways the question about safety and location is the ultimate geographic query, and geographers have studied this issue for a very long time and with significant results. Gilbert White, as Director of the Institute of Behavioral Science at the University of Colorado, focused on people's propensity to continue living in the floodplains of major rivers and analyzed human behavior in the face of natural hazards in more general terms as well. A Hazards Research Laboratory forms an integral part of the Department of Geography at the University of South Carolina, and many other academic programs in geography, in the United States and elsewhere, include a natural-hazards "track" that allows students to specialize in this complex field. In this time of environmental change and potentially abrupt climate swings, they have their work cut out for them.

Danger—real, perceived, or denied—forms a significant factor in the composite power of place, and not all dangers are natural. Although the focus in the pages that follow is on environmental hazards and their regional variance, the perception of risk attaches to place at all levels of scale. In any city, there are neighborhoods regarded as "safer" than others. In any country, there are cities whose crime rates figure prominently in their imagery. All highway networks have sectors more dangerous than others. But such realities are the stuff of frequent media coverage, their implications reinforced by statistics. These, in turn, affect perception and behavior.

But less immediate environmental dangers tend not to be on everyone's mind, not even in pre-Katrina New Orleans despite repeated warnings, in the scientific literature as well as in the media, that the city and its environs faced catastrophe in the event of a hurricane's direct hit (Fischetti, 2001). When nothing serious happens for a long time (on the human time scale, not the geologic one), cautions tend to be ignored and daily concerns rather than distant risks take precedence. As a result of a combination of historic and amnesic conditions, more than two billion people live today in areas of high environmental danger, millions of them by choice. Accelerating climate change is now worsening the odds for many of them.

HAZARDS FROM THE HEAVENS

Ultimately, of course, no place on Earth is completely safe. Our planet has been bombarded throughout its history by asteroids large enough to penetrate its atmospheric shield and strike the surface with devastating effect. The last really big one, about 65 million years ago, ended the age of the dinosaurs and opened the geologic era that witnessed the emergence of primates. Consider that it was only about 10 kilometers (six miles) in diameter when it hit the surface of Mexico's Yucatan Peninsula at about 90,000 kilometers per hour (55,000 miles per hour) and set most of the planet on fire, and you realize how vulnerable the Earth is. Nor was this the first time the Earth's evolutionary history was altered by powerful impacts causing mass extinctions. Geologists know of several earlier ones and are finding additional evidence suggesting that such collisions occur, on average, about every 100 million years. Humanity would have been unlikely to survive any of them, but even the much smaller asteroids that have struck the planet since—and do so with shorter intervals—would have devastating consequences.

Flying across northern Arizona, you can see evidence of a collision that occurred when the Earth was already inhabited by humans: Meteor Crater, about 1200 meters (4,000 feet) in diameter, its floor 180 meters (600 feet) deep inside a rim that rises nearly 60 meters (200 feet) above the surrounding plain. Estimated to have struck about 50,000 years ago, when North America had not yet been reached by our migrating ancestors, the meteor that caused this huge cavity was only about 60 meters across—about 10 car lengths—but its impact was undoubtedly noticed around the world. A giant cloud of pulverized rock reached beyond the stratosphere, was propelled into Earth orbit, and darkened skies across southern North America, the Mediterranean, and inner and eastern Asia, perhaps for years. Now some scientists are postulating that this was not the only recent impact of its kind in (or over) North America. In 2007 a group of geoscientists at a meeting of the American Geophysical Union theorized that a huge comet exploded in the atmosphere somewhere over northern North America about 13,000 years ago, eradicating the first wave of human migration from Asia and their culture, wiping out the mammoths and other fauna, and triggering a thousand-year return to ice-age climate (Kerr, 2007).

This would explain why the global warming that had been driving back the glaciers for several thousand years was suddenly interrupted by what environmental scientists call the Younger Dryas, a millennium of frigid conditions long attributed to other causes, so that this event—if it happened—did not just affect North America, but the entire Northern Hemisphere.

At present, the evidence for this mega-event is still being debated, but in geologic perspective, 13,000 years ago is the blink of an eye, and if that postulated catastrophe did occur so recently, we should obviously approach the risks from space more urgently just when we are spending the money needed on expensive weaponry and wars instead. It is reasonable to infer that the smaller the asteroid, the greater the frequency of impact or near-impact. Nothing like the meteor that struck in Arizona is known to have reached the Earth since, although it is possible that one or more large meteors splashed down somewhere in the global ocean. The comet that may have exploded overhead 13,000 years ago did not leave an impact crater, but this only underscores that the record on the Earth's surface does not fully represent the frequency of cataclysm.

As it happens, the Earth got a wakeup call just a century ago when, in the early morning of June 30, 1908, residents of present-day Russia's Krasnoyarsk and Evenkiyskiy regions in central Siberia saw what looked like a brightly burning moon streak across the sky in a northerly direction, clearing the forested horizon before exploding in a flash of fire. When search parties reached the scene, they found no crater, but a huge patch of flattened trees lying in a radial pattern some 32 kilometers (20 miles) across in the basin of the Tunguska River. If this was a meteorite, it had left no metallic evidence, but it was clear that something had exploded just before reaching the ground. Scientists theorize that it was an icy comet big enough to survive its fiery passage through the atmosphere, its final blast causing the destruction on the surface below, a miniature version of what may have taken place 13,000 years ago over North America.

It is not difficult to imagine what would have happened had this comparatively small icy comet (if that is what it was) exploded over a major urban area, or even above a populated rural area. Death and dislocation sowed from space would have had a lasting influence on human emotions, but in short order the Russian Revolution, two World Wars, and the Cold War occupied the world's attention.

To scientists, however, "Tunguska" was indeed a wakeup call. As astronomers became ever more aware of the billions of orbiting comets and meteorites and the potential for collision with planet Earth, a program called Spacewatch was launched to track as many "Earth-Crossers" and "Earth-Approachers" as could be identified. By the late 1990s, it was already possible to predict the trajectories of some that could pose a future risk. The first of these to come to global attention was the asteroid 1997 XF11, with an estimated diameter of about 1.5 kilometers (1 mile), whose projected orbit put it on a potential collision course with Earth in 2028. Later calculations modified that prediction, but not before serious discussions had begun over the feasibility of pulverizing approaching comets with explosives or diverting them from their collision course by attaching rockets to them, firing the engines, and changing their orbits. Today, with limited funding and growing awareness of the dimensions of the risk, scientists are sounding an alarm: they are seeing far more asteroids posing a potential risk than they are able to keep track of.

No place on Earth, obviously, is safe from extraterrestrial bombardment; the impact-cratered moon reminds us of the dangers from space. But the risks from air, sea, and land far outweigh those from the Solar System—at least over the short term. The perils of nature on the surface of the planet still define the power of place.

CORE, PERIPHERY, AND EXPOSURE

The distribution of danger on planet Earth displays none of the core–periphery dichotomies cited in earlier chapters, and for obvious reasons: environmental opportunities and advantages in the places that impelled human clustering did not usually display evidence of the hazards they entailed. When migrants streamed into the lower basins of China's great rivers, they learned to adapt to the vagaries of floods and droughts, disadvantages far outweighed by the fertility of local alluvial soils and the expectation of good crop yields. It is safe to conclude that none of them considered their vulnerability to sea level rise caused by global warming. When the Japanese chose Tokyo (then called Edo) as the site of their new capital in 1868, its record of recurrent earthquakes was well known, but political and cultural considerations overrode the risks, and in any case the city was already Japan's largest and had survived its repeated misfortunes. Had Japan's nineteenth-century planners been aware of the implications of Tokyo's location near the convergence of three of the Earth's major tectonic plates, they might have considered a contingency locale, which is now a topic of national discussion (figure 5.1). And had they realized that the "seventy-year rule"—major earthquakes had been recorded in 1633, 1703, 1782, and 1853—would prevail into the twentieth century, they would undoubtedly have reconsidered their choice. In 1923, the Great Kanto Earthquake set off a firestorm followed by a tsunami that, in combination, killed an estimated 143,000 people. Today, Tokyo lies at the heart of the world's largest conurbation and is a global node of finance and commerce, a mixture of skyscrapers and traditional buildings crisscrossed by countless kilometers of gas lines. All of Japan, and much of the

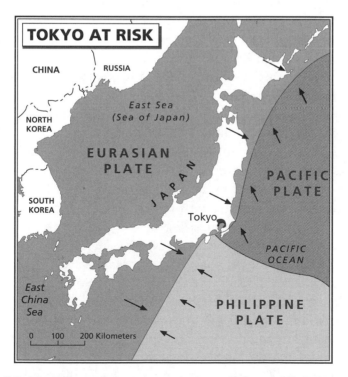

Figure 5.1. The Tokyo-Yokohama conurbation, still the world's most populous metropolitan area, lies near the convergence of three tectonic plates in one of the Earth's most dangerous locales.

global core, held its breath at some time during 1993, when the seventy-year anniversary of the Great Kanto Earthquake passed. Ever since, the question has been how long Tokyo's good fortune will hold, and how well the city's "earthquake-resistant" high-rises will perform when the time comes.

A century ago, the geographer Alfred Wegener set in motion research that ultimately revealed the crust of planet Earth to be made of mobile slabs, some geologically old, others young, some large, others small. He called his hypothesis *continental drift*, because the movement of continents was key to it; today we know that the continents are carried on those slabs, and the theory is known as *plate tectonics*. But a map of the world's known (and named) tectonic plates is more than a geologic curiosity (figure 5.2). Where moving plates converge, the crust shakes and fractures and is crushed into mountains, and earthquakes and volcanic eruptions as well as spectacular scenery mark the zone of collision. Where plates diverge, the fissures allow huge quantities of lava to pour forth onto the surface. Much of the latter happens at the bottom of the oceans, where new crust forms and intense heat produces a submarine animal life still only partially known. So, in a very general way, suboceanic plates tend to be geologically young and continental plates are older.

A map of the global distribution of recent earthquakes thus provides a partial answer to the question relating to safety raised earlier (figure 5.3). As is clear from a comparison of figures 5.2 and 5.3, the margins of tectonic plates are comparatively dangerous places to live; the interiors of continental landmasses, situated on large tectonic plates, are safer in this context (notably Australia, most of Africa, and central and northern Eurasia). In the global core, the highest risk zones lie in East Asia, western North America, and the eastern Mediterranean. In the periphery, the highest risk areas lie in the rest of the so-called Pacific Ring of Fire, as well as in South and Southeast Asia, the former outlined by the mountainous belt extending from Iran via Kashmir and Tibet to Malaysia and Indonesia. Compare figures 5.3 and 1.2, and it is clear that the great majority of those at highest risk from earthquakes (and volcanic eruptions) live in the global periphery. The western margins of the Pacific and Philippine Plates, notably, imperil hundreds of millions from eastern China to Indonesia.

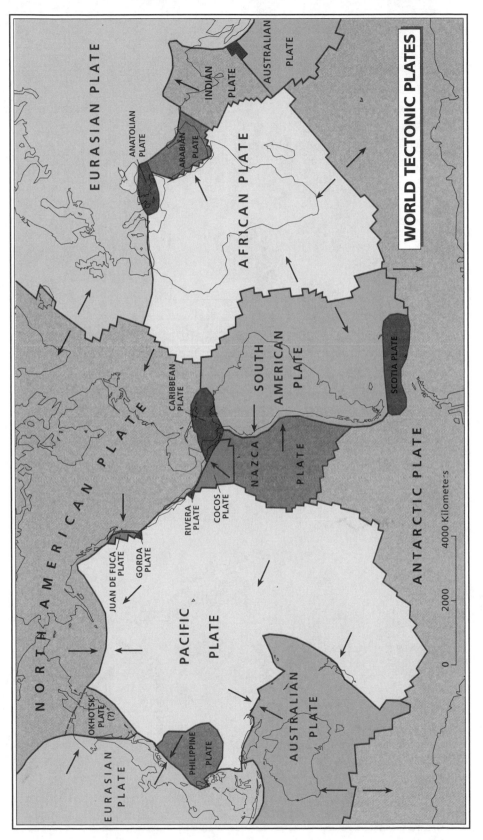

Figure 5.2. Tectonic plates large and small comprise the Earth's crust. All are in motion.

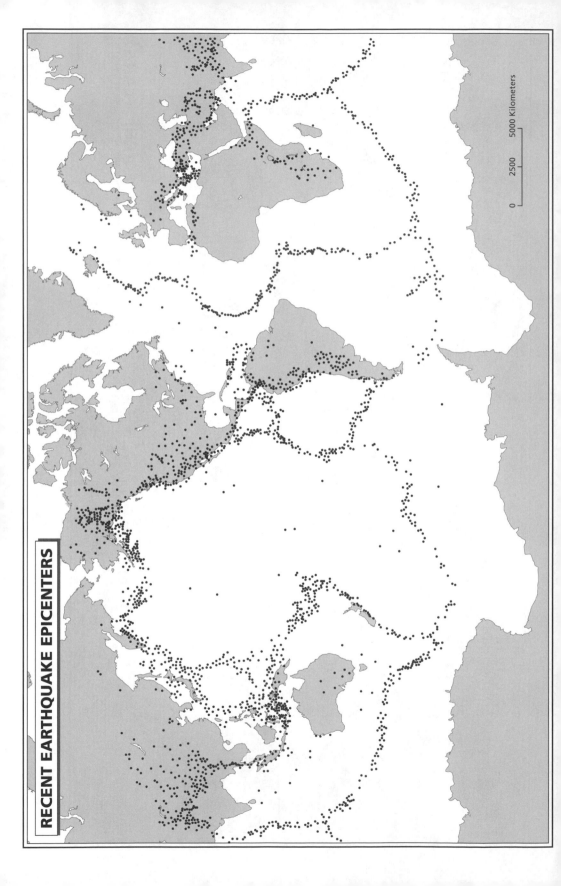

RECENT EARTHQUAKE EPICENTERS

5000 Kilometers

0   2500   5000

Figure 5.3 also implies that continental areas relatively remote from plate-collision zones are comparatively safer. In North America, it is the West that experiences the greatest risk. Canada east of the Rockies and the U.S. Midwest, East, and South have a much lower incidence of earthquakes and no recent volcanic activity. In South America, the zone of convergence between the South American and Nazca Plates puts the whole Andean rim in danger (Chile, in particular), but earthquakes are rare in Brazil and volcanism unknown. The great Eurasian landmass, underlain by the giant plate of the same name, is much more stable in the north than in the south, but peninsular India, on its own plate, is also quite steady. It is where the Indian Plate is colliding with the Eurasian Plate, along the great mountain chain of which the Himalayas form part, that the danger is greatest.

Where earthquakes and volcanic activity are *not* routine facts of life, their infrequent but sometimes dramatic occurrences are all the more consequential. Despite the zonation of danger implied by figure 5.3, extreme events (earthquakes more often than eruptions) can strike anywhere on Earth. The vulnerability of the West notwithstanding, several of the most severe earthquakes ever to occur in the United States struck southeast Missouri in 1811–1812 and coastal South Carolina in 1886. The Missouri quakes (there were several in a series) may have had a higher magnitude even than the San Francisco Earthquake of 1906; they changed the course of the Mississippi River near the Tennessee border and created a large lake in the area. The Charleston earthquake is reputed to have shaken the ground in New York City and rung church bells in Chicago. But perhaps the most talked-about historic earthquake in a relatively stable place occurred in Lisbon, Portugal, on November 1, 1755, at a time when the city's churches were crowded to honor the dead on All Saints Day. Two shocks, about 40 minutes apart, were accompanied by a tsunami and followed by a fire that roared through the city; about 30,000 people, most of them attending church service, died, and some 9000 buildings, including virtually all of the city's houses of worship, were destroyed. Portugal at the time was wealthy from its colonial

Figure 5.3. The outlines of the tectonic plates shown in figure 5.2 can be observed in this map of the distribution of recent earthquake activity. When plates collide or diverge, the crust shakes or ruptures.

ventures and the city was swiftly rebuilt, but the soul-searching went on for generations and, in religious circles, still continues.

Because the human population of the global periphery is much larger than that of the core, a far greater number of people there are at risk from extreme natural events. Moreover, victims in the periphery are, to a greater degree, left to fend for themselves, even in today's world of emergency programs and helicopter rescues. When the Lisbon earthquake struck, Portugal's capital was one of the focal points of colonial-era globalization, and riches from Brazil's plantations, the African slave trade, and gold and silver from various parts of its empire were enriching the state as never before. The city was swiftly and handsomely rebuilt with assistance from other colonial powers. But little or nothing is known about other eighteenth-century natural disasters in remote regions of the still-evolving colonial periphery. Lisbon had global connections and mattered in the imperial scheme of things. Indigenous towns in distant locales did not.

Vestiges of that pattern persist in the current wave of globalization. Imagine a catastrophic earthquake in Tokyo or some other core-area city: Tokyo's financial and industrial complex is connected to virtually every other commercial center in the world. The destruction of Tokyo's corporate and manufacturing infrastructure would have economic repercussions around the globe. Several hundred thousand casualties would mobilize a worldwide relief effort, sustained as long as necessary even as Tokyo was rebuilt with massive international help. It is hardly necessary to ask whether a similar response would follow a catastrophic earthquake in Lagos, Dhaka, Manila, or other cities in the periphery far below Tokyo's rung on the ladder of globalization. Place obviously makes a difference.

Is the gap narrowing? Undoubtedly. The aftermath of what happened in coastal China on July 28, 1976, probably could not happen today. On that date, twin earthquakes struck near the coastal city of Tangshan, then a city of about one million located about 160 kilometers (100 miles) east of Beijing. The shocks devastated not only Tangshan but also the nearby port of Tianjin; damage reached as far as Beijing itself. The death toll, never confirmed by Chinese authorities, may have exceeded 700,000, making this the deadliest natural disaster of the twentieth century by far. However, China's sclerotic regime (Mao Zedong died just six weeks later) and its still-closed communist society concealed not only the magnitude of the devastation but also the incompetence of a relief effort so ineffective that it engendered widespread revulsion among a people not given to risky expressions of emotion. No significant international aid was accepted, and countless thousands died for lack of medical attention. The world at large was generally unaware of the dimensions of the catastrophe.

Today, not even regimes like those of Myanmar, North Korea, or Zimbabwe could conceal the magnitude of major natural disasters. Some regimes still refuse or limit international assistance from certain sources, as the Iranian government was forced to do by conservative Islamic elements following the December 26, 2003, earthquake that flattened the city of Bam, killing more than 40,000, when an American offer of official aid was turned down. But satellite surveillance now makes it all but impossible for even the most secretive juntas to hide from the world their calamities, natural or man-made (women tend not to be the cause). And natural disasters occurring in remote areas of the global periphery, while they may not prompt an international response equivalent to those striking the core, now can be assessed from space and relieved with high-tech methodology ranging from GIS and GPS equipment to airborne field hospitals and satellite-guided access.

Nevertheless, the perils of the periphery continue to afflict locals living with natural hazards as well as human malevolence. When a major earthquake struck near the town of Muzaffarabad in remote mountainous Kashmir (between northern India and Pakistan) in 2005, while children were in school and markets were open, some 90,000 people perished instantly, many more were grievously injured, and widespread destruction flattened entire towns and villages and disrupted the already-tenuous road system. Bad weather followed, slowing the rescue effort, and hundreds of thousands were left in the open, unattended by doctors and without food, water, or shelter. As the death toll rose, Pakistan's government agreed to receive relief supplies, but refused an offer of helicopters (Bauer, 2006). Weeks of slow negotiation between Pakistan and India aimed at opening the disputed border between their respective areas of control over Kashmir finally resulted in an agreement to allow aid to pass through. American assistance was permitted but limited, given the magnitude of the disaster, and Islamist groups active in the region also organized to provide help, but selectively. In no way, however, could the world's capacities be mobilized to alleviate the suffering. Three months after the shock,

UN relief workers still complained of interference and obstruction, and the fate of a million locals had faded from the world's attention. Political discord, ideological competition, suspicion, corruption and indifference prevailed over local needs.

Earthquakes tend to be localized events, wreaking havoc in the immediate area above their epicenter source, the devastation decreasing in concentric zones. Severe damage can occur in one part of a city while other areas are only slightly affected or not at all, depending on the properties of bedrock, on the cushioning effect of existing fault systems, and, of course, on the quality of construction. In Japan, modern skyscrapers stand on giant shock absorbers. In the United States, building codes in San Francisco and other Western cities require earthquake resistance; Eastern cities (Charleston's experience notwithstanding) do not. But earthquakes can spread devastation far beyond their epicenters when they occur beneath the sea rather than below the land. The world was reminded of this geographic reality on December 26, 2004, when an undersea earthquake with a magnitude of 9.0 originated where the Australian, Indian, and Eurasian tectonic plates converge, below the waters of the Indian Ocean west of northern Sumatra. As figures 5.2 and 5.3 indicate, earthquakes as well as volcanism relating to plate collisions occur at sea as well as on land. For this particular undersea quake, the natural circumstances combined to generate not only the usual damage on land nearby, but also a tsunami consisting of a series of huge ocean waves traveling at 800 kilometers (500 miles) per hour that devastated coastal areas near and far and killed some 300,000 people. Six hours after the quake struck, people perished on the shores of East Africa. While the damage was greatest in coastal areas of northern Sumatra, where the provincial capital of Banda Aceh was virtually erased, the tsunami was also catastrophic in Sri Lanka, Thailand, India, and probably Myanmar (which failed to report casualties) as well as on countless Indian Ocean islands in its path, including India's Andaman and Nicobar Islands and the Maldives.

Although tens of thousands of globals were in the path of the tsunami as vacationers or on business, more than 99 percent of the casualties were locals living on or near Indian Ocean shores. Even as prominent political leaders and entertainers joined the massive international relief effort, questions were raised regarding the absence of an adequate early-warning system in a maritime region known to be susceptible to tsunami events at a time when the technology is available. Indeed, the United States had tsunami experiences in 1946, when an earthquake offshore from Alaska generated a tsunami that smashed into Hilo, Hawaii, killing 156 people, and 1960, when an earthquake in southern Chile produced a tsunami whose waves were still 7 meters (23 feet) high when they reached Hawaii 15 hours later, but from a less damaging direction. None of these alerts generated the creation of a global warning system, and geologists after the 2004 tsunami described it as a "100,000 year event," perhaps dissipating the temporary sense of urgency. One imagines that a catastrophic tsunami event in the North Atlantic Ocean, should it occur, would result in a different response.

As rehabilitation of the tsunami-afflicted coastal Indian Ocean zones continues, versions of our original question arise: Why would people rebuild and resettle in areas so vulnerable to nature's wrath? Will children who survived it but lost parents or siblings ever recover any sense of security? To the former, the record in California is instructive: emigration from the State increases after every major earthquake event. Globals are likely to have a choice; locals are not. As to the latter, the 2004 tsunami, while exceptional, is only the latest in a series of environmental crises going back through countless generations, encoded in the alleles of locals for whom inescapability and vulnerability are tenets of life.

VOLCANISM: GLOBAL REACH, LOCAL THREAT

Imagine a June morning in Costa Rica some time in the future. You are on vacation, having been attracted by the country's superb scenery and outstanding national parks. The weather forecast last night was for clear skies and relatively cool temperatures. You wake up and check the time. It is nearly 8:00 A.M., but your room is pitch black. No light filters in around the edges of the hotel-room drapes, as was the case early yesterday. You rise and push the curtain aside. It is nearly dark; light-sensitive streetlights and automobile headlights are on. But there are no clouds, and no stars in the darkened sky. Switching on the balcony light, you look down at the tiled floor—but see no tiles. A fine, gray dust covers tiles as well as grout. The birds, so noisy yesterday morning, are quiet. You grab the remote and turn on CNN.

A scientist is pointing to a map of Southeast Asia, saying that "this is not the first time" something like this has happened. Next comes a Google close-up of a string of islands east of Java, followed by a grainy photograph of a forested volcano rising from the water. The darkness outside your room has causes half a world away. An explosive eruption in Indonesia is about to change the routines of the planet.

It has indeed happened before, and there is no reason to assume that it will not happen again. Some progress has been made in the assessment of risk from recurrent earthquakes and periodic volcanic eruptions, but the kinds of events that would lead to the circumstances just described occur suddenly and without warning, as the 2004 tsunami did. Scientists are still debating the dimensions of an explosive volcanic eruption simply referred to as "Toba," involving the violent explosion of a large volcano of that name on the island of Sumatra about 73,500 years ago. There can be no doubt that Toba's explosive eruption shrouded and darkened the Earth for many years; it left a caldera 90 kilometers (55 miles) long and 50 kilometers (30 miles) wide. Hundreds of millions of tons of rock were pulverized in an instant and drifted like a giant black shroud across the skies, blocking the sun for perhaps as long as two decades. Early humanity was migrating out of Africa and across Eurasia, and some anthropologists theorize that a great deal of genetic diversity must have been lost in Toba's deadly aftermath, calling it our "evolutionary bottleneck." Geologists refer to Toba's explosion as a "500,000-year event," something that happens, on average, about every half-million years. That, however, is scant reassurance. Nature has a way of negating averages derived from computer models.

No one in the world yet knew about Toba when, on April 5, 1815, one of many volcanoes in the Lesser Sunda Islands (east of Java) rumbled to life. That, too, had happened before, and few of the island's 12,000 inhabitants paid much attention. The Tambora volcano on the island of Sumbawa in what was then the Dutch East Indies had been known to be active, but gave no indication that it would soon affect most of the world. Yet a week later, it did not just erupt as it had previously, but disintegrated in a series of explosions that could be heard 1600 kilometers (1000 miles) away, killing all but a few dozen of the island's inhabitants and covering the Indonesian archipelago with volcanic debris. A giant plume of dark soot representing tens of millions of tons of powdered bedrock rose above the islands, and colonial reports describe fields covered by poisonous ash and black dust, waters clogged by trees and cinders, and air rendered toxic by a fog of acid chemicals. Tens of thousands perished in ensuing famines as darkness enveloped the region. Not until the outlines of Tambora could be discerned again did it become clear that the entire crest of the mountain, 1300 meters (4000 feet) of it, was gone.

Meanwhile, much of the plume of soot that penetrated high into the stratosphere was beginning to blanket the Earth, blocking sunlight and changing weather. What began as a relatively narrow band of ash and dust gradually widened into a globe-girdling membrane that blocked sunlight and darkened skies. By the middle of 1816, it was clear to farmers virtually everywhere that this would be a year without summer, a growing season without growth. In Europe, food shortages arose quickly, prices rose, riots ensued, and armed criminals stole supplies. In North America, corn would not ripen, the livestock market collapsed, and the diaries of New Englanders describe deprivations unheard of even in bad harvest years. "A frost in May killed much of the spring planting and snowstorms in June compounded the problems. . . . [Even] on Cape Cod, ponds froze to a half-inch thickness in May, corn rotted on the stalks and flour reached $15 a barrel in Barnstable, a seven-time increase over normal prices. Snow was back in early September" (Coogan, 2007). Less is known about Tambora's impact elsewhere in the world, but we can only guess at the consequences of a similar occurrence today, on a planet with nearly *seven* times as many inhabitants as it had when the mountain exploded.

A map showing the global distribution of active volcanoes displays an obvious, but variable, relationship to that of world tectonic plates (figure 5.4). The relationship is especially clear in Southeast Asia and elsewhere along the Pacific Ring of Fire, but isolated intraplate volcanoes remain active, as well, on land (such as Mt. Cameroon, Africa's largest active volcano) and on the ocean floors away from mid-ocean ridges. The map may not be totally reliable, because some volcanoes that appear to be inactive and are designated as "dormant" can come to life even after long periods of quietude. Elsewhere there may be other potential volcanic activity, not revealed by familiar landforms, gathering strength below the surface (for example, beneath remaining glaciers) to some day surprise us all.

Volcanoes can pose risk to millions even at great distances, but their threat is immediate to locals living on their slopes or at their feet. And

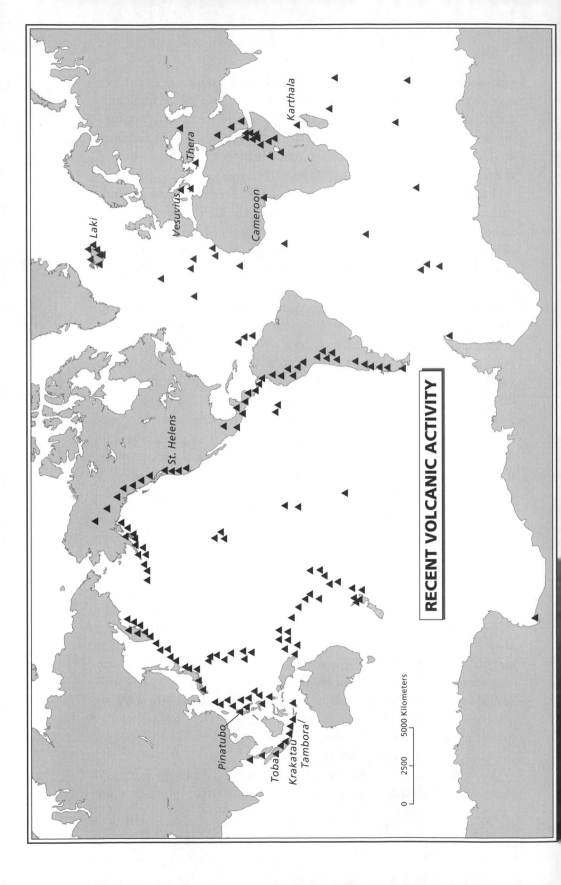

RECENT VOLCANIC ACTIVITY

Laki

Vesuvius

Thera

Karthala

Cameroon

St. Helens

Pinatubo

Toba

Krakatau

Tambora

0   2500   5000 Kilometers

such hazards are not always signaled by those familiar, cone-shaped, cratered, sometimes snow-capped mountains looming over the landscape. In certain areas, for example where tectonic plates are pulling away from each other, deep fissures open in the crust and lava pours out in huge quantities while vast clouds of toxic gases spew into the atmosphere. This is what happened in Iceland in 1783–84 along a 25-kilometer (16-mile) fissure known as the Laki Volcano. Over a period of eight months, more lava gushed from this fissure than from any volcano in recorded history. The eruption unleashed massive amounts of deadly hydrofluoric acid, sulfur dioxide, and hydrochloric acid and killed about 10,000 locals, about one-fifth of the island nation's population (Stone, 2004). Acid rain fell on livestock as well as people: half the horses and cattle and three-quarters of the sheep died. Famine ensued, raising the human death toll and fraying social bonds in this close-knit society.

Recent research on the Laki eruption reveals that this was no local event, and that its impact was global. From scientific studies of the time, from weather observations, newspaper reports, farmer's diaries and business records it has been possible to piece together what happened. Because of unusual weather conditions that summer of 1783, the plume of poisonous gas and acid in suspension emanating from Laki drifted southeastward, fed by successive eruptions from the fissure. Expanding as it drifted, it soon reached Britain and Ireland, then was reported days later in Europe, North Africa, the Middle East, and even India. The scorching 1783 summer under this lethal chemical cloud was followed by what may have been the most frigid winter of Europe's Little Ice Age. Everywhere, observers described the atmosphere as a "fog" or "haze" the Sun could not penetrate; farmers reported a "deadly dew" on their crops and terrible skin conditions on their livestock. Computer models now indicate that the gaseous Laki plume blocked enough sunlight, as far away as North Africa and South Asia, to disrupt seasonal rainfall patterns for several successive years. Famine struck the Nile Valley, India's monsoon failed, and reports of disastrous crop failures emanated even from Japan

Figure 5.4. Recently active volcanoes—and some ancient ones that made (and in some cases changed) history. Volcanoes discussed in the narrative are identified by name.

(Barone, 2005). Some scientists are suggesting that Laki's toll should be counted in the millions, not thousands, which raised the question as to the impact of a similar eruption today (Laki remains an active volcano, one of its ice-covered vents erupting as recently as November 2004). Had the 1783–84 eruption happened just two centuries later, it would have closed airports in Western Europe for months, with economic and other implications difficult to imagine.

It has now been 125 years since the most recent of the great explosive eruptions that punctuate human history shook the planet: Krakatau. In 1883 this volcano in the Sunda Strait between Sumatra and Java exploded with a roar audible 4600 kilometers (2900 miles) away, killing all on the island and generating tsunamis reaching heights of 40 meters (130 feet) that drowned some 34,000 locals along nearby shorelines. It sent a massive volume of pulverized rock into planetary orbit, causing measurable global cooling and producing the legendary bright red sunsets for which Krakatau is perhaps best remembered today. According to one recent account, this natural disaster had significant cultural and political consequences as well, triggering the rise of Islamic militancy in this area of the (then) Dutch East Indies, a legacy that endures to this day (Winchester, 2003). But if Krakatau's bang was louder than Tambora's, its impact on the wider world was far less consequential. Like so many active volcanoes whose slopes and environs are settled by villagers, farmers, and fishers attracted by fertile soils, streams, and natural harbors, Krakatau was active and known to be a risk, but memories of warnings in the form of rumbles and smoke plumes fade quickly. And although the science of prediction has made major strides over the past half century, there are enough false alarms to persuade many locals in immediate danger to resist evacuation until it is too late.

Among the reasons behind this reluctance is a lack of awareness of the dangers that life near a volcano entails. When you are born in the shadow (or in sight of) a mountain that rumbles and smokes now and then but changes little over a lifetime, and with whose risks your parents and grandparents have lived long before you grew up here, the notion of authorities compelling you to leave every time the volcano grows moody is hard to accept, especially if you live on the surrounding flatlands some distance away. Living on the slope may mean having to run for your life if lava starts flowing from the crater, but on the plain nearby, surely, there would be ample time to get away? When the Indonesian volcano Kelud threatened to erupt in 2007, some locals had to be evacuated at gunpoint.

In fact, countless victims of volcanic eruptions do not die as molten rock descends on them or ejected rocks fall on them, but perish in the hot, fast-moving gases that rush down the mountain, incinerating everything on its slopes and fanning out over the countryside below, even boiling the water of nearby lakes and seas. One of the most dramatic events of this kind occurred on the Caribbean island of Martinique in 1902, when Mount Pelée, the volcano overlooking the capital of St. Pierre, disgorged an avalanche of scorching gas racing downward at several hundred kilometers an hour at temperatures exceeding 400 degrees centigrade, "dark, billowing, reddish-violet fumes...destroying everything...public buildings, private homes, the Grand Hotel" (Scarth, 2002). St. Pierre had been known as the "Paris of the Caribbean," in many ways the region's most stylish and cultured city. In minutes, all but one of its 27,000 inhabitants were cremated, the townscape reduced to heaps of ash. In the harbor, water boiled at the surface, glue between planks melted, and boats sank at anchor. Ever since, gaseous emanations of this kind have been referred to by scientists as "Pelean," the deadly incandescent shroud appearing suddenly and often with little portent. But read the many analyses of this disaster, and it is clear that the mountain gave ample warning. For some weeks, St. Pierre's literate and well-informed public had been involved and concerned, yet few residents left the city for reasons of safety.

Living with the hazard of sudden volcanic impact, therefore, is not just the fate of locals in remote reaches of the global periphery. From Thera to Pinatubo and from Vesuvius to Laki, volcanic eruptions have killed those living in their immediate vicinity and changed the course of human history in areas beyond. Major volcanoes tower over cities from Tokyo to Seattle and from Naples to Manado, putting ever larger numbers of people at risk and threatening nodes in the global network of interconnections. A cluster of active volcanoes on Russia's Kamchatka Peninsula has the potential to disrupt crucial air routes between America and Asia. As in the case of earthquakes, massive volcanic activity can occur in locales not usually seen as threatening: the Yellowstone area poses a major potential volcanic hazard in the heart of North America. Ashfalls following the 1980 collapse of Mt. St. Helens in Washington State led to renewed realization that the atmosphere (as well as the ruptured crust and endangered life) is part of the comprehensive picture of volcanic hazard. This notion was reinforced more recently when volcanic activity on the island of Montserrat drove residents away, buried large areas under ash, and made forecasts of Caribbean weather patterns and wind directions part of media reportage. Local volcanic events can have regional and even global consequences.

POWER OF THE ELEMENTS

Imposing volcanoes and spectacular mountains give visual meaning to the concept of power of place, but sun-drenched, dune-fringed, wave-lapped shorelines conceal an even greater menace. A tranquil beach setting can be transformed in a matter of hours into a scene of raging winds, rising waters, and torrential rains permanently altering the natural landscape and destroying what was built on it. Wind and water imperil hundreds of millions living in environs every bit as dangerous as the slopes of volcanoes or the valleys of quake-prone mountains. The difference is that the Earth's coastal and near-coastal population is far larger than that concentrated in and near mountains.

People persist in living in flood-prone areas along coasts as well as in river basins for the same reason they cling to their dangerous montane abodes: when the sea stays back and the river remains within its channel, the living is good. Alluvial soils are to floodplain populations what volcanic soils are to farmers on the slopes: fertile and productive. Successive generations of farmers have lived in the Mississippi-Missouri lowland for generations; after the river system flooded disastrously in 1993 at a cost of 50 lives, more than 55,000 homes, and more than $17 billion in crop and property losses, "people and activities...busily reestablished themselves in the inundated zones following the great flood—blithely confident that such a disaster would not repeat itself in the foreseeable future" (de Blij et al., 2004). Geographers who have studied human responses to flooding as well as other hazards report that human behavior does not reflect growing awareness of rising risk, because people tend to make optimistic rationalizations for continuing to live in the danger zone—whether they are locals in the periphery or globals in the core. In the great flood of 1993, called a 500-year event by hydrologists, the

Mississippi at the Gateway Arch of St. Louis crested at an all-time high of more than 15 meters (nearly 50 feet), exceeding flood stage by more than 6 meters (20 feet). After the waters subsided, farmers as well as flooded-out urban residents made the decision to return to their properties, many of them on the assumption that this was a "once in a lifetime" event. Today, properties are bought and sold as before in the very areas inundated less than 20 years ago, the memory of the disaster fading fast.

It is the continental coastlines where the greater danger looms, and where far larger numbers of people are at risk. What happened more than a half century ago in the Netherlands may be remembered as a turning point, even though current predictions of rising sea levels were not yet in prospect. On the last day of January 1953, a hurricane-strength storm arose off Scotland and tracked toward the Netherlands, striking on February 1 at spring tide with winds in excess of 150 kilometers (95 miles) per hour. The water breached the dikes of numerous polders in the southwest, flooding 162,000 hectares (400,000 acres) of land, killing more than 1800 people and tens of thousands of livestock, and causing incalculable property damage. While many crucial dikes held to prevent even worse, the vulnerability of a nation living substantially below sea level was dramatically exposed. In response, the Netherlands government imposed a "disaster tax" and, drawing on Marshall Plan funds and other resources, began a comprehensive scheme to fortify its already-reinforced coastline against onslaughts from the North Sea. The gigantic Delta Plan now shortens the Dutch coastline by 720 kilometers (450 miles), buttressed by a storm-surge barrier that contains 61 enormous sluices normally open but closed when necessary. An ingenious and colossal system of movable barricades closes the otherwise unobstructed New Waterway linking Rotterdam to the open sea in time of danger.

But boat into the port of Amsterdam, and you enter a lock and are lowered from sea level into the North Sea Canal, and as you sail eastward you see the roofs of houses standing lower still behind a dike topped by a roadway. Have lunch at an outdoor "terrace" restaurant on one of Amsterdam's many squares, and you soon forget that sea level is at the top of the restaurant window high above, and that the sea is not much more than 25 kilometers (15 miles) away. So superbly effective is the system of water control in this delta of the Rhine and Maas Rivers that its failure is simply unimaginable.

It is exactly that—the unimaginable—that must be contemplated by millions at the mercy of nature within reach of the global ocean, because the power of nature looms large over this variant of place. The planet is in a climatic transition with precedents, except that the precedents lacked the massive human contribution now playing a role in it. When a previous round of global warming drove back vast continental glaciers from the present-day Midwest into northern Canada, climate swung wildly from coast to coast, leaving evidence ranging from now-desiccated lakes filled by meltwaters and powerful, fierce storms to meters of rock ground to dust by the ice, swept up and redeposited by raging winds. More recently, when the Little Ice Age pushed farmers out of Iceland and Scandinavia, Europe's climate fluctuated ruinously, generating not only the coldest of cold spells but also the hottest of summer heat waves and crop-killing droughts. Again in the present time of climate change, such increasing extremes mark an overall warming whose global consequences will include rising sea levels as well as a larger incidence and intensity of coastal storms and the melting of mountain glaciers, and whose regional impacts are likely to intensify heat and drought in tropical Africa, the Mediterranean, and the American Southwest, the melting of Arctic permafrost, and the shrinking of equatorial rainforests. If, as the UN-sponsored International Panel on Climate Change suggests, Western and Nordic Europe will experience significant warming, then powerful storms of the kind the Netherlands experienced in 1953 are likely to be in the offing. It is worth remembering that the 1953 storm was equivalent to a category 1 hurricane, and that the massive storm barriers built in its wake have not yet been tested by anything stronger.

When I was in the Netherlands in 1989 with a television crew from the ABC network, the quick-witted producer, taping the segment on the Dutch engineering marvel that keeps the country dry, had his shorthand for what he saw: a "submarine culture" where, even then, the 1953 calamity had faded from memory—"Bangladesh with money" is how he described it. But in Bangladesh, nobody lives below sea level. Yet Bangladesh was the scene of eight of the ten costliest natural disasters during the twentieth century, including a cyclone (as hurricanes are called in that part of the world) in 1991 that pushed a wall of water 6 meters (20 feet) high across the islands and flatlands in the delta of the Ganges-Brahmaputra Rivers, killing an estimated 150,000 people. More than three times as many had died in floods in 1975, but no system of barriers and dikes could protect the teeming farmlands of the south, virtually at sea level and open to the funnel-shaped Bay of Bengal. So the Bangladesh government, with international assistance, tried the next best thing: building a series of concrete, storm-proof shelters on pillars to which storm-trapped villagers could flee. Unfortunately, not many locals could reach those shelters already built when the 1991 storm struck; tens of thousands were needed when dozens were available. And those farmers who managed to survive there found themselves marooned for days, even weeks following the storm. The dangers of deltas, homes to millions, exemplify the geography of jeopardy.

And deltas are by no means the only low-lying, high-risk places on the margins of the continents. The edges of the Earth's landmasses today are already flooded, sea level having risen nearly 200 meters (about 600 feet) over the past 18,000 years or so as the planet warmed at the end of its most recent glaciation. In the first half of this geologically brief time, as ice sheets that covered much high-latitude land sent huge quantities of meltwater into the oceans, gently sloping coastal plains were inundated, land connections (such as those between mainland Europe and Britain and New Guinea and Australia) were flooded, and much of the archeological record of our early coastwise migrations was lost. Breaking waves built offshore sandy "barrier" islands and pushed them landward, leaving a worldwide legacy of naturally protected "intracoastal" waterways between mainland and open sea. Today, from West Africa to East Asia and from North Carolina to Texas, those offshore bars are populated by millions in settlements ranging from fishing villages to retirement communities and from tourist facilities to second homes. The poor and the wealthy, the permanent and the seasonal, all congregate in some of the highest-risk settings on Earth—at a time when rising sea levels seem poised to write the final chapter in the saga of the present warm spell.

While the danger to these vulnerable residents from high-tide storms, hurricanes, tsunamis, and sea-level rise is extreme, the reality is that all inhabitants of low-lying coastal areas are at growing risk, and entire island states, such as the Maldives in the Indian Ocean and Kiribati in the Pacific, confront the prospect of submersion. But a 2007 joint study by geoscientists at New York's Columbia University and geographers at the London-based International Institute for Environment and Development argues that all places below 10 meters

(33 feet) above mean sea level are now susceptible to increasing extremes of weather and climate, including two-thirds of all cities with populations exceeding five million. As to individual mainland countries, the study suggests that China has the largest number in danger, with 144 million people, or 11 percent of its population, living close to sea level. But other countries face proportionately greater dangers still, including the vulnerable Netherlands and Bangladesh; the Thames Barrier, Britain's ingenious and hitherto-effective flood-control system, could not protect London from inundation under the circumstances forecast by the study.

How likely is the worst-case scenario predicted by geographers and others? The precedents are not encouraging. Over the past two million years, the planet has been experiencing the kind of cold–warm–cold oscillations characteristic of an ice age, and we are presently experiencing a still-short warm phase after a long glaciation. During the previous warm phase, it got even warmer than it is today, and sea level rose as much as 3 to 5 meters (10 to 16 feet) above present levels—without the human contribution to global warming now being made (Hansen, 2004). Had modern civilization arisen during that previous warm phase, we would have built our megacities well inland from where they are today, along coastlines making the continents look quite different (figure 5.5). Now, with human as well as natural forces at work, we may be in for a gigantic reconfiguration of human habitation.

As in other contexts, there is nothing equal about the Earth's distribution of jeopardy arising from climate change or weather extremes (figure 5.6). In all dimensions, the richer countries and communities will be able to cope far better by diverting and reallocating resources the poorer ones do not have. Even so, it is already clear that even wealthier societies can fail in emergency situations, as was the case in Europe (especially in France) during the 2003 heat wave that killed an estimated 30,000 people, most of whom were elderly. When Hurricane Katrina struck New Orleans in 2005, the impact fell disproportionately on the poor, who were concentrated in the especially vulnerable, lower-lying areas below the historic high ground near the Mississippi River, and who suffered the greatest loss of life. In Subsaharan Africa, where drought, cropland degradation, and freshwater scarcity are symptoms of long-term climate change, environmental stress severely affects the rural poor, creating economic conditions

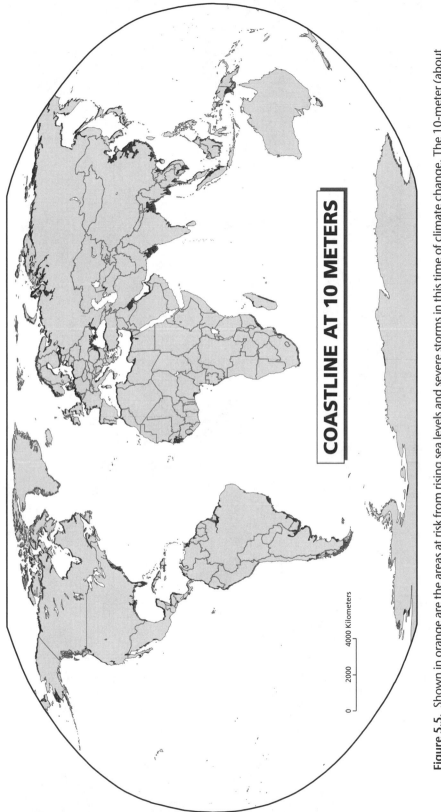

Figure 5.5. Shown in orange are the areas at risk from rising sea levels and severe storms in this time of climate change. The 10-meter (about 33-foot) contour is often taken as the worst-case scenario; this map suggests that relatively little territory would be lost. But take a magnifying glass and see the implications for East China, Western Europe, and the Southeastern United States, among other urbanized regions.

COASTLINE AT 10 METERS

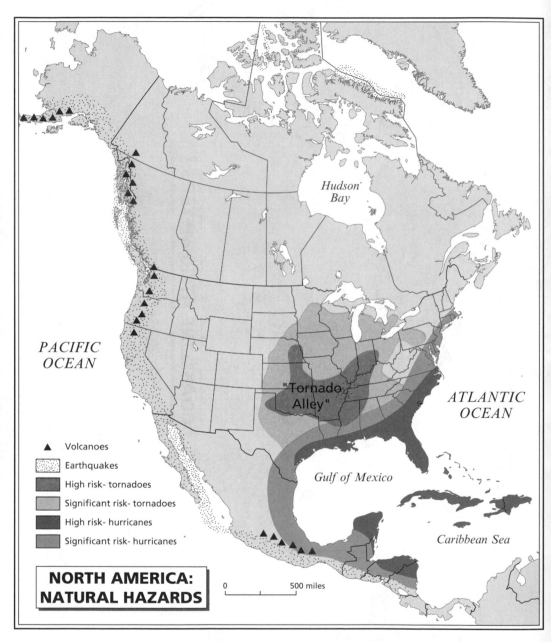

Figure 5.6. Not much of North America's more densely populated area is comparatively safe from natural hazards. Hurricanes in the east, tornadoes in the center, and earthquakes in the west are just some of the natural hazards threatening large parts of the continent.

that can contribute to disastrous social dislocation; environmental factors have been blamed for exacerbating crises in Darfur and Somalia (Homer-Dixon, 2006). By making enraged mobals out of desperate and frustrated locals who invade their neighbors' domains or who stream into already-burgeoning cities, ecological causes have destabilizing political consequences ranging from rural insurgencies to urban gang warfare. Add religious opportunism into the mix, and such circumstances can reduce "national" governments to weakness and irrelevance, threatening regional order in the afflicted areas.

Until recently, it seemed appropriate to distinguish between the sudden impact of an event such as a high-category hurricane or a flood and the apparently slow progress of global warming. Current research, however, suggests that climate can change quite abruptly, in decades or less, and that such changes have happened in the past and without human influence. "Winter temperatures plummeting six degrees Celsius and sudden droughts scorching farmland around the globe are not just the stuff of scary movies. Such striking climate jumps have happened before—sometimes within a matter of years," writes a prominent scientist, echoing the view that the current warming phase will trigger extreme events not confronted in modern times (Alley, 2004). Recent research is suggesting that the Sahara's most recent drying out (it has happened before, a cyclic process that relates directly to the repeated cold–warm–cold switch of the latest ice age) may have transformed this vast region from savanna to desert in a matter of 50 years. It happened about 5000 years ago, a fateful transformation that sealed Africa's eventual cultural division into Mediterranean and Subsaharan regions.

We humans, as individuals, are on this planet so briefly that we have neither the time nor the mobility to experience the full or even partial range of the power of nature. Farmers in Bangladesh live with dangers unimagined by farmers in France. The shaking ground familiar to many Indonesians is not a part of life in Brazil. The Russia of the Urals does not live in fear of the volcanoes towering over Kamchatka. Every place in the world has its own combination of risks. The variability of the power of nature spells acute and immediate danger for some, comparative safety for others, but sanctuary for none.

6

PLACES OPEN AND SHUT

The power of place manifests itself in continua of opportunity and risk, advantage and privation. On the global map it is revealed in patterns of health and sickness, wealth and poverty. On the ground it is demarcated by barriers and barricades, patrols and controls. Reflecting on the impress of place on the fortunes and misfortunes of the planet's nearly seven billion human inhabitants, it is worth noting that, for all their vaunted mobility, only about 200 million live outside the country of their birth, or less than 3 percent of the total. Some academics (as well as politicians) refer to the present as the "age of migration." The figures indicate otherwise. The overwhelming majority of us die under the governmental, linguistic, religious, medical, environmental, and other circumstances into which we were born. The constraints on transnational and intercultural migration remain powerful and, in some respects, are increasing rather than softening, roughening rather than flattening the global playing field. Place, most emphatically place of birth but also the constricted space in which the majority of lives are lived, remains the most potent factor shaping the destinies of billions.

As a result, those destinies are closely tied to the fortunes and misfortunes of the state that imparts "nationality" on citizens born within its borders. One of these involves relative location. There are numerous reasons why approximately 70 percent of the poorest-of-the-poor are citizens of African states, but one of these reasons may not be immediately obvious—until one takes a close look at the continent's regional geography. Africa has more landlocked countries than any other continent or geographic realm in the world, and almost as many (14) as the rest of the world put together (and still another one may join this group if voters in a future referendum in Southern Sudan opt for independence). Unless a landlocked country has a combination of good management and a relatively rich resource base, as Botswana does but Zimbabwe does not, it is far more susceptible to any regional malaise than a coastal state. As economic geographers have long pointed out, a coastal state trades with the world; a landlocked state trades with, or through, its neighbors. When those neighbors are well off, as in the case of Switzerland (always the example), then the landlocked state does well. If they are not, the landlocked state suffers doubly from its isolation and from its abutters' failures. Compared to the world at large, the peoples of Paraguay, Belarus, Tajikistan, Nepal, and Laos are not among the rich. So it is with Mali, Chad, Burundi, and Zambia.

Landlocked states got a bad start in life, but they are not the only countries suffering from consequences of comparative isolation. The world map shows plenty of examples of coastal states that exhibit the same failures as landlocked ones despite their maritime access. East Timor (Timor Leste, as the locals prefer) is an island state; Cambodia has a window on the Gulf of Thailand; Somalia has one of the world's longest coastlines; struggling Guyana overlooks the same corner of the Atlantic as thriving Trinidad and Tobago. Remoteness from the mainstreams of change can affect coastal as well as landlocked countries, and it is a dimension of the power of place that has locational and psychological aspects. Austrians don't fret over their country being landlocked the way Bolivians do. Many young New Zealanders respond to the remoteness of their affluent, well-governed country by emigrating to places where "the action is." Looking at the world map, though, there can be no doubt that remoteness afflicts more African countries than any other world realm, and that a combination of spatial and psychological factors creates a power of place in which isolation is a pervasive element.

PLACE AND AUTHORITY

Since the world's approximately 200 states vary enormously in territorial size and human population, the impress of place is a matter not only of location but also of dimension and scale. Smallness and singularity are not inevitably coupled, but they are often linked. Everyone in the Maldives lives under the threat of sea-level rise, but even the Netherlands has slivers of land some tens of meters above sealevel. Everyone in the Comoros is at risk from an eruption of Mount Karthala, but even Indonesia has a large volcano-free island in Borneo. Virtually everyone in Oman is born into a Muslim family, but Nigeria is half Muslim, half non-Muslim. Almost all Uruguayans grow up speaking Spanish, but neighboring Brazil is multilingual. No one is safe from malaria in Togo, but millions live beyond its reach in India.

Some countries are so large that they encompass an enormous diversity of natural and cultural environments and incorporate huge populations, but many more are so small that they are designated as microstates, such as Liechtenstein, or ministates, such as Swaziland and Bhutan. What large and small have in common is that their boundaries designate the limits of governmental authority and reach, affecting all within their enclosures. The very few remaining globals, impoverished locals, and desperate refugees of Zimbabwe are all afflicted by the mismanagement of their state by a regime that has failed at every level. Chile's emergence from dictatorial rule is emblematic of the virtues of democracy and the benefits of open economies, raising the country's international stature and thinning the ranks of the poor. Such generalizations, however, cannot be made for megastates. China's communist system oversees an unprecedented economic transformation, but the successes written in Pacific Rim cityscapes are contradicted by harsh failures in the interior countryside. China's money-laden globals are negotiating corporate boardrooms from Australia to Zambia, but China's locals lose their homes in historic districts of Beijing and their land in remote villages of Gansu without adequate recourse to a legal system hampered by one-party rule. India is a world within a world, its cultural landscapes ranging from high-technology office parks on the "Silicon Plateau" of Bengaluru (the new name of Bangalore, America's outsourcing bane) to the changeless villages in rural Bihar, where the holy Ganges is the lifeline for millions. In north and south, east and west, India presents vastly different faces, so that a lifetime in the state of Assam (Asom) gives little inkling of what daily life is like in the Punjab, and mountain dwellers in Himachal Pradesh face environmental, economic, and medical challenges quite unlike those facing inhabitants of tropical Tamil Nadu.

A state is thus a place only in the legal sense; in all other respects it is an assemblage of places often more disparate than some groups of individual countries are. In many ways, India's West Bengal State has more in common with neighboring Bangladesh than it has with most of India itself. Visit the markets of Kashi in China's western Xinjiang Autonomous Region, and the cosmopolitan social landscape of Turkestan leaves a far stronger impression than the cultural imprint of Han China. Nevertheless, the borders on the map, now more and more often demarcated on the ground, define not only the spatial limits of state sovereignty but also the authority of the state over the behavior of its citizens.

This behavior includes migration—not only across those borders, but also within them. The magnet of urbanization attracts migrants in all parts of the world, but most of this migration is internal. The numbers are uncertain; while it is comparatively easy to enumerate regulated international migration, reliable data for internal movements are hard to come by. Some governments still make it difficult for their own citizens to move from one part of their country to another, requiring permits and payments. China's Maoist regime restricted such movement severely on political grounds; post-Mao governments have tried to keep control of it for social and economic reasons, fearing disorder in the Pacific Rim region. During the apartheid era, South Africa's rulers tightly controlled internal migration for economic as well as political purposes; following the country's transition to democracy, its new government sought ways not only to deal with vastly increased internal movement but also a huge influx of illegal migrants from collapsing Zimbabwe. No freedom to relocate internally exists in North Korea, Myanmar, or Turkmenistan, current examples of countries whose autocratic regimes construe such movement as a risk to their supremacy.

When citizens are free to move within their countries, they do so in large numbers—compared, that is, to their international cohorts. That such movement is linked to, and constrained by, the cultural regionalism of those countries is confirmed by what the map shows. In the multilingual United States, where English is nevertheless the lingua franca, one family in seven moves every year. In multicultural India, with nearly four times the U.S. population, internal relocation involves a far smaller fraction of citizens, inhibited as it is by caste, language, religion, cost, and other social factors. In Canada, where internal mobals have been able to move without obstruction for generations, this has not expunged the country's cultural bifurcation

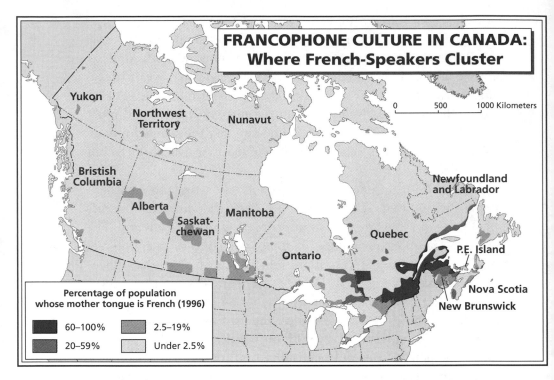

Figure 6.1. Canada is a bilingual state, but those who speak French at home are concentrated in the southern part of the Province of Quebec and adjacent areas; small clusters lie farther west. From Canada Census data.

(figure 6.1). Cultural clustering remains a powerful factor of destiny and a strong impediment to internal migration.

POLICIES AND DESTINIES

Governments, by proclaiming "official" languages and "state" religions, by promoting "national" educational standards, and by pursuing medical goals (among many other objectives), continue to have enormous impact on the destinies of their citizens in this globalizing world, because the overwhelming majority of all global inhabitants will live their entire lives under the management of the country of their birth and no other. In the 1990s aftermath of the collapse of the Soviet Union and in light of the success of the expanding European Union, there was much speculation as to the apparently decreasing relevance of the state as the key constituent in international affairs, but such predictions were premature. By opening or closing their societies to globalizing influences ranging from technical to cultural and from economic to medical, governments can equip or impair their citizens for what is now the inevitable transformation of the world. The growing need for capability in English as well as at least one other language has led many governments to institute English-language instruction as part of school curricula; according to Chinese educators, some 400 million students in China are today getting English instruction at some level. But other governments have taken no such initiative, and in democracies whose States or provinces control educational policy, the result may be a patchwork of progress and stagnation. As noted in chapter 3, certain national governments proclaim a state religion, thereby closing the door to a church–state separation that has proven conducive to progress wherever it prevails and consigning believers in other faiths to lesser status and various forms of disadvantage.

Still, governmental decisions in such areas as education and religion, while important for the futures of their young citizens, do not normally have life and death consequences. But when governments take initiatives in the public health arena, they touch the destinies of millions. One of the most tragic examples of misguided government policy and its consequences concerns South Africa, whose post-Mandela leaders, virtually alone in the world, long denied the link between HIV and AIDS. The country's ministers of health for years insisted that AIDS could be staved off and treated through proper nutrition even as the government was forced by marches and civil disobedience to begin making effective drugs available to sufferers. As recently as 2006, a UN official at the World AIDS Conference described South African government theories on the source of the disease as "more worthy of a lunatic fringe than of a concerned and compassionate state" (Legassick, 2007). By denying medical evidence and defying public opinion, the South African government stood by as this, the most modern state in Subsaharan Africa, became one of the worst-afflicted societies in the realm, with 22 percent of all persons 15 to 49 years of age infected, a figure that, given its government source, is regarded by many researchers as an underestimate. As elsewhere in Subsaharan Africa, the AIDS epidemic in South Africa disproportionately afflicts women, who are four times as likely to be HIV-infected as men (UNAIDS, 2006). And the recorded rate of infection is still rising, so that average life expectancy in South Africa, already below 50, continues to decline. One result of the administration's disastrous management of this emergency is that an additional two to three million South Africans are infected but, accepting government misinformation, are not concerned and do not believe that they can transmit the virus to others.

The distribution of HIV/AIDS in Southern Africa regionally reveals more than just government failure on the issue in South Africa alone. In 2007, the worst-afflicted country in the world was neighboring Swaziland, a ministate ruled by an all-powerful king and his mother in which political parties are outlawed and where estimates of infection range between 33 and 43 percent. Lesotho and Botswana, also neighbors of South Africa, likewise have higher infection rates, and Botswana has the unhappy distinction of being one of the few countries in the world where male life expectancy (35) exceeds that of females (33), both being among the lowest recorded in modern times and reflecting the extreme impact of AIDS in Africa on women. Given the fact that Botswana has one of Africa's few upper-middle-income economies by World Bank standards, with a per capita gross national income of more than $10,000 in 2007 (South Africa's exceeds $12,000), it is clear that averaged national incomes reflect neither the state's capacity for intervention nor the individual citizen's ability to secure medical help. As South Africa's HIV/AIDS epidemic worsened, then-President Thabo Mbeki said in his public speeches that the fundamental cause of the disease was poverty, and while misleading, he was right in the sense that the poor have always been least able to obtain treatment for disease, and not just in South Africa and not just for AIDS. The government's misfeasance had least effect on the relatively well-off white sector in the South African population, more effect on locals in the Asian and Coloured communities, and by far the strongest impact on the black majority, numerically as well as proportionately comprising the bulk of the poor. If South Africa's dismal data were computed for this majority only, the country would rank alongside its smaller neighbors in every social index ranging from percentage infected to life expectancy.

What this underscores is the significance of scale in the context of all dimensions of destiny. With two-thirds of the entire world's HIV-positive adults and children in 2006, nearly three-quarters of all deaths, and millions of orphans, Subsaharan Africa is the world's worst-afflicted realm. Southern Africa is the regional epicenter of HIV/AIDS. South Africa is the deadliest large country; rural areas in three of its provinces (Eastern Cape, Free State, and KwaZulu-Natal) have the highest death rates; and ministate Swaziland (population one million) has the highest rate of infection overall. But even in Swaziland there are communities more severely affected than others.

Just how crucial government policy is when it comes to a health crisis of epidemic proportions in the global periphery was demonstrated in Uganda, once at the epicenter of the AIDS crisis in tropical Africa. Without massive financial resources or medical facilities to cope with the emergency, Uganda's government embarked on an intensive campaign of propaganda, education, and intervention—the last in the form of widespread distribution of condoms even in the most remote parts of the country. President Museveni himself joined the campaign, urging citizens to have themselves tested and to refrain from irresponsible sexual behavior while appealing to foreign donors for medicines and supplies. This effort resulted in a dramatic reduction of infection rates, giving hope to other African governments trying to combat the scourge with inadequate means.

Arrive in South Africa or, indeed, any other severely afflicted country as a global visitor, and you are not likely to be confronted by direct evidence of the crisis. HIV/AIDS is called the "slim disease" in many African languages because its symptoms include a loss of weight leading to a skeletal appearance late in the course of the disease, but in the cities and towns, in hotels, on the highways, and in the national parks, life seems to go on as it does anywhere else. An occasional billboard urging condom use and sporadic media commentary may be the only reminders that one is in a region suffering under a public health calamity so severe that labor shortages result from it in countries where unemployment is simultaneously a critical problem. As in the days of apartheid, globals travel the business and tourist routes and rarely or never see the battle being waged in the traditional rural areas, in the townships, and in the clinics.

LOCALE AND PRIVATION

Such features of scale and separation are not, of course, unique to modern South Africa or to Subsaharan Africa generally, and among the globals on those fast-track routes there are some who come to help rather than to profit or play. Among these, the economist-geographer Jeffrey Sachs believes that the state, even the oft-failed African state, is key to the reversal of fortune of those whose destinies it so strongly affects. More effective—and more liberally financed—state planning would not only improve national economies but also enhance the prospects of those now trapped in poverty. From agricultural technologies to health interventions, governments must lead a recovery they are best positioned to achieve. Sachs promotes his views by word and deed, pressuring leaders to improve their performance and directly supporting village budgets to illustrate how effective even small subventions can be. Having dealt with governments and locals in many parts of the world, Sachs has worked on the issue at all levels of scale (Sachs, 2005).

The dismal record of many African governments has discouraged other globalizers from pursuing this course, notably another economist, William Easterly, who argues that Western support for crooked and venal regimes only strengthens their hold over the people whose destinies they control. They point to the hundreds of billions of aid dollars that have flowed into Africa since decolonization without having reversed the realm's inexorable decline (Easterly, 2006). These scholars assert that the downside of destiny is so intractable that it is delusional to believe that any amount or kind of intervention can change it. There is nothing new about this argument, which was once applied to Asian economies that subsequently prospered. But in its latest incarnation, it comes dangerously close to equating extreme poverty and Africanness. If 70 percent of the world's poorest-of-the-poor are concentrated in a geographic realm that comprises only 12 percent of the global population, what does that say about Africans' failures?

What it reflects is a reluctance to acknowledge the particular and punitive combination of environmental, ecological, historical, cultural, economic, and political debilitations that afflict Subsaharan Africa and raise even higher than elsewhere the barriers to progress. Certainly Africa's own widespread failures of government and leadership are among these impairments, but what is often negated is the weight of the historic baggage Africa carries when the world is moving ever faster (de Blij, 2004). African destinies have been shaped by outsiders for centuries, and continue to be. Colonial governments built culturally emblematic cities complete with modern central business districts (CBDs) and attractive suburbs, but they also controlled inward migration by locals. After decolonization, the pent-up drive to relocate made Africa the fastest urbanizing realm on the planet, making Lagos and Nairobi synonymous with chaos and crime. Things were not any better in the countryside. Ask an African farmer trying to sell his or her crops on this "flat" world's markets, and you will hear how hard it is to compete with produce subsidized by rich and formerly colonial governments trying to buy the votes of their farmers through aid ranging from tax relief to tariff walls (to be sure, neither do African governments make their farmers' lives easy). Pervasive poverty has many causes, global as well as local, but its cost to Africa and thus to the world, from environmental damage to health crises and from persistent conflict to lost talent, is incalculable.

MOSAIC OF FATE

While there can be little doubt regarding the validity of the data, the various averages and indices that illustrate the general circumstances of life in rich as well as poor countries conceal variations that matter. They matter in the global core, where two countries with approximately the same gross national income (GNI) may have very different internal distributions of that income, so that one country has a sizable poor underclass and far wider income disparities than the other. They also matter in the periphery, where similar data on health conditions (for example, number of doctors or number of hospital beds per thousand inhabitants) say nothing about accessibility or cost.

These variations tend to be spatial as well as structural, geographic as well as systemic. If there is a symbol of globalization, and perhaps of the "flat" world imagined by many globals, it must surely be the gated communities that have made their appearance even in the poorest of states. These had their predecessors, of course, during imperial times, when the enclaves of colonists presented comfort and security enabled by power and control. Today they beckon not only the expatriates of global business but also the newly rich domestic globals, often with huge illustrated billboards promising exclusivity, security, self-sufficiency, and facilities covering demand ranging from spas to sports. Given the urban geographies of cities in the periphery, such enclaves may be buffered by distance from poorer neighborhoods, but often the advantage of proximity to the CBD prevails over the seclusion that comes with distance and a long commute, so that privilege and privation exist cheek by jowl, different worlds separated by a wall, fence, or canal. Vastly divergent destinies are separated by a barrier and a few meters of soil.

Another pernicious practice is as old as commerce itself: corruption. These days, countries of the world are ranked by various agencies in terms of the levels of corruption they endure. Again, such rankings conceal not only very different symptoms of the problem, but also the geography. It is reasonable to link corruption to government; rulers and appointed as well as elected leaders (and not just in the poorest states) have stashed away countless billions in foreign bank accounts, and information on such thefts forms a large part of the "corruption index" assigned to individual states. While corruption at this level affects every citizen for obvious reasons, it is corruption in other forms that afflicts ordinary people: corruption by extortion. As a local, try opening a bank account, ordering a telephone, passing a driver license test, or even just traveling a road, and you may be forced to pay an overcharge, bribe, or "toll" that does not merely go into the pocket of the clerk, technician, or outlaw involved, but gets disbursed to networks of profiteers who enrich themselves at the cost of the public. Living with such corruption becomes a suffocating way of life that saps confidence and initiative.

Corruption, of course, is a crime, and globals tend to think of it as a particular problem in the periphery, where its impact is especially grim. But certain states in the global core also suffer severely from it. In Italy, a founding member of the European Union, organized crime represents the largest single segment of the national economy. Extortion, usury, racketeering, and other forms of villainy infect the Italian economy, and "businessmen prefer to make a pact with the Mafia rather than denounce the blackmail" (Kiefer, 2007). A combination of colluding politicians, countless public contracts, and conspiring businesses creates opportunities for graft unmatched in the heart of the European Union. The geography of this malaise reveals a higher incidence of it in Italy's poorer Mezzogiorno, from Campania, Calabria, and Puglia to Sicily, than in the richer and more international north, but it is a national, not merely a regional, problem.

To oppose what is routine, from the big-time politics of patronage to the "petty" corruption of daily life, can be risky and even dangerous, and especially so in the poorest countries where a veneer of democracy conceals ruthless protection of vested interests by insiders willing to use all tactics to maintain their advantage. And yet every thoroughly corrupt society has its courageous and incorruptible opponents of the status quo, who use whatever means available to expose wrongdoing, and who do so in the face of imprisonment, exile, or worse. These are the lawmakers, businesspeople and technicians, officials, media people, and teachers who are the hope for the future in countries where destiny weighs most heavily on locals.

Confronting this insidious side of the power of place can be a daunting experience for the uninitiated. For many years, globals arriving at Lagos airport got a taste of what Nigerians cope with when passing through customs and immigration "formalities" and retrieving their luggage. Those unfamiliar with what was then the standard shakedown procedure, and who found themselves without the small (and not-so-small) denomination bills with which to pay off those in control of entry and baggage delivery, had nowhere to turn; police, if in evidence at all, turned a blind eye. On final approach, a palpable tension settled over those passengers aware of what lay ahead; those unaware would soon feel the first pang of what expatriates often described as "culture shock." What those airplane riders experienced, however, was very much like the apprehension felt by locals in cars and buses traveling on rural main roads often waylaid by petty criminals. Living with corruption and extortion at the local level on a daily basis has a suffocating effect on the public. The concept of the failed state means different things to different people. Having nowhere to turn is the symptom at the local level.

In the aftermath of the dreadful Sani Abacha dictatorship (1993–1998), Nigeria's new and democratically elected government addressed corruption and extortion problems in high-profile ways, thereby exposing how this, Africa's most populous state, had been— and continued to be—mismanaged at every level, its institutions weakened and eroded and public confidence at a low ebb. In 1999 a president, Olusegun Obasanjo, was democratically elected and immediately faced poverty-generated crises including Muslim fundamentalism in the north and fuel-price riots in the south. When he was reelected in 2003, he tightened the scrutiny of federal and State investment projects to ensure open bids and financial transparency. He also ordered a check on the offices of State governors. By 2006, of the country's 36 State governors, 33 were under indictment or formal investigation for "financial irregularities." On Transparency International's corruption index, Nigeria in 2007 still scored a mere 2.2 out of 10—the third-lowest score in Subsaharan Africa and one of the lowest (worst) in the world. It matters all the more because Nigerians constitute nearly one-fifth of the realm's total population.

When Americans hear about Nigeria in the media, the news is likely to focus on the country's large oil reserves centered in and near the Niger River delta, the discord between the federal government trying to keep order and locals seeking to gain a larger share of the proceeds, occasional kidnappings of foreign oil-company employees by members of the Movement for the Emancipation of the Niger Delta (MEND), and deadly fires caused by attempted thefts of oil from pipelines leading to export terminals. Nigeria's oil wealth has not brought it prosperity, which raises the general question of why countries rich in resources can nevertheless sink into the deepest poverty. Global resource distribution is one key aspect of the mosaic of fate represented by the world's boundary framework: some countries found themselves with riches ranging from diamonds to "black gold," as oil is sometimes called, but others have very little in the way of saleable commodities. It would seem that the larger a country is, the better its chances of having a bigger share of the world's resources, but it does not always work out that way. Mali is about 70 times as large as Kuwait, but Kuwait has a sizeable share of the world's oil reserves while Mali has a little gold and some salt. Once again, geography, in the form of location, matters. Some countries lie astride rich mineralized zones. Others are less fortunate.

Perhaps the word "fortunate" is not appropriate in this context (certainly not in the case of Nigeria). Africa's natural resources were among the attractions that drew colonizers to its shores; further discoveries made many of those colonies profitable and set a pattern of exploitation that continued after they became independent states. When a country depends on commodity sales to fund its needs, however, this suppresses other kinds of productivity and creates a dependence that can prove fatal should commodity prices drop. Even if they do not drop, revenues from sales of oil, gold, or other saleable products must be invested in ways that will diversify the economy and protect other industries, including less glamorous agriculture, against the inflationary forces that commodity sales generate. But such income arrives in cash easily spent on megaprojects and even more easily diverted to personal use by those in control, so that resource wealth has political implications, too: it tends to entrench autocratic regimes. It also makes struggling toward representative government and efficient administration more rather than less difficult.

In Nigeria's case, oil was discovered in the delta shortly before independence, so that no colonial pattern of energy exports had been set when sovereignty arrived in 1960. The tragic story of Nigeria's collapse is all too well known: an oil-fueled boom in the 1980s was accompanied by heavy borrowing on future income, wasteful mega-projects, skyrocketing corruption, and neglect of industries that had once formed the cornerstone of the Nigerian economy. Then the world price of oil crashed and so did Nigerian standards of living, and poverty spread like an infectious disease. The World Bank and other international financial institutions stepped in to help Nigeria institute needed reforms that had the unavoidable effect of mak-ing life even more difficult for locals caught in the downward spiral. Meanwhile, billions of dollars were stolen by Abacha and his gener-als, whose murderous suppression of protest in the Niger Delta may have helped oil-company operations but caused worldwide revulsion. Not until the return of democracy and the oil-price recovery after the turn of the century did Nigeria's economic prospects brighten some-what—even as its democratic institutions still proved shaky during the election of 2007.

The Nigerian case is especially significant because it confirms that governance is crucial when it comes to resource windfalls. In many other economically poor but well-endowed countries, colonial powers laid out the facilitating infrastructure, created the system of resource exploitation, and turned the economy over to their local successors, who usually failed to sustain it. Nigeria's bonanza came after the British had left behind a mixed economy, and the institutions of its government proved to be incapable of meeting the challenge. A more recent example is Sudan, whose recently discovered oil reserves made an oil exporter out of a long-term importer, with terrible consequences for locals near and far—near the oilfields, where villagers were summarily forced off their lands, and far away in Darfur, where the regime's newfound power translated into impunity. Valuable natural resources can be a curse as well as a boon (Collier, 2007). They generate revenues, but they also fuel strife.

CONFINES OF CONFLICT

No part of this planet is immune from the conflicts humans generate, but certain places are historically so prone to strife that their very names symbolize trouble: the Balkans (*balkanization* has become a term for hostile fragmentation); Palestine and environs, where the latest and current confrontations are only the most recent in millennia of contention; the Horn of Africa, where resurgent Islam has buffeted ancient Christianity for centuries; the Transcaucasus, where empires and ideologies have collided since time immemorial; the Western Rift Valley region of equatorial Africa, where cultural conflict has claimed millions over generations.

The locals caught in these conflicts, which are often latent until stoked by external forces, often adapt by constructing distinctive, variegated, and eclectic cultures. Language, religion, music, dance, diets, dress modes, and other cultural attributes confer on each generation a sense of endurance and continuance that sustains confidence in times of strife. Historically, their options were limited by weakness and isolation, and their survival depended on local cohesion rather than state protection. Today, a growing number respond by becoming mobals. Troubled Armenia, on the flanks of Transcaucasia and adjoining its nemesis Turkey, annexed by the Soviet Union, freed by its collapse and now in discord with its neighbor Azerbaijan, has historically generated a large diaspora. Currently, an estimated 20 percent of its locally born population live abroad. Their remittances and other forms of support have been vital to this impoverished, landlocked state. Along with poverty, violence forms a powerful push factor in the genesis of migration.

In this globalizing world, conflicts attract unprecedented attention because the diffusion of technologies ensures the widespread dissemination of information. Even the generals of Myanmar are unable to effectively conceal their armed campaigns against the country's minorities, and the uprising led by Buddhist monks in September 2007 could be seen in real time on television. But such information does not always elicit coordinated international action. It took unconscionably long (and ultimately American leadership) to stop the latest carnage in the Balkans as more than 200,000 locals lost their lives, many in concentration camps, in the collapse of Yugoslavia. The locals in Rwanda, Burundi, and the eastern Congo were less fortunate still, their destinies shaped by colonial imperatives, cultural discord, demographic crises, political truculence, natural habitat, and physical remoteness. Today's catastrophe echoes earlier ones: "In four months in 1972, an estimated 100,000 Hutus were slaughtered in Burundi by the minority Tutsi elite.... [T]ens of thousands of women and children were dragged from their homes and schools and clubbed to death.... [A]pproximately 3.5 percent of the country's total population was liquidated in a matter of weeks, yet the OAU and the UN took no action, and raised little effective protest" (Best and de Blij, 1977). Beginning in 1994, the epicenter of civil war was Rwanda, where Tutsi and Hutu exacted a terrible toll on each other and spread the conflict into neighboring countries. To the locals in this strife-endemic area today, migration still is no option, and effective international intervention again has not materialized. Escaping on foot from the arena of conflict means entering a refugee camp that is likely to be the target of marauding gangs; peacekeeping efforts by the Organization of African Unity (OAU) and the UN were essentially to no avail. By the middle of the current decade, the estimated death toll among locals in this relatively limited area was 3.5 million, a searing indictment of the "international community" and a reminder that geography—physical as well as human—still figures dominantly in their destinies.

A map of the world's theaters of recurrent conflict suggests that the effects of landlocked location extend beyond economics and commerce (figure 6.2). Although coastal states are as vulnerable to ethnic and cultural strife as landlocked states are, access facilitates remediation, as was the case when a British-led coalition intervened in and ended a civil war in Sierra Leone in 2000 (earlier, failing Somalia's coastal location had invited an intervention that was doomed by the dimensions and intractability of its problems). When a state is landlocked, regimes are able to act with greater impunity, and combatants can better avoid scrutiny. A civil war raged for more than three decades in the Southern Sudan, resulting in two million deaths and four million internal refugees; again, international involvement was deterred by the relative location of one of the world's most land-locked arenas of conflict. An agreement brokered through interna-tional mediation ended the war, but raised a new problem: the peoples of Sudan's southern provinces soon will be allowed to vote on inde-pendence. Approval would create yet another landlocked, very poor country. Meanwhile, the more recent conflict in deeply landlocked Darfur, spilling over into (also landlocked) Chad and Central African Republic, further evinces the role of remoteness in the persistence of state-fueled strife. While Sudan is not landlocked, its govern-ment, supporting militias that played crucial roles in the dislocation of more than one million of Darfur's people and the deaths of more than 200,000, held the trump card in terms of access: to get to Darfur, you first have to touch down at Khartoum. International interven-tion could not occur without the cooperation of the state that has the most interest in constraining it. The locals who are the pawns in the struggle suffer the consequences.

International intervention is one way to mitigate conflict in strife-prone places; what other solutions might be tried? A recent study argues that endemic strife prevails in certain areas "due to the struc-ture of boundaries between groups rather than as a result of inherent conflicts between the groups themselves.... [D]iverse social and eco-nomic factors trigger violence when the spatial population structure creates a propensity to conflict, so that spatial heterogeneity itself is predictive of local violence" (Lim et al., 2007). When ethnic or cul-tural groups are intensely mixed, they tend not to engage in violent conflict; neither do groups that are clearly separated. It is group size, partial separation, and poorly defined boundaries that foster conflict: "Geography is an important aspect of the dimension of social space." Although the authors do not propose policy options, they clearly believe that interventions in historically strife-afflicted areas should include the restructuring of place: "conflict might be prevented or minimized by political acts that create appropriate boundaries suited to the current geocultural regions rather than the existing histori-cally based state boundaries. Such boundaries need not inhibit trade or commerce...but should allow each cultural group to adopt inde-pendent behaviors in separate domains. Peaceful coexistence need not

WORLD AREAS OF RECURRENT CONFLICT

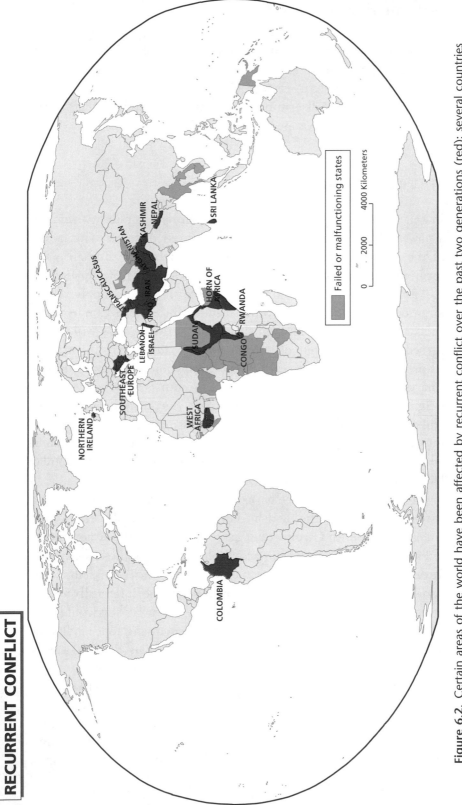

Figure 6.2. Certain areas of the world have been affected by recurrent conflict over the past two generations (red); several countries regarded as failed states are among those afflicted, including pre-intervention Afghanistan and post-colonial Somalia. Other countries (gray) are seen as being under stress and as "candidates for failure" by the World Bank and other agencies.

require complete integration." In practical terms, such social-spatial engineering may be possible in places like Bosnia and perhaps Iraq, but it is unattainable in eastern Congo and western Sudan, where reaching the scene, disarming the combatants, and protecting the locals is all that can be hoped for.

STILL ROUGH COUNTRY

In this twenty-first-century world, therefore, accessibility remains a powerful and fateful factor in the destinies of locals. The failure of the international community to intervene in the human disaster in interior Equatorial Africa is as much a matter of logistics and cost as it is of will; maps showing passable all-season supply routes, airports, landing strips, and other facilities in eastern Congo reveal the magnitude of the logistical challenge there (as far as will is concerned, Rwanda had one of Africa's better road systems throughout its prolonged ordeal, but few peacekeeping vehicles traversed them). The same locational and environmental circumstances that concealed Belgian and other foreign excesses during the rule of King Leopold still camouflage agonies that would otherwise mobilize multinational intervention. Millions of locals perished in the Congo and Cambodia while the world's attention was focused on the fate of the Soviet Union, Yugoslavia, and Afghanistan.

Accessibility should also be seen in the context of scale and scope. It was one thing for the British to intervene in coastal Sierra Leone, smaller than South Carolina, but quite another for the Americans to attempt something similar in accessible Somalia, almost as large as Texas. When, in advance of the 2003 intervention, Turkey closed the door to American ingress into California-sized Iraq, it fatefully altered options as well as strategies. Military routes from Turkey would have had to cross through the Kurdish domain, endowing that landlocked and potentially independent entity with potentials the Turks were unwilling to countenance. Inaccessible North Korea may have two coastlines, but its lengthiest and heavily demarcated land border is with its ally China, and its other boundary is the sealed Demilitarized Zone, so its regime can subject millions of wretched locals to famine and starvation for political ends without revealing what is happening. Relevant also is the map of Myanmar: this isolated country's lengthy coastline and river routes do not translate into international linkages. Indeed, it is the Chinese who are penetrating the ruling junta's cocoon by creating opportunities in the interior. Along their boundary with the Shan State, one of Myanmar's minority districts, local trade and cross-border migration are changing the cultural landscape.

The world still is a patchwork of spaces open, accessible, and interconnected while others remain closed, remote, and isolated. Barriers in the former are receding, and locals as well as globals make the most of it. The pitfalls miring the poor and powerless still corrugate the world of the latter. The global playing field has undoubtedly leveled in the core and in significant corridors of the periphery, but "given the global facilities that exist today...many people find it hard to enter the global economy at all. The concentration on those who are gainfully engaged in trade leaves out millions who remain excluded—and effectively unwelcome—from the activities of the privileged.... [Global] inequality not only is terribly large, but is also getting marginally *larger*" (Sen, 2006).

It is the privileged, the globals, whose resources create options of which billions of locals can only dream, who have not only the advantage of security but also the luxury of choice. In his commentary on identity, Sen argues that people see themselves as members of a variety of groups: citizenship, place of residence, geographic origin, gender, class, politics, profession, employment, food habits, sports interests, taste in music, social commitments, and so forth, that make us members of "collectivities" that endow us all with particular identities. He cites several examples: the Bangladeshi Muslim who is "not only a Muslim but also a Bengali and a Bangladeshi, typically quite proud of the Bengali language, literature, and music, not to mention the other identities he or she may have connected with class, gender, occupation, politics, aesthetic taste, and so on." He sees himself as "an Asian, an Indian citizen, a Bengali with Bangladeshi ancestry, an American or British resident, an economist, a dabbler in philosophy, an author, a Sanskritist, a strong believer in secularism and democracy, a man, a feminist, a heterosexual, a defender of gay and lesbian rights, with a nonreligious lifestyle, from a Hindu background, a non-Brahmin, and a nonbeliever in an afterlife." To emphasize the point, he argues that a person could be "a British citizen, of Malaysian origin, with Chinese racial characteristics, a stockbroker, a nonvegetarian, an asthmatic, a linguist, a bodybuilder, a poet, an opponent of abortion, a bird-watcher, an astrologer, and one who believes that God created Darwin to test the gullible."

Such multiple identities, however, reflect the destinies of globals and their comparative freedom of choice. Their privileges arise from the good fortune of their place of birth, their natural and cultural environs, the prosperity, stability, and social norms of their society, prevailing educational and medical standards, and other attributes of the global core and its wider sphere. Not many locals in rural Africa will wonder whether God created Darwin to test the gullible, and millions of Bangladeshis have little time to nurture their pride in the Bengali language, literature, or music. While an American global who is also gay may make homosexual rights the focus of his various identities, a local in Sudan is likely to find herself debilitated from malaria and other endemic maladies, inadequately nourished, over-worked, in danger of male violence, at risk from militants, her life centered on the survival of her children and her thoughts on the next day, not her sexuality or the future of democracy. "Deciding on what our relevant identities are," in Sen's words, is an entitlement of the privileged, not a universal accessory.

Locational, demographic, religious, linguistic, medical, economic, and social factors combine to formulate an aggregate power of place that is further defined by natural and environmental conditions. So variegated is this spatial mosaic that human adaptation is infinitely diverse. Such adaptation creates a preference for familiar surround-ings that persuades the overwhelming majority of us to stay in or near the place we know best, even under threat of armed conflict or at risk from natural hazards. When a small minority of migrants do make their move, these intercultural mobals often find their way blocked by barriers and regulations. The global playing field remains far from level.

7

SAME PLACE, DIVERGENT DESTINIES

Dramatic media pictures of desperate would-be mobals clinging to overcrowded boats, climbing over border fences, or running across unguarded wasteland confirm statistical data: males are in the vanguard of unregulated as well as legal transnational migration. Less graphic photography of the average business-class section of a 747 flying from Los Angeles to Hong Kong would reveal that most of the comfortable globals en route are male as well. But scrutinize a daytime picture of an African or Asian village, and you are likely to notice that among the locals, women outnumber men, whether working in the fields, carrying water or firewood, preparing food, or tending children. If the Earth seems flat, this is far more so for males than for females.

Even in the same village, in the same house, the destinies of boys and girls diverge startlingly, and not only in rural villages in the global periphery. Equality of the sexes in employment, income, political influence, and other circumstances is an elusive goal even in the richest countries of the global core. Northern European countries are often cited as having progressed furthest in this respect, but even there, the playing field (for example, in religious hierarchies) is not completely level. Nor does growing wealth guarantee progress in closing the gender gap. Male dominance is a deeply embedded tradition that has a way of trumping fairness: in modern Japan, where women have made significant strides by many measures, the Minister of Health and Welfare in July 2007 publicly referred to the role of women as being "birth-giving machines" (*Economist*, 2007d). When China in the late 1970s embarked on its economic reforms, one key to success was deemed to lie in bringing its population spiral under control. China's "one child only" policy had the desired result, but in effect it frequently meant one *male* child only as tens of millions of pregnancies were aborted to ensure a male heir. Millions more female

WORLD CHILD MORTALITY

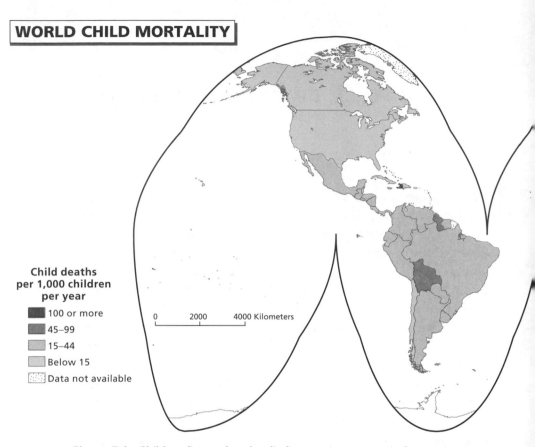

Figure 7.1. Children five and under die from various causes in far greater numbers in the periphery than in the core. The darker the orange on this map, the higher the annual mortality, but despite the regional contrasts, the situation is significantly better than it was just one generation ago. Data from Table G-1 in H. J. de Blij and P. O. Muller, *Geography: Realms, Regions and Concepts*, 13th ed. (New York: Wiley, 2008).

infants were and are abandoned, giving rise to an international adoption industry that is almost exclusively female. Today, economically booming China has a demographic surplus of some 20 million males, with troubling implications for the future. Similarly obscene sex ratios in northern India reflect the grim realities of life for many females in the world's other demographic giant (Corbridge and Harriss, 2000). The divergent destinies of females and males often actuate before birth.

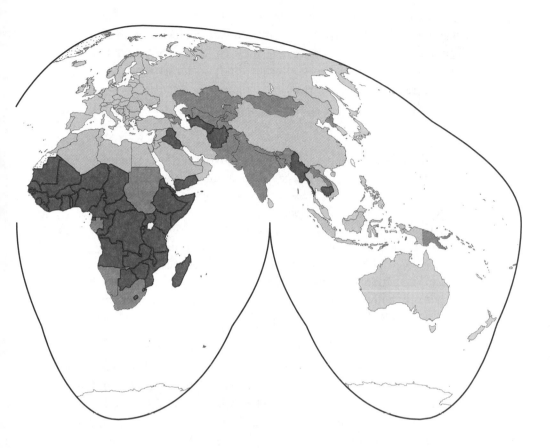

Once born, however, the inequalities that last a lifetime tend to be concealed by official statistics. Infant and child mortality are among the social indices that mark any society's level of development, but all too rarely are these reported by gender. Data on poverty are also generalized, yet it is clear that women bear the brunt of it: where households are poor and children do not have a good prospect of survival, women are regarded primarily as bearers and raisers of children, locking them in a cycle of privation from which they cannot escape. Although substantial progress has been made in many countries of the periphery in lowering the mortality of infants and children, the situation in much of Subsaharan Africa still is dreadful, as it is in such Asian countries as Pakistan, Myanmar, and Cambodia (figure 7.1).

Of those children that do survive, the males tend to have better access to what limited health and education facilities are available. From the start, and on average, male children are better taken care of than are females. Boys in traditional societies tend to get more and better medical attention and treatment, get the better share of available food, and get accustomed early in life to privileges denied to girls.

> In the village, girls are inducted early into the cycle of female poverty and overwork that has trapped their mothers and previous generations. Money for school fees is often short; what is available first goes to pay for the boys. As soon as she can carry anything at all, the girl goes with her mother to weed the fields, to bring back firewood, to fetch water. She will do so an average of perhaps twelve hours a day, seven days a week, for the years she remains capable of working. But the national statistics, at the end of the year or at the end of her punishing life, will say nothing about her contribution to village or country. (de Blij, 1996)

In the closing decade of the twentieth century, mortality rates for children 1 to 5 years of age showed the results: in Pakistan, 54 girls per thousand died annually as compared to 37 boys; in Bangladesh, the ratio was 69 to 58; in Thailand, 27 to 17 (United Nations, 2000). Although the gap has narrowed over the past generation, it is still there, and it is by no means confined to the poorest of poor societies.

The educational results can be seen in the varying literacy rates for males and females. In India, for example, the literacy rate for males in 2008 approached 70 percent, but for women it was barely more than 40 percent. English may be seen as India's lingua franca and the key to India's success in information technology industries, but only an estimated 5 percent of Indians are bilingual, and of these, the majority are males. In neighboring Bangladesh, the situation is even worse: male literacy exceeds 50 percent, but female literacy hovers around 30 percent. Imagine this: in Sudan, one of Africa's largest countries and located in the crucial transition zone between Muslim and non-Muslim realms, female literacy in 2008 was about 14 percent, more than 20 percent lower than that of males. The poverty trap is directly related to the education gap.

THE LONGEVITY GAP

Given these monumental disadvantages, how is it that life expectancies for women are normally higher than those for men? In the overwhelming majority of countries of the world, women on average live years longer than men, in some cases (the Baltic countries, Russia) a decade longer or even more (figure 7.2). This global longevity gap widened between 1950 and 2000 from less than 5 to nearly 7 years and is attributed to several causes, among them the survival of the fittest during those early years of nutritional and medical disadvantage. During the first year of life, male mortality averages 25 percent higher than female mortality. But because about 105 males are born for every 100 females, the numbers are about even by the time reproduction starts. Different hormones and chromosomal factors also play a role, but women may also be intrinsically stronger than men. In addition to benefiting from measurable socioeconomic progress in poorer societies, "women seem to have been less inclined to adopt some of the unhealthy habits often associated with affluence: smoking in particular, but also excessive consumption of food and alcohol, fast driving (and high accident rates), and high levels of work-related stress" (Sivard, 1985). Those prescient words certainly applied to post-Soviet Russia, where male life expectancy declined dramatically in the years following the collapse of the communist empire as a result of alcoholism, accidents, drug abuse, suicide, and untreated disease. In the general social disorder accompanying Russia's difficult transition, even female life expectancy dropped, but not nearly as far as that of males.

As the map shows, the longevity gap is larger in the global core than in the periphery, although it is growing faster outside the core in certain parts of the world than in others. Where life expectancy for men exceeds that for women (today only four countries, all in Subsaharan Africa, display this condition), or where men and women have equal life expectancies (five others, three in Africa and two small island states), something serious is amiss, and, as noted in chapter 4, in Subsaharan Africa this relates primarily to the AIDS pandemic. Africa's disastrous decline in life expectancies for men as well as women has also narrowed the longevity gap to what is regionally the narrowest in the world.

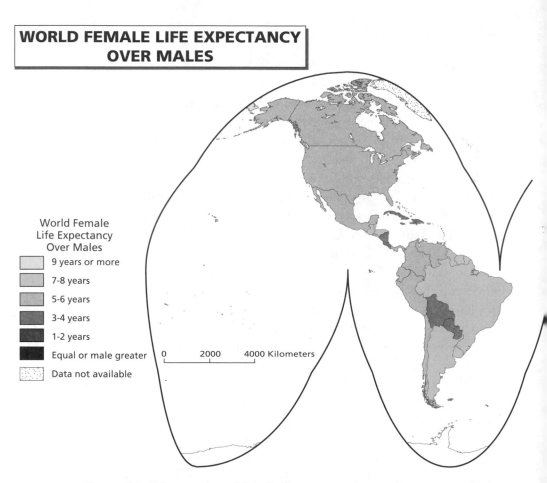

WORLD FEMALE LIFE EXPECTANCY OVER MALES

World Female
Life Expectancy
Over Males

- 9 years or more
- 7-8 years
- 5-6 years
- 3-4 years
- 1-2 years
- Equal or male greater
- Data not available

0   2000   4000 Kilometers

Figure 7.2. Where male and female life expectancies are the same, nearly the same, or where men live longer on average than women, something serious is amiss. Data from Table G-1 in H. J. de Blij and P. O. Muller, *Geography: Realms, Regions and Concepts,* 13th ed. (New York: Wiley, 2008).

The longevity gap should also be seen in terms of the risks of childbirth. Pregnancy and childbirth pose greater health risks to women in the global periphery than in the core, risks that, on average, were recently rated by the United Nations as 23 times greater. The good news is that the range is narrowing: in the two decades ending the last century, although a dozen countries in the periphery still suffered more than 500 deaths per 100,000 childbirths, another dozen, in the core, reported fewer than 10 per 100,000. The bad news is that the contrast still remains agonizing, with women in some countries

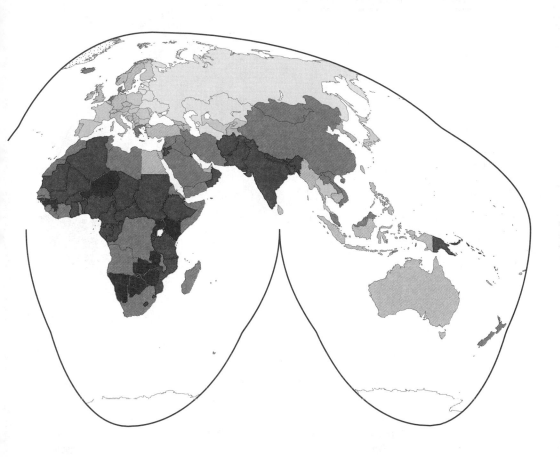

of the periphery dying in childbirth at a rate 20 times as high as that prevailing in certain countries of the core (figure 7.3).

Longer life is advantageous only if the circumstances of life are acceptable, and in the global core millions of widows live satisfactory lives in relative comfort and security. But in virtually all cultures, men tend to marry women who are younger, so married women can expect to outlive their husbands, often by a decade or more. Hundreds of millions of women in less prosperous societies face grave difficulties following the deaths of their spouses. As family ties loosen, countless women who have spent lifetimes sustaining their families find themselves alone in their last years, in poverty and without sufficient (or any) support from a deceased husband's residual resources. In this man's world, even a woman's comparative longevity has its downside.

WORLD MATERNAL MORTALITY

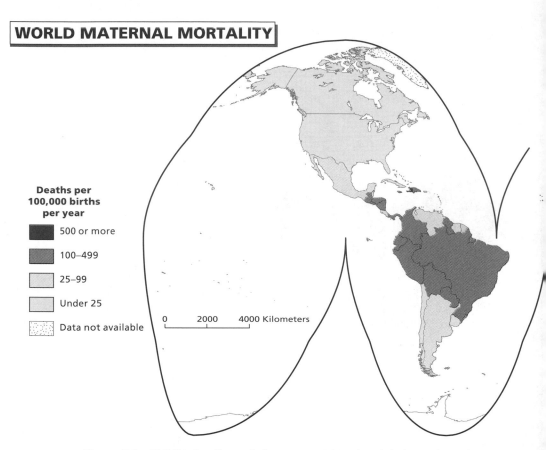

**Deaths per
100,000 births
per year**

500 or more

100–499

25–99

Under 25

Data not available

0   2000   4000 Kilometers

Figure 7.3. Childbirth still entails far greater risk in the global periphery than in the core, annually ranging from over 500 per 100,000 births in much of Africa to under 25 in Europe, North America, Japan, and Australia. Data from *Maternal Mortality in 2005*, published by the World Bank and based on estimates from WHO, UNICEF, UNFPA, and the World Bank.

QUALITY OF LIFE

Geographers often refer to tangible social environment as a cultural landscape, suggesting that the material representations of culture, from public buildings to simple dwellings and from decorative gardens to farm fields, are products of prevailing traditions forged over time. As such, they also reflect natural conditions (flat-roofed desert houses, high-pitched roofs under rainy climes) and the availability of building materials (wood, stone), creating preferences that may outlast changing technologies.

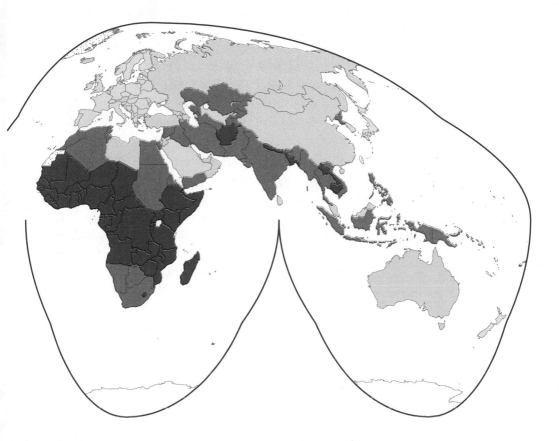

Whatever its genesis, the exterior fabric of the cultural landscape is largely made by men. The edifices of religion, a key component of cultural landscapes, represent the dominance of popes, bishops, imams, and monks. Chinese geomancers, whose instructions determine the favorable orientation of buildings, are male. Engineers, planners, and builders still are mostly male as well. The cultural landscape "is created and dominated by males; men are traditionally associated with the outdoors.... [T]he home is the indoor, female space, which is less well known" (Lloyd et al., 1982). Studies of male activity and mobility in rural areas show that women spend far more time within, and in the immediate vicinity of, their dwellings than men do, even when women manage to engage in some commerce or trade. Imprisoned by family obligations, inferior education, inadequate legal protections, and unavailable support in the form of credit or pension, women in the poorer areas of the global periphery are the most local of locals.

They are not, however, alone in experiencing the localizing pressures of the man-made world. Although males comprise the majority of transnational migrants, females in large numbers also cross international borders to seek term employment as domestic workers, often with the active encouragement of governments eager for their remittances. The major source for this cyclic "contract" migration, the Philippines, is only the best-known among "sending" countries whose policies weaken these aspiring mobals' bargaining power, colluding with "destination" governments, keeping their wages low and limiting their options by restricting their chances of relocating permanently. Even in the postindustrial societies of the global core, where women participate far more in the mobility that comes with modernity, research shows that women tend to take jobs closer to home and try to secure working hours that allow them to attend to domestic burdens, resulting not only in a subtle pattern of occupational segregation but also in wage differentials that persist in the richest of societies (Hanson and Pratt, 1995). Compared to the plight of many women in rural areas of the periphery, these may seem minor biases, but they do confirm that the world is "flatter," in general, for men than it is for women, whether in the core or in the periphery.

Although much statistical information underscores this disparity, no overall measure of "quality of life by gender" has been devised for the countries of the world in the mode of Transparency International's "corruption index" or annual surveys of cities' rankings according to their "livability" qualities. Gallup and Pew, among other organizations, poll for levels of "happiness" and "satisfaction," their results asserting that richer societies are also more contented, but neither organization maps those results by gender. The United Nations keeps track of human rights conditions in its member countries, but such records also do not consistently reflect gender differences. In any case, it would be difficult to measure quantitatively such widely varying quality-of-life issues as a woman's right to drive a car or to travel without a male family member's permission, on the one hand, and domestic violence or female genital mutilation, on the other.

What is known fragmentarily is dismaying. Domestic violence, overwhelmingly instigated by males, is a global, cross-cultural phenomenon. It occurs among the rich as well as the poor and in industrialized as well as traditional societies. Surveys show that the incidence of such violence is astonishingly high. In a large UN study of divorce in a high-income European Union member state, physical violence against the wife was cited in nearly 60 percent of all cases. In a more recent study of social conditions in a Bangkok shantytown, more than 50 percent of women reported regular beatings by their husbands. A study from Brazil reported two dozen unpunished domestic murders in one small State alone; it was stated that the murdered wives had been killed "justifiably" by their husbands. In India, "suicide rates for married women are higher than anywhere else and an alarming number of young Indian brides are daily reported burned to death in kitchen accidents. Such tragic 'accidents' usually occur to young women whose parents have failed to remit adequate dowry payments" (Wolpert, 1999). In Turkey, "honor killings" of "disgraced" female family members, usually by fathers or brothers, are an issue in the formal discussions relating to Turkey's prospective entry into the European Union; in Europe itself, this practice, perceived as a tenet of Islamic tradition, affects intercultural relations (Howland, 2001). Even modes of dress can lead to violence or worse. In Iran, gangs of Islamic zealots rough up women deemed to wear apparel that is too "revealing"; in Pakistan in 2006, government efforts to protect women against "misinterpretation" of Islamic Hudood laws were not enough to stop an extremist from killing a provincial government minister because her gauzy head covering was not sufficiently "Islamic."

The variable geography of religious dogma, as noted in chapter 3, makes life difficult for intercultural migrants as well as their hosts. Male dominance is an even older imperative than religious obsession, and together they form a nefarious mix that continues to afflict women, even in modern societies. The Talmud instructs the Orthodox Jew to thank his maker every day that he was not born a woman. The Bible has it that Eve was made from Adam's rib, joined him in eating the forbidden fruit, and was punished for all time through pain in childbirth and enduring subordination. The Quran is suffused with sexual repression and depictions of women as unclean temptresses whose form and face must be hidden. None of this would matter if ancient holy books were not taken literally or seriously by significant segments of society, but they continue to be, with disproportional impact on women. The segregation of sexes that naturally flows from

Quranic teachings invariably disadvantages women. The established male hierarchies that dominate Christian sects are only now cracking slightly. Male dominance reinforced by religious authority has created a power structure even in avowedly secular societies that is, more or less, the global norm.

Sharia, the body of Islamic laws, may be the most malevolent expression of this dominance, although local interpretations of Sharia rules vary widely. Invariably, however, Sharia law, however interpreted, disadvantages women. Salman Rushdie has focused the world's attention on the case of Imrana, a woman in northern India who was raped by her father-in-law. The Islamist seminary in her area, where the ultraconservative Deobandi sect in whose religious schools, or *madrassas*, the original Taliban were trained, ruled that she must leave her husband because, as a result of the rape, she was now "unclean." Without recourse and at the mercy of the mullahs, Imrana complied, which left her destitute: the husband was under no obligation to support her and, in any case, there is no alimony under Islamic law. "In [Muslim] honor-and-shame cultures like those of India and Pakistan, male honor resides in the sexual probity of women.... [T]he belief that a raped woman's best recourse is to kill herself remains widespread and deeply ingrained. [Pakistan's] government...has allied with the West in the war on terrorism, but seems quite prepared to allow a war of sexual terror to be waged against its female citizens" (Rushdie, 2005).

This sexual terror has other heinous manifestations. One is a practice referred to as female genital mutilation, a procedure also called female circumcision, still performed, in this first decade of the twenty-first century, on as many as two million girls under the age of 11 every year. It involves the complete or partial removal of the clitoris, often with crude equipment and without anesthesia, and frequently leads to infection, infertility, or increased difficulties in childbirth. Variations of it take place in several areas of the world, including many countries in Southwest and Southeast Asia and Africa. The World Health Organization's estimates suggest that between 70 and 90 percent of all women in Somalia have been subjected to female circumcision, but the practice also takes place in Sudan and Egypt. Regarded as barbaric by many observers, it is defended in cultures where it endures as an ancient ritual designed to ensure the virginity and suitability of women for marriage and as a "control" on women's attitude toward sex. Such arguments are hard to accept for even an extreme cultural relativist, but initiatives to ban the practice lead to another issue: who should determine what is permitted in a particular society? Seen as a violation of fundamental human rights by some, it is treated as a matter of cultural sovereignty by others. No such argument, however, can counter the inequality between the sexes represented by this hideous procedure.

What is beyond doubt is that its elimination must come from within the societies where it prevails; pressures from outsiders tend to raise objections and defenses. Already, adverse publicity and public opposition has caused some governments in countries where the procedure continues to occur to seek ways to curb or eliminate it. In Egypt in 1996, a television program showed a harrowing sequence of a girl, screaming in pain and bleeding profusely, being circumcised by a robed male in religious garb. The outcry that followed led to the government's injunction against the procedure, but with little effect: a nationwide survey in 2005 revealed that 97 percent of married women had been subjected to it (*Economist*, 2007e). A majority of Egyptians, including about two-thirds of all mothers, still support the practice, largely because conservative clerics proclaim it to be religiously sanctioned and future husbands demand it. While about two-thirds of all the operations in recent years have been performed by physicians, the remainder continue to be done by traditional practitioners. But in 2007 it was a trained doctor, not a religious medicaster, who precipitated the latest uproar when a girl died under anesthesia awaiting circumcision. In response, Egypt's minister of health issued a comprehensive prohibition on the procedure, a secular ruling that had the support of leading clerics. However, in this era of Endarkenment (see chapter 4) and promises of postmortem debauchery in paradise, it will be a long time before this and other religion-inspired, sex-biased excesses fade into history.

Compared to such iniquity, quality-of-life issues such as women's right to travel independently or to drive automobiles seem trivial, but the continuum of suppression encompasses almost endless innovation. Whose original idea was it, one wonders, to encase the feet of young girls so that their growth would be stunted, painfully deforming and crushing growing bones to satisfy a prurience that made invalids of these women later in life? "Foot-binding" was an obsession among rich and powerful Chinese men that endured into the early twentieth century. It was unrelated to religion but evidence of the Han culture's prevalent male dominance; women who were chosen for the procedure were in no position to escape. Communist doctrine and ensuing economic reforms ended this kind of mistreatment, but substituted or instituted others, as China's current gender imbalance shows.

Saudi Arabia, because of its energy riches, pivotal location in the Arab realm, religious importance—cradle of Islam, site of Mecca, center of Wahhabism, source of funding for Muslim causes worldwide—as well as its global linkages, is always in the limelight. Behind the facades of modernization that mark Saudi cultural landscapes, however, lie real-life gender gaps that are among the widest in the world. The Saudi regime consists of a hierarchy of some 6,000 "princes" vying for power and privilege (note that "princesses" are not in the picture). When the country held its first-ever political elections (for municipal councils) in 2005, women were not allowed to vote. The prohibition against women driving in Saudi Arabia must be one of the most often-cited examples of the gender gap in Islamic countries, and indeed, it is proof that national economic prosperity and individual wealth do not necessarily improve the rights and opportunities for all. Tradition remains a powerful brake on modernization. Saudi clerics advising the "royal family" invoked the Quran as justifying the relevant law, but Saudi women did make their point some years ago. During the commotion created by the Gulf War in 1990, foreign troops, including vehicle-driving female soldiers, were temporarily based in Saudi Arabia. Emboldened by their presence, several dozen Saudi women, many of them educated abroad, got into the family car and drove through the streets in defiance of the law. Their campaign was short-lived: all were arrested, and the ban on female driving was confirmed in the courts. The cultural geography of Saudi Arabia looks a lot flatter from a male perspective than from that of a female.

While no comprehensive quality-of-life index can be constructed for the world at large, there is no doubt that gender discrimination, ranging from overt to subtle and revealed by indices ranging from personal freedoms to aggregate incomes, afflicts virtually all societies to some degree, and all states without exception. On Wall Street, the supposed epitome of free-market competition, top female executives are disappearing, according to media reports charting high-rank corporate appointments. Referring to one high-profile dismissal, more than one commentator wondered whether "her status as a demanding woman in a male-dominated industry tipped the scale against her" (Thomas, 2007). From violence in the household to professional promotion, from unpaid labor to unequal wages, women still face higher barriers in this globalizing world. In the context of gender, the world is not only far from flat; in some ways it is getting measurably rougher.

RULERS AND RULED

Women form a slight majority of the planet's population, but one would not think so when looking at the makeup of the approximately 200 governments leading the states of the world today. Whether democratic or autocratic, the great majority of countries are led by males. Men are invariably in the numerical lead in parliaments, legislatures, congresses, assemblies, and judiciaries. Even when there would seem to be no barriers to female candidacies, men dominate the political scene. In the United States, all twelve initial candidates for the nomination by the Republican Party for the 2008 presidential election were (white) males. All but one for that of the Democratic Party were male, and the sole exception was the wife of a former president, a politician only in the wake of her service as First Lady. Countries, like corporations, proclaim to be looking for female leadership. Why is the world of representative government still so—well, unflat?

It is not that women have failed to prove their capacity for leadership or their ability to exercise power as effectively as men. Few men put their stamp on their countries as effectively as did Catherine the Great on Russia. The only leader of India to suspend democratic government and assert autocratic power was a woman prime minister, Indira Gandhi. The only modern leader of the United Kingdom to embark on full-scale war to secure a threatened distant dependency was a woman, Margaret Thatcher. If the purported world-flattening principle that "capabilities create intentions" does indeed prevail, then many more capable women would be governing nations today. As things stand in 2008, only one Subsaharan African state has ever been led by a woman, the current and elected president of Liberia, Ellen Johnson-Sirleaf. Only two South American countries have female leaders, Michelle Bachelet of Chile and Cristina Kirchner of Argentina. Of 40 European states, just two are led by women:

Germany's Chancellor Angela Merkel and Finland's President Tarja Halonen. In Southeast Asia, the sole female leader is President Gloria Macapagal-Arroyo of the Philippines. No woman has ever held the leading position anywhere in North America (other than a few months in Canada), East Asia, or Australia (New Zealand, on the other hand, has had Helen Clark as prime minister since 1999). While these numbers may change slightly, national governance remains an overwhelmingly male prerogative. Looked at in the context of history, just 46 of the world's states have ever been led by a female.

Among the dozen geographic realms of the world, only one can claim to contain a majority of countries with experience in female leadership: South Asia. Indira Gandhi's role as prime minister of India was eventful and fateful. In 2007, India elected Pratibha Patil its first woman president, a largely ceremonial yet significant position. In Bangladesh, women continue to play leading roles in traditionally chaotic political struggles for primacy; Prime Minister Khaleda Zia in the 1990s used the power of her office to ensure a modicum of stability; today she and her long-time (female) opponent are both imprisoned. In Islamic Pakistan, Benazir Bhutto, the daughter of a former (and executed) president, returned to her country from exile to organize opposition parties against the leader of the military coup that ousted her father, and between 1988 and 1999 she repeatedly held the position of prime minister. She paid for that initiative with her life. Sri Lanka elected Sirimavo Bandaranaike as president in 1959, and following her party's defeat elected her once more in 1970. Her daughter, Chandrika Bandaranaike Kumaratunga, won a landslide victory in the 1994 presidential election, inheriting a rebel insurgency she tried forcefully but ultimately unsuccessfully to defuse through concessions as well as military offensives.

The most consequential four of South Asia's seven countries, therefore, have been effectively led by women through difficult times (only the kingdoms of Nepal and Bhutan and the tiny Republic of Maldives have not). Indeed, Pakistan and Bangladesh are the only countries to hold this distinction among Muslim states. Why is this the case? A combination of factors includes the enduring power and influence of prominent families who sometimes anoint female members for the role, the veneration of upper caste and class, the admiration of education and personal appeal (especially in the case of Benazir Bhutto and also Sonya Gandhi, the Italian-born leader of India's

Congress Party who declined a run for the national leadership), and, undoubtedly, notions of pliability that were surely negated by the forceful leadership of Gandhi and Kumaratunga. Still another factor, sadly, is political violence and assassination, thrusting widows into the fray. Thus the appointments of Gandhi and Patil in India did not reflect a broader penetration of the Indian political establishment by women. In 2007, women occupied only 9 percent of the seats in India's Parliament, and less than 4 percent at the ministerial level; women held less than 3 percent of the seats in the Supreme and High Courts. In Pakistan, women also constitute but a small minority in high-level representative government, and even in Bangladesh, where both the Awami League and the Nationalist coalition opposing it have been led by women, this does not reflect significant progress for women overall. Endemic violence is what infuses Bangladeshi politics. Both party leaders are family members of assassinated former presidents, and thus inherited their political capital. Their rivalries are personal: the leader of one party accuses the dead husband of the other party of having orchestrated her father's killing. By comparison, the political system of democratic Sri Lanka, the country's deadly insurgency notwithstanding, is stable and durable, although even there, the best of the realm's social indices do not translate into adequate representation for, or participation by, women. The South Asian anomaly, unfortunately, is no paradigm for the rest of the world.

If national leadership remains largely elusive, the situation is somewhat better, and in some countries significantly better, at the representative level. In elected national parliaments and congresses in the world's democracies, women may not yet have achieved parity with men but their numbers are rising. Data from the United Nations show that, in mid-2007, women held 47 percent of seats in Sweden's legislative house, the highest representation worldwide with the exception of the Bahamas, where 8 of 15 Senate seats were held by women in 2007 (figure 7.4). When states have a "lower" and "upper" house, as in the United States with its Congress and Senate, the upper house tends to have the greater power, so representation at this level is key. Figure 7.4 reports single-house representation for states with one house only; in states with lower and upper houses, it displays representation in the upper house. In bicameral governments, women's representation usually is stronger in the lower than in the upper house, but with some interesting exceptions, including

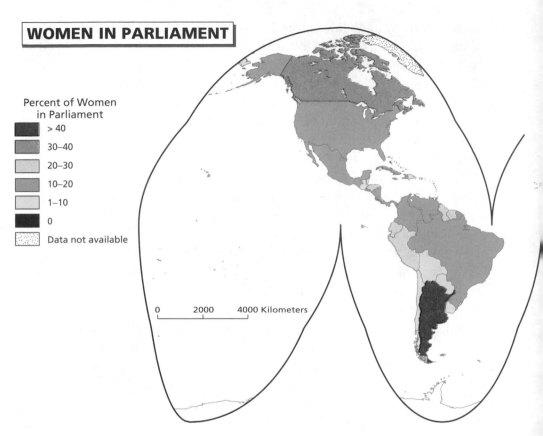

WOMEN IN PARLIAMENT

Percent of Women in Parliament
- > 40
- 30–40
- 20–30
- 10–20
- 1–10
- 0
- Data not available

0   2000   4000 Kilometers

Figure 7.4. The percentage of women in national parliaments or representative assemblies is higher in several countries of the global periphery than it is in many countries of the core. Some major democracies lag far behind. From data compiled by the Inter-Parliamentary Union (IPU): "Women in Parliaments: a World Classification," June 30, 2007, and available at http://www.ipu.org/wmn-e/classif.htm.

Canada, Argentina, South Africa, Australia, and Ireland, where the reverse is true. Since these states also rank among the more progressive in general political terms, this may constitute a signal that lower-house strength can translate into higher office once it reaches a certain threshold.

Comparing figure 7.4 with earlier versions reveals considerable and nearly worldwide progress toward gender balance in representative government. For much of the twentieth century, women's representation was strongest in a cluster of countries in traditionally progressive northern Europe. Today, while Sweden, Finland, Norway,

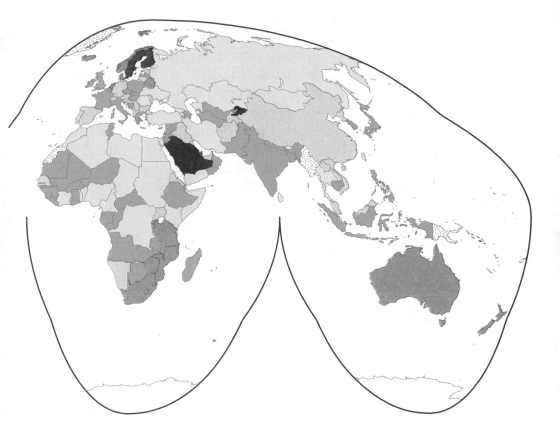

Denmark, and the Netherlands still rank in the highest category, they have been joined by such states as Rwanda, Costa Rica, Cuba, Moçambique, South Africa, Australia, and Canada. In other countries, women's representation has doubled, even tripled, in one generation (in Turkey's 2007 elections, it went from 24 to 50, from under 5 to nearly 10 percent, in a single election cycle).

Such progress in many relatively young democracies (and even in some states without real democratic traditions, such as Moldova, Turkmenistan, and North Korea) seems to suggest a global leveling of political playing fields—until it comes to certain older countries with democratic traditions, one of which has proclaimed policies designed to bring democracy to the wider world. A surprise is the United Kingdom, a bulwark of representative government, where women in 2008 held just 19.7 percent of the seats in the House of Commons; the United Kingdom ranks just below North Korea but slightly above

France. A bigger eyebrow-raiser is the United States, where women hold 16 senatorial seats (out of 100) and 71 out of 435 seats (16.3 percent) in Congress. Obviously, even the global core has its rough patches. As to other noteworthy aspects of figure 7.4, women occupy only 9 percent of seats in avowedly democratic India's two enormous legislative houses, a proportion essentially unchanged from 2001, and the same proportion as in bicameral Brazil. Compare such data to those for Tanzania (30 percent), Peru (29), Afghanistan (27) and Vietnam (26), and it is clear that in the political world of gender, the small and poor have something to teach the large and powerful.

BARRIERS ABOLISHED

In the United States, any eligible citizen can seek elected office, and all citizens can vote. Approximately half of all voters are women. If the playing field was level anywhere, surely it must be so in this open democracy? Yet in 2008, only nine of the country's 50 state governors were women, so male dominance is not confined to the House and Senate. How has this male dominance developed, and why does it persist?

The answer lies in the past as well as the present, and it applies to much of the rest of the world as well as the United States (Opdycke, 2000). Today the idea that anyone can run for office or vote may seem normal and routine, but women in the United States did not achieve full enfranchisement until as comparatively recently as 1920 through the Nineteenth Amendment to the Constitution: "The right of citizens of the United States to vote shall not be denied or abridged by the United States or by any State on account of sex." This was a half century after the U.S. government had approved the Fifteenth Amendment, which granted the vote to all *male* citizens "without regard to race, color, or previous condition of servitude." By the time women became able to vote (and could seek office), male dominance of political institutions and networks was deeply entrenched. So was male domination of corporate America, and money drives politics. It is no accident that the percentage of women who have reached the top of the corporate ladder in America is even smaller than that for governors and senators. In 2008, just 2.4 percent of the country's Fortune 500 corporations were led by female CEOs. The "glass ceiling" is as enduring as unequal pay for equal work is persistent, and will take generations to nullify.

It may be surprising that proportional representation remains so elusive in this bastion of democracy, but even in countries that enfranchised women earlier than the United States, progress in this arena is slow. Women's enfranchisement, in any case, is essentially a twentieth-century phenomenon (figure 7.5). Iceland, often referred to as the world's oldest democracy, did not enfranchise women until 1915. Finland, where women have made as much progress in virtually all spheres as anywhere in the world, was among the first—as recently as 1906. New Zealand lays claim to having been the first state in the world to formalize women's right to vote, in 1893.

Scrutiny of the map reveals some interesting linkages between enfranchisement dates and major political-ideological events. Australia followed New Zealand's lead in 1901, the year the state was formally established; the United Kingdom trailed its Commonwealth by 17 years. China never enfranchised women until the communist takeover in 1949. Japan did so following its defeat in World War II and the creation of its new Constitution under U.S. auspices in 1945. Pakistan gave women the vote immediately upon independence (and separation from India) in 1947, but India delayed until 1950. Portugal was the last European country to do so when, during a turbulent decade of military coups and colonial wars, its "Revolutionary Council" promulgated a socialist Constitution that enfranchised women in 1976 (Portugal's former colony, Brazil, had done so more than 40 years earlier). Islamic Turkey, under the guidance of its modernizing founder Kemal Ataturk, enfranchised women in 1934, nearly two decades before Greece (1952). In Turkey's case, however, this affected mainly a modernized but small urban elite, because in the country at large patriarchy remained firmly entrenched. Saddam-era Iraq made the decision in 1980, nearly 20 years after Iran (1963). Women voted for the first time in parliamentary elections in Kuwait in 2006. But other countries in the Muslim world still have not fully enfranchised women, including not only Saudi Arabia but also Libya and Qatar.

Given the comparative novelty of women's enfranchisement and the entrenchment everywhere of male-dominated power structures, the growing presence of women in national parliaments across the world is encouraging if slow. In the United States, where such

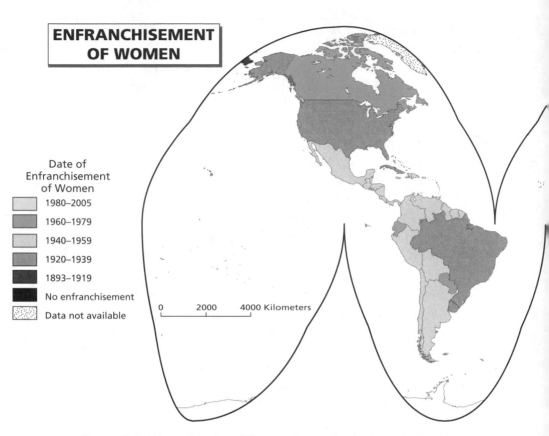

Figure 7.5. Women's enfranchisement began in the late nineteenth century and is still not universal. Data from the Inter-Parliamentary Union (IPU) and available at http://www.ipu.org/wmn-e/suffrage.htm.

representation is still modest, it has nevertheless tripled over the past two decades, as it has in the United Kingdom. It has more than doubled in Canada, New Zealand, and Argentina. During the present century, women are likely to achieve representative parity in several countries, and more women will become national leaders. How will this change the world? In the words of one scholar, "The few women who have attained the highest positions in male-dominated governments have not avoided confrontational politics. Yet in broad opinion surveys women have revealed attitudes significantly different from men's. When women have had a chance to use power in settings where there is a deep feminist consciousness and social commitment to justice—as in the Nordic countries—government policies are

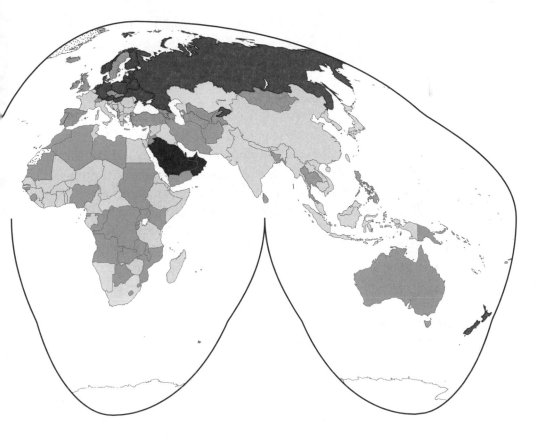

noteworthy for their emphasis on equality, development, and peace" (Sivard, 1985). But the Nordic countries are no more representative of the world than the South Asian realm discussed above. In their comparative luxury of limited diversity, modest dimensions, high living standards, and overall social well-being, they have achieved a "flatness" that facilitates the kind of social progress reflected by stronger female representation in their governments, but that combination of circumstances is still rare. Perhaps the more encouraging European case is the Netherlands, whose population is larger than Denmark, Finland, and Norway combined, whose cultural geography is far more variegated, and whose major issues, ranging from Muslim immigration to its relations with former colonies and from EU integration to its antiterror role in Afghanistan, represent a wider spectrum of challenges. That the percentage of women in the country's bicameral parliament has risen from just below 20 to more than 35 percent in the past two decades suggests that Dutch voters, having tried the option, liked what they got and went for more. Dutch politics are as contentious, divisive, and emotional as they come, and women have proven their capacity not just for competition, but also for effective leadership.

Obviously, a male-dominated political world misses out on the talents and perspectives of countless women who, in a truly flat world, would perhaps "make the difference" male politicians keep promising. The heroics of some of those women come to world attention, but most will never influence the course of global events. In Myanmar, Aung San Suu Kyi, leader of the country's National League for Democracy, has endured indignities and worse while spending 12 of the past 18 years under house arrest for her opposition to the male junta (one never hears of female juntas) misgoverning her country. Yet Myanmar is a member of the Association of Southeast Asian Nations (ASEAN), where the generals are received as though they constitute a representative government, and where deals are hammered out that help perpetuate their misrule. While the United Nations on September, 15, 2006 added Myanmar to its short list of countries deemed a threat to international peace and security, the junta strengthened military ties with North Korea, economic links with China, and security cooperation with India. Meanwhile, the fate of women in this blighted country ranks among the worst on Earth.

If enfranchisement and other barrier-eliminating actions have not brought sufficient flatness to the world's political landscapes, what else lies behind the inequities revealed by the map in figure 7.5? Some states, including India, designate a number of seats in parliament as women-only, but even measures of that kind have failed to significantly alter a pattern that is changing but slowly. What lies behind the figures is a combination of factors conditioning societies everywhere, rooted in the realties of the distant as well as recent past and persisting despite modernization and globalization. When religious dogma segregates men and women and reserves state politics as a male domain, it formalizes inequalities far older than religion itself. When eight of nine judges on the Supreme Court of an avowedly democratic country are males making decisions stipulating reproductive rules for females, the echoes of that distant past are not difficult to hear. Some day in the distant future the divergent destinies of men and women (they always will diverge) and their inevitably diverse priorities may be equably represented by certain governments. The first steps on that road toward a flatter world have been taken over the past century. But today, from the most isolated village to the most connected country, the inequalities of gender still distort visions of place.

8

POWER AND THE CITY

The city is humanity's most enduring symbol of power. States and empires rise and fall, armies conquer and collapse, ideologies come and go, but the world's great cities endure. If there is a force that can vanquish a city, it is natural, not artificial. Ancient cities that anchored early states in Southwest, South, and East Asia fell victim to climate change as deserts encroached on their hinterlands. Modern cities on low ground at the water's edge would not survive the sea-level rise that could accompany sustained global warming. But no political upheaval or economic breakdown would end the life of a major city—not even destruction by atomic bombs. Hiroshima and Nagasaki were rebuilt because the advantages and opportunities offered by their sites and situations were unaltered by the catastrophes that struck them. Silk route terminal Chang'an morphed into Xian and Tenochtitlan became Mexico City because their locational benefits, sites, and regional networks outlasted their violent transitions. Not for nothing is Rome known as the Eternal City.

With the maturation of the modern state came the notion of the "capital" city, focus of its administrative system and emblematic of its power. Cities had always dominated their hinterlands, but now their power radiated far afield. From Athens to Amsterdam and from Madrid to Moscow, these national capitals became imperial headquarters that launched colonial campaigns near and far. London was synonymous with this early wave of globalization, but Paris also lay at the heart of a global network of power and influence. In these capitals, cityscapes substantiated national achievements through elaborate palaces, columned government buildings, decorative triumphal arches, spacious parade routes, and commemorative statuary. Museums bulging with treasure attested further to the primacy of the culture, leading one observer, long ago but memorably, to designate such centers as "primate" cities (Jefferson, 1939). The trappings of this primacy reappeared in the architecture of colonial headquarters from Dakar to Delhi and from Luanda to Lima, incongruous Greco-Roman-Victorian-Iberian imprints on administrative offices, railroad stations, post offices, even prisons half a world away from Europe. More than ever before, the city in the global periphery was the locus of authority and transculturation.

Today those colonies are no more, but the cities persist, and many of them are linked in a new framework of power defined by the processes of globalization. Urban geographers refer to such cities as "world" cities because they form part of a global urban network that links them more efficiently internationally than locally. For example, London has stronger links to New York than it has to Leicester or Liverpool; Miami interacts more with São Paulo than with Jacksonville or Orlando. (Such interactions, or course, refer to connectivity involving globals, their corporations, and their finances; to locals laying bricks for contractors, the issue is rather less relevant.) One significant result of this globalizing influence is that world cities tend to become comparatively less effectively linked to their "own" countries as they are increasingly enmeshed in this global capitalist system. This symbolizes a new kind of power that transcends state boundaries and sustains a world economy much as the old colonial cities represented imperial interests. But not all major cities are world cities: Milan has the linkages to qualify, but Rome does not. São Paulo does, but Rio de Janeiro does not. Mumbai does, but not Dhaka.

This does not mean that cities not ranked as world cities have no vestiges of power. Cities, globally linked or not, are magnets for mobals, markets for manufacturers and farmers, centers of learning, sources of information, clusters of talent. This historic kind of domination over nearby hinterlands continues. But the era of globalization has diversified the urbanized world rather than homogenized it. The urban terrain is rougher than ever.

If the city—whatever its rank—is synonymous with enduring power, whether political, religious, ideological, or economic, it also signifies inequality, because cities harbor social extremes in close juxtaposition. Even when one is inured to scenes of rural poverty, the searing contrasts between the well-off and the indigent in cities of the periphery are jarring. Cities in the global core also have their rich and poor, but nothing in London, Los Angeles, or Tokyo compares to the divergence of fortunes visible in Manila, Jakarta, or Kolkata. The key question is whether globalization, largely transmitted through the world's urban network, is mitigating or worsening these conditions. Does urbanization, with all its attendant opportunities and possibilities, ultimately level the global playing field? Are those jarring intra-urban opposites an inevitable but temporary symptom of a society on the way to better times? Will rural areas benefit as urbanization proceeds?

MOMENTOUS MILESTONE

In March 1994 a spate of newspaper and television reports around the world announced that a significant moment had come and gone: the planet's urban population, for the first time in human history, now exceeded 50 percent of the total. Some agencies that keep track of such data did not agree: the American Association for the Advancement of Science waited until after the turn of the century to make a similar announcement. By the end of the first decade of the twenty-first century, there is no longer any doubt. Human communities have existed on Earth for perhaps 150,000 years; they did not cluster into villages until after the recession of the last glaciation, when the domestication of plants and animals began a cycle of occupational specialization without end. By about 8000 years ago, some of those villages, more favorably situated, were growing faster than others. In a remarkably short time, essentially egalitarian cultures had been transformed into stratified societies as urbanization and state formation inaugurated a series of revolutions still going on today. Not only have urbanites become the majority among the Earth's recently exploding population, but the United Nations will before long admit its 200th member state. Ancient states often had uncertain borders; today, hundreds of thousands of kilometers of marked and sometimes fenced political boundaries compartmentalize the world. And this process, too, still continues: in August 2007 a submersible planted a Russian flag on the seafloor under the ice at the North Pole, staking a future claim to the resources under the seabed, a claim sure to be contested by Canada and the United States among others. Meanwhile, even as the global population explosion is approaching its end, regional populations are beginning to shrink, and the international mosaic of states is stabilizing, the urban spiral continues unabated. Projections suggest that people in the world's cities will outnumber those still in the country-side by more than two to one by the end of the present century.

What caused the decade-long uncertainty about the crossing of the global urban threshold? Various agencies collect data from different sources. The United Nations relies on data from (and projections based on) the national censuses of member states, but such information is not always reliable and can be badly dated. Conducting a census is expensive when there are other pressing national needs, and there are times when governments are reluctant to gather data that may, for example, reveal the numerical strength of ethnic or religious minorities. Other agencies use methods ranging from sampling techniques to satellite information to estimate population changes; in some countries, urbanization proceeds so fast that no ten-year census could keep track of it. Add to this the obvious problem of definition—what, exactly, makes a citizen an urbanite?—and things become even more difficult. Different countries have different standards when it comes to enumerating urbanization. When does a village qualify to be designated a town? In Canada, the official definition of a village limits it to 1000 inhabitants; anything larger is a town. In the United States, that limit is 2500. But in India, a place can have up to 5000 residents and still be designated a village. And in Japan, a clustered settlement cannot be officially designated "urban" until it has 30,000 inhabitants or more. This sample of differing criteria suggests why generalizations about global urbanization are difficult to make.

Clearly, sheer size is not a satisfactory criterion when it comes to urbanization. Perhaps a better way to standardize the urban definition is to relate it to the most common occupation of a settlement's inhabitants. For example, if most of them are farmers, the place is rural, no matter how large it is; but if most are involved in commerce, manufacturing, or other industries, it is urban, no matter how small it is. But it would be enormously costly and problematic for countries, especially in the global periphery, to secure such information. Some governments simply designate as urban not only a city, but also a large part of its still-rural surroundings, as China did when it expanded the "municipality" of Chongqing to provincial dimensions, then proclaiming that Chongqing, now nearly the size of South Carolina, is "the largest city in the world" with 28 million inhabitants. No doubt Chongqing, which incorporates much of the Three Gorges Dam project, is territorially the largest city in the world, but less than half its population live in urban environs, and the real city at the center of the "municipality" probably has no more than seven million residents. In any case, despite such statistical deceptions and even by the most conservative calculations, there is no doubt that the Earth's human population passed a momentous milestone around the turn of the present century, with uncertain implications for the future.

TOWARD AN URBAN WORLD

The urbanizing spiral even proportionately outraced the global population explosion itself. As recently as 1800, only about 3 percent of the world's population lived in towns of 5000 or more, so that the number of urban residents grew 17-fold in the two centuries during which the planet's population grew from about one billion to six billion. Today, urban growth continues even in countries and regions where overall population increase has been reversed, as in Europe, Russia, and Japan. Even if the Earth's population stabilizes toward the end of the century, as many demographers project, urbanization will continue. The world is on the threshold of change as consequential as any in the history of civilization.

From maps of urbanization today, we may be able to get a glimpse of the future. The planet's most thoroughly urbanized regions substantially define the global core, with South America, as a geographic realm, constituting the significant exception in the periphery (figure 8.1). South America's high level of urbanization arises from several causes: the early agglomeration of wealth and power in the colonial cities and the nature of land ownership, the subjugation and numerical overwhelming of indigenous populations by burgeoning immigration, the concentration of industrialization, and the comparatively early slowdown of the rural population explosion in territorially large countries with relatively modest populations. The map shows that the few countries with large Amerindian populations (Bolivia, Peru, Ecuador) have lower levels of urbanization than those with almost exclusively Iberian ancestries (Argentina, Uruguay, Chile). Nowhere else in the global periphery has the Europeanization of former colonial dependencies gone as far as it has in South America, and its regional urbanization reflects this.

The combination of circumstances that propels South America's urbanization comes at a high cost, especially in Brazil, its most populous and territorially largest state occupying nearly half of the continent and sharing borders with all but two of its countries. In a number of ways, Brazil provides insights into the likely future of urbanization elsewhere in the periphery. For all its well-known accomplishments in multiculturalism, Brazil remains a country of stark, appalling social inequalities. As a geographic realm, urbanizing South America is often cited as exhibiting the sharpest division between affluence and poverty, and Brazil is reputed to have the widest gap of all. In fact the data, while troubling, are not uniquely disproportional: there are other places in the world where similar asymmetries prevail. But none of those other places matches Brazil's combination of opportunities and potentials. Consider this: Brazil is nearly three times as large territorially as India but has less than one-sixth of India's population. The distance from Brazil to U.S. markets is one-third that of China's. In terms of connections to and relations with its regional neighbors, Brazil is in a far better position than either India or China. Still, today the richest 10 percent of Brazilians own two-thirds of all the land and control more than half of Brazil's wealth (Knapp, 2002). The poorest one-fifth of the people live in the most squalid conditions prevailing anywhere on Earth, even including the megacities of Africa and Asia. According to UN reports, in this age of adequate available (but not everywhere affordable) food, about half the population of Brazil suffers from some form of malnutrition and, in its poverty-stricken Northeast, even hunger. There is nothing flat about the human geography of Brazil: some of the world's most architecturally magnificent central cities are ringed and sectored by the most wretched *favelas* where poverty, misery, and crime converge. This in a country richly endowed with mineral resources, an agricultural superpower, a leader in gasohol technology and production, and in possession of still-unopened frontiers.

Is Brazil a harbinger of the urbanized future? Is its chaotic megacity, São Paulo, a precursor for the global periphery about to be swept up in urbanization's accelerating wave? Is the fate of the Amazon region indicative of what lies ahead for what remains of the natural world in urbanizing Africa and Asia? Portents are not encouraging. Much of what ails Brazil is less the result of environmental, resource, or other limitations than of gross and pervasive mismanagement. When it became clear around the turn of the century that unemployment was rising while the global economy was booming and that the

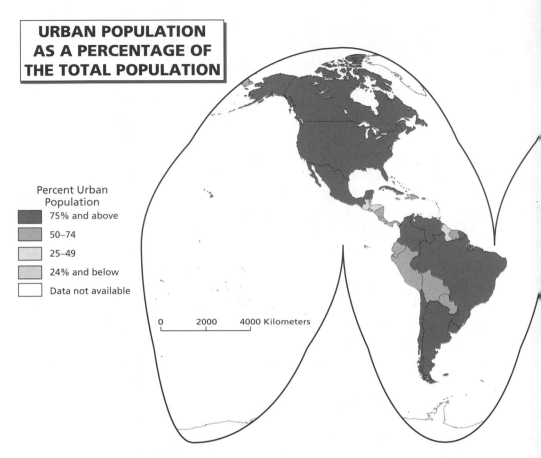

URBAN POPULATION AS A PERCENTAGE OF THE TOTAL POPULATION

Percent Urban Population
- 75% and above
- 50–74
- 25–49
- 24% and below
- Data not available

0   2000   4000 Kilometers

Figure 8.1. Although the global core is more highly urbanized than the periphery, the distinction is fading: South America already is more highly urbanized than Eastern Europe. Data from Table G-1 in H. J. de Blij and P. O. Muller, *Geography: Realms, Regions and Concepts,* 13th ed. (New York: Wiley, 2008).

number of Brazilians afflicted by poverty had doubled between 1980 and 2000, the voters ousted the government and elected a Workers Party leader, Luiz Inacio Lula da Silva, as president. Lula almost immediately initiated reforms of Brazil's inefficient social security system and the malfunctioning public workers' pension plan, but even before his reelection in 2006 his government came close to collapse for the same reason previous ones did: Brazil's endemic corruption. In 2007, Brazil's ranking on Transparency International's "corruption index" was 3.3, even lower than it was in 2004 and similar to that of India, China, and Saudi Arabia. So endemic are graft, bribery, and deceit that

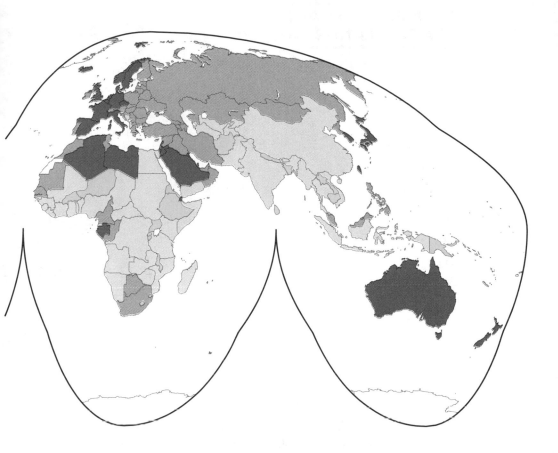

public confidence in government and its agencies, from tax collection to public transportation and from law enforcement to public education, remains at dangerously low ebb even during the term of a popular president. When serious disorders erupted in several *favelas* in Rio de Janeiro in 2005, the government's response was insufficient, and large parts of the city remained out of control for weeks. When gangs controlling the drug trade attacked buses and other public transport facilities in São Paulo in 2006, they held the city hostage for days, proving the ineffectiveness of the authorities. Chaos in air traffic control and airports led to accidents that killed hundreds, but long-needed remedies, even if promptly instituted, will require years to take effect.

The answers to the foregoing questions, therefore, are likely to be affirmative. As figure 8.1 shows, much of the global periphery has yet to go through the urbanizing spiral that has carried South American

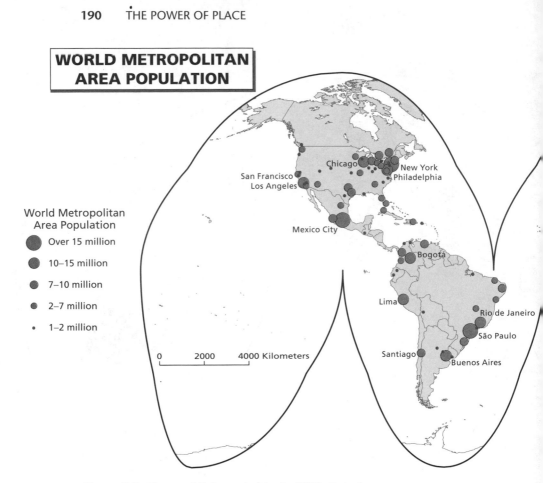

WORLD METROPOLITAN AREA POPULATION

World Metropolitan Area Population
- Over 15 million
- 10–15 million
- 7–10 million
- 2–7 million
- 1–2 million

0   2000   4000 Kilometers

Chicago
New York
Philadelphia
San Francisco
Los Angeles
Mexico City
Bogotá
Lima
Rio de Janeiro
São Paulo
Santiago
Buenos Aires

Figure 8.2. The world's largest cities in 2008. Data from numerous sources.

urbanization close to levels prevailing in the core, and the govern-ments of states in which the burgeoning megacities evolve will be even less capable of controlling and guiding the process than Brazil's has been. Many of these cities are mushrooming among the poorest of the poor in Africa and Asia: in the first decade of the twenty-first century, Subsaharan Africa had the world's highest rate of urbanization and South and East Asia were close behind. Only 34 percent of the popu-lation of Subsaharan Africa, least populous of these three geographic realms, was clustered in urban places, so the high rate reflects a com-paratively small base; but teeming South Asia is only 30 percent urban and Southeast Asia just 39 percent. In terms of sheer numbers, East Asia (43 percent) has seen the greatest increase in urban population in recent decades, although, for all its great and growing cities, China in

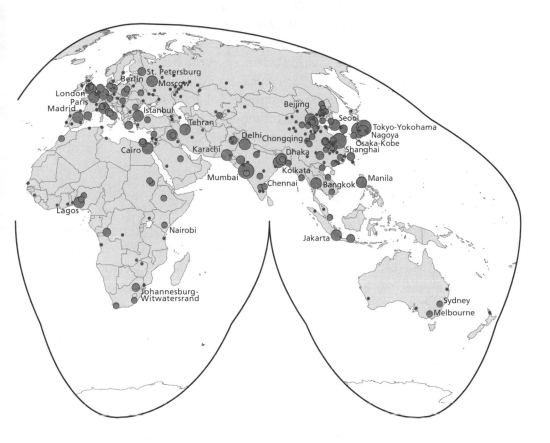

2008 was still only 37 percent urban, lagging behind every other country in the realm, including even Mongolia. Officially, 80 percent of
Japanese live in urban places, but given Japan's stringent definition of
urbanization, the comparative figure is probably closer to 90 percent.

A map displaying the current distribution of cities of the world,
therefore, is but a still picture of a changing pattern (figure 8.2). In the
global core, the Tokyo-Yokohama conurbation, the Bosnywash mega-
lopolis of eastern North America, and the old cities of Europe will see
comparatively little of this change: there will be infrastructure modernization and some spatial reorganization, and migration will alter cultural
fabrics, but neither explosive growth nor sudden implosion will affect
them. As noted above, only irreversible environmental impacts might
alter this forecast, but the magnitude of any such events would do more
than change the planet's urban geography. Neither will the map change

significantly in urbanized Middle or South America. In the former, the dominance of Mexico City, already at the heart of one of the world's largest conurbations, will continue, and outside Mexico only Panama City and possibly post-Castro Havana appear to have significant potential for growth. No rival to São Paulo is likely to arise in South America (with about half of São Paulo's numbers, Buenos Aires is closest), but several smaller Brazilian cities, including Belo Horizonte, Porto Alegre, Salvador, and Manaus, may in time surpass Rio de Janeiro.

THE NEW MEGACITIES

Thus, the most dramatic changes to be reflected in a future version of the map in figure 8.2 will occur in the four least-urbanized realms of the world today, and here the potential for unanticipated developments is far greater. The biggest question mark hovers over Subsaharan Africa, where China, with its massive financial reserves and its growing need for commodities, is a growing presence. If this, plus the rising number of multinational initiatives to help African states and societies, has a sustained effect, one of the consequences will be even faster urbanization than is already occurring, and Lagos, Subsaharan Africa's sole and chaotic megacity in 2008, will have rivals in such already-burgeoning places as Kinshasa, Abidjan, Addis Abeba, and Nairobi. Other potential growth poles include Luanda and Accra and, in the transition zone between Subsaharan and Islamic Africa, Khartoum, but still others may emerge and mushroom in unexpected locales.

Subsaharan Africa's health-related problems notwithstanding, its population of nearly 800 million, by far the fastest growing on the planet, is projected to exceed one billion by 2020. Its political geography is fragmented into about four dozen countries, creating political and administrative discontinuities that will inevitably affect urbanizing processes. Most of Africa's colonial-era borders may not be effectively demarcated, but its cultural geography is so diverse that transnational mobals do not easily blend into the general population. The recent example of Zimbabwe is a case in point: the abhorrent policies of the regime of President Robert Mugabe have generated a desperate emigration of an estimated three million refugees by 2008, the great majority of them into neighboring South Africa. Those not intercepted by border patrols or farmers somewhere along the Limpopo

River, the natural boundary between the two states, try to reach the urban complex of Gauteng astride the Witwatersrand, at whose center lies Johannesburg. But South Africa itself suffers from severe unemployment problems, and illegal migrants often are quickly identified by locals and repatriated by authorities. Were it not for international borders, South Africa's major cities, their growth controlled during the apartheid period but burgeoning through internal migration following liberation, would rival Kinshasa if not Lagos.

Only one of Subsaharan Africa's nearly 50 countries has a population exceeding 100 million. Nigeria's total, the subject of much speculation, is reported as 134 million (United Nations, 2006) and 141 million (World Population Reference Bureau, 2007), and other approximations go even higher. The uncertainty is such that it confounds even usually reliable sources: in the same month, in mid-2007, the *Economist* reported Nigeria's population as 127.1 million in its annual *World in Figures* and as 146.2 million in its *World in 2007*. Whatever its demographic dimensions, in the early twenty-first century Nigeria was the only Subsaharan African country to incubate a megacity to match those elsewhere in the global periphery. Lagos, once the British colonial headquarters and later the first capital of Nigeria, now contains more than 10 percent of Nigeria's population. It is a home-grown city: the overwhelming majority of Lagos residents are Nigerians, with transnationals in a small minority, underscoring the role of Africa's political compartmentalization in the evolution of its urban system. An urban tradition prevailed in the southwestern quadrant of Nigeria long before the colonial conquest, and Lagos reflects a pattern common to other countries with megacities: internal migrants tend to move from smaller to larger cities and eventually to the largest, rather than migrating directly from countryside to metropolis. Nigeria has a network of such smaller cities; the country's second-largest city, Ibadan, lies in the Lagos hinterland (figure 8.3).

Lagos, however, reflects governmental failures even more vividly than does São Paulo. The lack of administrative integrity and competence that has long afflicted Nigeria as a state is replicated by the long-term mismanagement of Lagos, whose disorderly growth now puts it beyond the control of even the most capable government. Laws, rules, and regulations, from zoning to traffic and from markets to property, are routinely ignored. Violence, like corruption, is endemic, and repeated money-for-guns initiatives have done little to improve

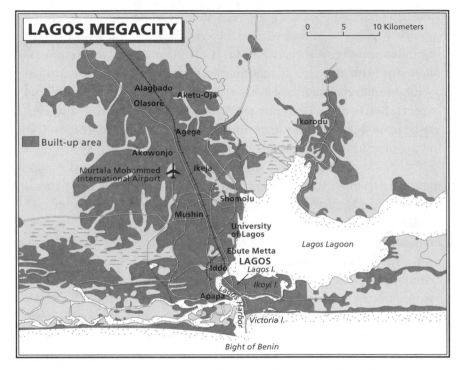

Figure 8.3. The vast urban region of Lagos, Subsaharan Africa's first megacity. The scale reflects the enormous dimensions of the built-up area.

public safety. Garbage-strewn shantytowns encircling dilapidated inner-city housing are among the world's most severely polluted, amenity-deprived slums. Heat and humidity, squalor, congestion, and frequent disorder confront new arrivals as well as long-term residents. Unlike São Paulo, Lagos lacks a large and modern core; the CBD on Lagos Island, the water-buffered aggregation of office and residential high-rises at the entrance to Lagos Lagoon, is undersized for an urban cluster as large as the population of the Netherlands.

Which revives the question of power and the city. Power in the sense of authority is not necessarily reflected by dimension: megacities are hampered by their own congestive chaos. For all its size, Lagos does not evoke an image of control and command, energy and bustle. Visual evidence of the presence of international corporations is sparse given the enormity of the place. Cultural assets gracing smaller towns in Nigeria are overwhelmed by more pressing demands of daily life. And yet Lagos continues to grow, a city often referred to as the Calcutta of Africa but lacking Calcutta's (now Kolkata's) charm. Of course, Lagos has its well- and better-off residents, their abodes fortified against the impoverished majority, but the world may indeed be flatter here than in most mega- cities of the world in the sense that the overwhelming majority are needy and the masses living in the older corrugated-iron-roofed shacks of Iddo are not significantly better off than the more established arriv- als on the outskirts north of Agege. Lagos attracts because its jobs in the port and in the industrial zones beckon and because circumstances in other Nigerian cities and towns, and in the rural areas, create power- ful push factors—and because Nigeria has a huge reservoir of domestic population unimpeded by political barriers in its move to the cities.

Other emerging African megacities display similar qualities, nota- bly Kinshasa, the capital of the Democratic Republic of the Congo, also containing about 10 percent of the country's population, and Abidjan, already oversized in a country of 21 million as a result of a combina- tion of domestic as well as cross-border migration. With a population approaching four million, Abidjan's fortunes have declined as its num- bers have risen. Once a showcase headquarters of French colonialism, endowed with an elegant and modern CBD and, upon independence, the unchallenged capital of Ivory Coast, the city had a history of tight control by efficient if not democratic managers. Ivory Coast was a one-party state during its first three decades of independence, and the policies of its autocratic president yielded stability and economic pros- perity. Abidjan grew modestly, but in the 1990s, following the death of its benefactor, political stability ended, turmoil ensued, two military coups followed, and Ivory Coast's long-suppressed north–south divi- sions (in part a Muslim–Christian division) erupted into a civil war. The breakdown of order produced an unprecedented migration into Abidjan, overwhelming the city's infrastructure and converting its outskirts into teeming shantytowns. Already housing nearly one-fifth of the country's population, Abidjan's explosive growth is converting an African urban exemplar into a chaotic megacity. Again the failure of national government has crucial implications for the fate of a city.

If power resides in the city, how is it that problems of such mag- nitude plague the very cities in which governments are based? In fact, neither São Paulo nor Lagos hosts a national administration, and in both Brazil and Nigeria national governments abandoned their megacity headquarters to escape to smaller cities in interior locations. Brazil's government was centered in congested Rio de Janeiro until

1960, when Brasilia became the new capital. Lagos lost both its functions as State capital in 1975 and as national capital in 1991, when the federal government moved to Abuja near the geographic center of the country. Ever since, municipal governments in both São Paulo and Lagos have complained that federal leaders neglect their problems, but the intractable nature of those problems is what drove those governments away in the first place. Even comparatively functional Abidjan was abandoned by Ivory Coast's first leader, who, late in his long presidency, tried to move his government to an interior village called Yamoussoukro. There he ordered the construction of a basilica on the scale of the Vatican, the *Notre Dame de la Paix* (Our Lady of Peace), amid a cluster of buildings that would house the government, arousing anger among non-Catholics in Abidjan, who rioted in the streets over the issue. Although Yamoussoukro remains the country's official capital, many agencies of government stayed behind, and some foreign governments, including the United States, refused to recognize it and kept their embassies in Abidjan as well.

ASIAN JUGGERNAUTS

Nothing in either South America or Africa, however, matches what is happening in Asia. For sheer numbers and diversity of form and dimension, the megacities of South, East, and Southeast Asia deliver the message for the twenty-first century: as the planet's greatest population concentrations urbanize, the world will enter a new era. To put this message in numerical context, China alone has a population larger than South America's and subsaharan Africa's combined. South Asia, set to overtake East Asia as the world's most populous realm in 2010, will contain nearly one-quarter of all humanity by 2025. Even before this area of the planet reaches urbanization levels half those prevailing in the global core, it is already synonymous with its megacities, the world of Mumbai, Delhi, Kolkata, Dhaka, Shanghai, Beijing, Manila, and Jakarta. Consider this: there are more people in Dhaka than in Greece. There are more people in Manila than in Belgium. There are more people in Delhi than in Chile. Mumbai will soon overtake Australia.

Some of these giant conurbations, and others still ascending (still others are not even on the map as yet) will come to rival the great conurbations of the global core, first in size, later in power. Among megacities in the global periphery, São Paulo and Mexico City already outnumber New York and London and match Tokyo, but neither begins to approach the dominance in global finance or business of this global trio. Nor, as noted above, do the policies of the Brazilian or Mexican governments do much to enhance their competitiveness. By contrast, China's modernizing, burgeoning cities project the capacity of the communist regime to steer the ship of state economically as well as politically, and the sheer size of India's urban economy will override the inefficiencies of its federal government. The ultramodern skylines of Shanghai and Beijing purposely reflect modernization as well as practicality. Mumbai and Delhi, carrying the heavier residual colonial imprint, are being transformed by international linkages and domestic economic growth into nodes in the network of globalization. Such cities have been labeled "gateway" cities because they open doors to penetration by foreign corporations and facilitate linkages between these and domestic multinational companies, but not all megacities are gateway cities (Short, 2000). In Africa, the gateway functions of Lagos do not match the city's dimensions and reflect the distressed state of the Nigerian economy. In South Asia, Karachi, Dhaka, and Colombo, for individually different reasons, do not function effectively as gateway cities. In the region of East Asia that is not part of the global core, China's Pacific Rim megacities are primary examples of gateway cities, but interior cities such as Harbin, Baotou, Chengdu, and Kunming, all growing toward five million, lose ground (and Pyongyang remains outside the global system for other reasons). And in Southeast Asia, Singapore, Bangkok, Kuala Lumpur, and Saigon outrank Jakarta and Manila. But whatever their size and status, the fast-growing nodes and linkages in the Asian urban network form the avenues of foreign infiltration some see as beneficial and others as detrimental to local and national economies and cultures.

URBANIZATION AND GLOBALIZATION

Is globalization the great leveler of obstacles to opportunities and possibilities for all, as its proponents argue, or does it raise the bar against mobals and locals? If there is no resolution to this argument, which has raged for years, it is clear that the key arenas of globalization lie in the cities. Certainly the process has impacts beyond the urban frontier, but the cities are where the action is. Globalization means so many things to so many people that it defies brief definition. The subplots are so many and so intertwined that some observers suggest the term should never be used without a qualifier, as in "economic" globalization, "cultural" globalization, or "political" globalization. Economic globalization is perhaps most effectively defined as "the integration of national economies into the international economy through trade, foreign investment (by corporations and multinationals), short-term capital flows, international flows of workers and humanity generally, and flows of technology" (Bhagwati, 2004). To proponents, the integration of national economies into the international economy spells modernization, mutual advantage, and expanding opportunities. To opponents, it describes a loss of tradition, community, and self-determination. Either way, channels of globalization lead to and through cities, whose very growth demonstrates the pervasiveness of the project.

Thomas Friedman, tackling the cultural issue and redefining "glocalization" to mean "how outward (a) culture is: to what degree is it open to foreign influence and ideas," argues that "the more you have a culture that naturally glocalizes—that is, the more your culture easily absorbs foreign ideas and global best practices and melds those with its own traditions—the greater advantage you will have in a flat world" (Friedman, 2006). Yet those global "best practices" are not always the hallmark of economic globalization. A lack of openness may explain "why so many Muslim countries have been struggling as the world goes flat," but citing Dubai as an exception brings to mind the abominable treatment of South Asian workers by Arab globals driving Dubai's spectacular modernization. And in the megacities of the globalizing periphery, access to the rewards of "glocalization" is not routinely unrestricted for locals seeking to participate in the process. Foreign corporations and domestic governments share an interest in controlling the proceedings for reasons ranging from migration to wage levels to the flow of ideas. As to the "glocalizing" impact, the cultural landscape of globalization, from the *maquiladora* cities of Mexico to the conurbations of Pacific Rim China, presents vistas of low-rise factories the size of football fields, enormous parking lots, drab, basic, and usually overcrowded apartment buildings, polluted waterways, and sun-obscuring smog. Tens of millions of locals and mobals prove their willingness to take the job opportunities globalization creates, but let us not misinterpret motivations. Not many walk to work celebrating their absorption of foreign ideas and global best practices.

The topic of political globalization has caused some heated debate. Some observers assert that globalization promotes democracy directly as well as indirectly: "Farmers are now able to bypass dominant classes and castes by taking their produce directly to the market thanks to modern information technology, thereby loosening the control of these traditionally hegemonic groups.... [T]his can start them on the way to becoming more independent actors, with democratic aspirations, in the political arena" (Bhagwati, 2004). Others argue that the problem lies less with farmers' opportunities than with weak governments in poor countries being overpowered by rich, corporation-driven governments in the global core that are taking control through "integration" of the world economy. Their view tends in some cases to be apocalyptic: "The capitalist elite has appropriated the process...and is pursuing its own objectives at the expense of broader society, culture and the environment. As it is currently practiced, globalization is perhaps the single greatest threat to human society" (Murray, 2006). Citing growing inequality in personal and family incomes and expenditures in states whose growth is driven by globalization, these critics argue that the process represents "growth without equity" and threatens a future of social unrest in many of the countries with fast-growing economies.

Oft-cited evidence comes from a calculation called the Gini coefficient (GC) that measures income in a country on a scale of 0.0 (everyone earns the same income) to 1.0 (one earner takes it all). Corado Gini was an Italian statistician whose pioneering contributions included a mathematical formula to measure the degree of dispersion of a phenomenon in a concentration, and his name is forever linked to the way economic gains are spread throughout a population. Banks and other agencies track the GC of individual countries, and this is the evidence often used to identify Brazil as exhibiting the world's sharpest division between affluence (of the few) and poverty (of the many). But some countries whose economies are caught in the rush of globalization are fast catching up and may, in some cases, have overtaken Brazil (the GC is difficult to establish, so indices are open to debate). China, for obvious reasons, had a very low GC in the early 1970s, before its economic boom began. By 1993, its GC had reached 0.41, and today it is approaching 0.50 (Brazil's in 2007 was 0.57). Various indicators suggest that India's GC, probably already underestimated at 0.38, is rising fastest in those of its States most affected by globalization and associated urbanization. The key reason for this growing

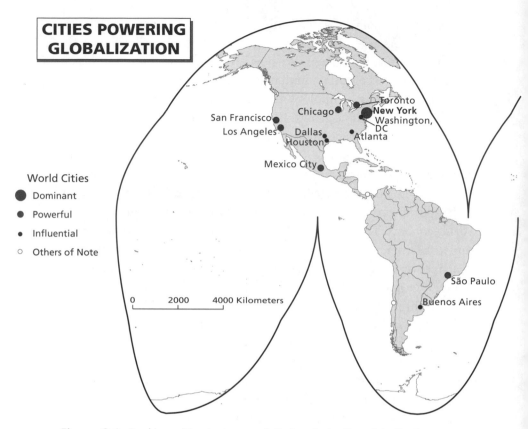

CITIES POWERING GLOBALIZATION

World Cities

● Dominant

● Powerful

• Influential

○ Others of Note

Toronto
New York
Washington, DC
Chicago
San Francisco
Los Angeles
Dallas
Houston
Atlanta
Mexico City
São Paulo
Buenos Aires

0   2000   4000 Kilometers

Figure 8.4. Ranking cities in terms of their role in the globalization process is problematic and tendentious. There is general agreement that New York, London, and Tokyo rank as the world's three dominant cities, but beyond this there is no consensus. This version, one of many, owes much to B. J. Godfrey and Y. Zhou, "Ranking World Cities: Multinational Corporations and the Global Urban Hierarchy," *Urban Geography* 20, no. 3 (1999), p. 268, as well as Grant and Nijman (2004), Short (2000), and Taylor (2004).

maldistribution of wealth lies in the contrast in incomes (and income growth) between urbanizing and rural areas. While the poorest of the poor are slightly better off as globalization transforms the overall economy, their world is getting rougher, not flatter, because they are being left ever further behind those in the cities.

Those who view this latest surge of globalization (European colonization was only one among several earlier manifestations) in a pessimistic light tend to argue that "the world system that . . . emerged some time ago, dominated by a certain number of Western metropolises or

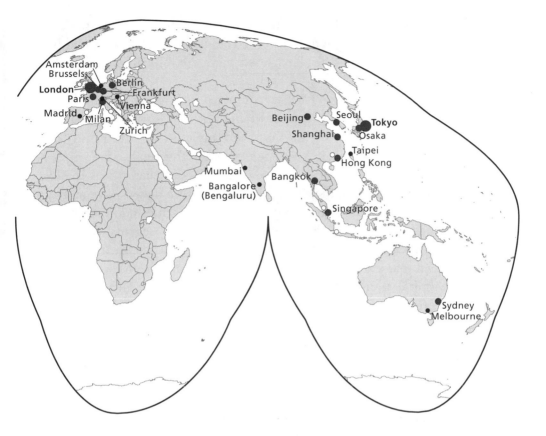

capitalist metropolises and their corporations, is still here; only its intensity and its scope have changed" (Ahmad, 2003). No doubt the cities are where the action is, but not all cities are equal. Even supporters of economic globalization concede that the concentration of corporate power and decision making in major cities has created a global urban hierarchy in which the top-ranked centers in the global core dominate the worldwide network of which they are a part. One way to measure this influence is to count the number of corporate global headquarters present (among, say, the world's top 500) and to assess their collective power as corporate command posts in the international business networks they anchor (Sassen, 1991). Still, the globalizing world changes fast, and while some cities surge, others lag. The three giants of globalization have long been New York, London, and Tokyo; in the next rank are cities with fewer world headquarters but more regional headquarters, including Paris, Los Angeles, Frankfurt, and, outside the global core, Singapore (figure 8.4). As you go down the rankings, it becomes difficult to distinguish among cities as top-500 companies disappear and the comparative size and strength of regional companies headquartered there are difficult to measure (Taylor, 2004).

More than one analyst has compared this picture with that prevailing during colonial times, when decisions—economic as well as administrative—made in European capitals were transmitted through "the colonial city" to dependencies at the mercy of imperial rulers; the world is no less flat today, they argue, than it was then. Gated communities and gleaming if faceless office towers have taken the place of exclusive expatriate suburbs and Gothic administration buildings. Corporate globals are the new colonial regents. But the picture is more complex than that. The stagnant "third-world city" to which many a colonial city gave rise essentially is no more. Globalization is transforming many cities and modifying all but a few others (even Lagos shows some evidence of this) in ways that reflect a new era rather than mirroring the old.

Those modifications take several forms, only one of which is the large inflow of mobals seeking the jobs globalization creates. The huge, immeasurable accretion of shantytowns encircling periphery cities affected by globalization represents a vast expansion of the region's informal economy; it also exemplifies the ripple effect of paid employment, no matter how modest. One or more family members earning a regular wage in a factory in Lagos, Dhaka, or Manila can enable other members of their extended family to decide whether to stay in their rural village through difficult times or to try their luck by moving to the burgeoning outskirts; even the most minimal but dependable support opens new opportunities. A vigorous debate continues on the related question of textile sweatshops, where workers (especially women) labor long hours at exploitive wages: should consumers in the global core boycott the companies' products, or do those factories represent liberating opportunities for the workers, whose prospects would be diminished by declining sales? Long lists of job applicants suggest the latter, but the issue highlights an abusive side of globalization abhorred by its critics. Is the employment terrain really flatter because such low-paid work is available at all, or does that low pay signify the deepening inequalities attributable to globalization?

IMAGE OF POWER

Even as megacities mushroom and the tentacles of globalization endow them with new infrastructures to facilitate operations, whole new urban geographies are in the making. The most obvious manifestation of this is the skyline phenomenon, since "ever taller" seems to represent the aspirations of globals from Kuala Lumpur to Taipei, both of which in recent years have held a record about to be claimed by Dubai. Coupled with this competition for height is modernism, with futuristic structures such as Shanghai's Oriental Pearl Tower and its 101-story World Financial Center, opened in 2008, demonstrating to the world the limitless technologies of their engineers. But in many ways most significant is the clustering of tall office, hotel, and apartment buildings in comparatively small, new kinds of CBDs where foreign companies' operations congregate along with banks and other financial institutions as well as domestic companies with regional linkages. Since multinational companies tend to do business with each other, there is efficiency in proximity (Grant and Nijman, 2002).

There was a time when "landscape of power" referred to the massive industrial complexes of resource-rich states whose steel-making capacity was one measure of potency; today that notion is represented by the globalizing centers of megacities, where corporate decision making, financial transactions, and producer services are the gauges of power. Some antiglobalizers in China refer to this as a new form of extraterritoriality, with urban districts as off-limits to locals as nineteenth-century colonial enclaves were inaccessible (by law) to all but authorized Chinese.

The impact of globalization has other ramifications. While the economic geographies of central cities may change functionally, and one business pattern may give way to another, indiscriminate and high-speed "modernization" can destroy cultural heritage without recourse. The impact of China's Pacific Rim globalization on its capital, Beijing, was already pervasive before the city was awarded the 2008 Summer Olympics, but the combination of objectives led to a wholesale sweeping away of historic neighborhoods, their inhabitants exiled to remote apartment buildings beyond the outermost of its several new eight-lane ring roads. On many streets, residents stubbornly continued with their daily lives until the bulldozers demolished their modest houses, but what the dramatic images of these scenes missed was the loss of neighborhoods—of clusters of residents with common histories and shared linkages with distant villages, whose visitors had a place to alight and adjust. It was a flattening indeed, but not of the kind globalization allegedly brings with it.

Urbanization and globalization will continue their linked and inexorable march, so the remaining question relates to the rural areas whose shrinking share of the world's population will witness changes no less dramatic than those occurring in the megacities. Will the countryside "flatten" as population densities in rural areas proportionately decrease, living standards rise, land pressure diminishes, pollution abates, and nature revives? Will an increasingly urbanized world come to regard the heritage of culture and nature in nonurban areas with greater prudence than has been the case in the past? Precedent is not encouraging. Urbanites demand far more of the planet than their rural counterparts, from energy resources to water, from metals to wood and from textiles to food. As the world passes its 50 percent urban–rural milestone, the urban half of the population is requiring more than ten times the consumables per year as the rural half. For individual countries or societies, the imbalance is even greater: the average American consumes more than 30 times as much in the way of resources in a given period as the average Bangladeshi does. When it comes to particular resources, an Israeli uses more than four times as much fresh water per day as a Palestinian. Another way to look at it is this: if the consumption patterns of America's highly urbanized society became global, it would take four more Earths to sustain humanity.

Accelerating urbanization of the world will not, therefore, level global playing fields. Apart from the direct impacts of vastly expanded conurbations—loss of farmland to expanding megacities, rapidly increasing and heavily polluted runoffs from growing shantytowns, ever-increasing waste production creating environmental hazards even in the very centers of conurbations—city dwellers put indirect demands on rural areas through behaviors ranging from eating habits to building practices. Urbanites, unless constrained by religious strictures, eat far more meat than do villagers, empowered as they are by higher incomes; the globalization of the McDonald's brand is essentially an urban phenomenon. As an economic success story, the penetration of global markets by McDonald's is emblematic, but in the countryside it has led to the widespread conversion of forest to pastureland in order to raise the livestock that are turned into hamburgers. Multinational builders and furniture makers also put pressure on forests, and while decisions on such matters rest with those who have stewardship over those forests, including national and provincial governments as well as private owners, the fiscal power of global corporations all too often overwhelms environmental valuations.

In many ways, the most consequential impact on rural areas arising from accelerating urbanization will involve energy needs and water supplies. Media reports focus on China's and India's quests for oil and gas, but the enormous expansion of coal-fired power plants gets much less attention. Even as the urbanized United States, historically the most profligate polluter of the atmosphere, is reconsidering the emission-free nuclear power option (about 20 percent of electricity in this country is generated by nuclear power plants), China is in the process of building hundreds of coal-fired plants to keep pace with urban demands, and India is not far behind. Already, China's cities are plagued by sporadic power outages, and China's demand is on course to exceed America's within a decade. But China's planners expect nuclear reactors to generate no more than 4 percent of total demand by 2020. Anyone who has spent time in a major Chinese city and failed to see the sun on a meteorologically clear day has seen the future.

In the countryside of the global periphery, urbanization's energy demands produce Dickensian scenes. In Shanxi Province, "coal-mining operations have damaged waterways and scarred the land. Because of intense underground mining, thousands of acres are prone to sinking, and hundreds of villages are blackened with coal waste.... Roads are covered in coal tar; houses are coated with soot; miners, their faces smeared almost entirely black, haul carts full of coal; the air is thick with the smell of burning coal.... [T]he number of people suffering from lung cancer... has soared over the past 20 years" (Bradsher and Barboza, 2006). Annually, thousands—yes, *thousands*—of miners die in unsafe coal mines around the world. In China alone, accidents kill more than 5,000 coal miners in an average year. Imagine the outcry if a fraction of this number perished in nuclear plant accidents. Yet the "safety issue" is a key weapon in the arsenal of the antinuclear lobby. The casualties of coal, below and above the ground, apparently are a price to be paid in the hinterland to ensure that the demands of the cities are met. The annual cumulative calamity in the periphery receives little attention in the media of the core, but even occasionally fatal coal-mining accidents in such locales as West Virginia or eastern Utah do not engender debate over the fundamentals. Urban power and rural weakness involve more than farms and forests. The power of the city is also a matter of life and death.

9

PROMISE AND PERIL
IN THE PROVINCES

If locals in rural frontiers are in the thrall of powerful globals based in a network of world cities, they are not without power themselves. In the global core as well as the periphery, countrysides are the sources and scenes of resistance to decisions and actions taken in capitals and corporate boardrooms. French farmers seeing their privileges endangered by economic reforms demonstrate, and occasionally riot, in the streets of Paris. Often their banners proclaim their causes, but sometimes they show the name of a French region or even the flag of a *département*, reminding the authorities that they are dealing with an entity that has emotional resonance as well as economic interests. Chinese villagers organize to protest grievances ranging from the summary expropriation of land for factory building by industrialists empowered by the Beijing government, to oppressive rule by bosses whose loyalties are to the Communist Party rather than to the locals they are supposed to serve. They decry a new two-China policy—not involving Beijing and Taipei, but dividing their country into eastern "haves" and western "have-nots." South Africans in rural KwaZulu-Natal stage rallies in support of their embattled deputy president facing charges in urban courtrooms including rape and corruption, certain that his trials constitute a political assault on the Zulu nation he represents and shouting not only for justice but also for secession.

Ours may be an era of globalization and worldly flattening, but we also witness the resurgence of another of humanity's ancient predispositions: the territorial imperative. The very Internet-enabled dissemination of information driving the breakdown of barriers among globals also spreads ideas about power and autonomy among locals that arouse the kinds of nationalisms and ethnic aspirations economic globalization is supposed to mitigate. On a planet fractured into nearly 200 countries, the European Union (EU) has taken a lead by enmeshing 27 of them in a multinational entity designed to integrate economies and coordinate laws, but the European paradox is that a widespread revival of chauvinism seeks to reverse this unifying, globalizing process. In several areas of Europe, there are provinces, regions, and other entities that press for more self-determination as opposed to international integration. It is a contradiction that has global implications, because "supranational" unions, associations, and agreements, from NAFTA to ASEAN and from Asia-Pacific Economic Cooperation (APEC) to the Gulf Cooperation Council (GCC), are designed to lessen rather than intensify discord and division among states, and to accommodate rather than agitate such regionalisms.

It may be that devolutionary initiatives such as those occurring in Europe have to do with scale and dimension. Europe, for all its global influence, is a realm of small countries making the best of limited and crowded space. The prospect of a United States of Europe, an actual economic superpower and a potential political one, whose government might some day supersede what remains of national sovereignty, tends to excite some European globals but terrifies many European locals. With national governments of member states participating more or less enthusiastically in the process, locals fall back on their provincial familiarities to cushion the impact. When they realize that the evolving system gives their provinces (or regions, communities, States) scope for political activism, cultural assertion, and economic self-direction, those provinces, especially when endowed with ethnic identity, become the bases for new and stronger identities. Thus, while lowering national barriers and facilitating the workings of globalization, the EU experiment simultaneously strengthens local territorial attachments and constructs new mental maps. The notion of an independent Scotland, for example, might never have reached the level of support it has among Scots today had the United Kingdom not joined the EU; Scottish nationalism was energized by the prospect of the Scottish "country" becoming a third-tier entity in the EU hierarchy when it was in effect a first-rank member, on a par with England and Wales, in the United Kingdom. Here, in other parts of Europe and, indeed, elsewhere in the globalizing world, the profiles of component parts of states have escalated, countering the trend globalization should promote.

Subnational entities, in this perspective, form the ultimate geographic expression of the power of place: they embody local objectives and aspirations in a national state enmeshed in globalizing processes, and their inhabitants succeed in countering the prevailing forces by asserting their historic and cultural identities. Being born into Basque, Corsican, Bosnian, Kurdish, Baluchi, Tutsi, Asomese, or any number of other societies embarked on such a campaign means that you are destined to be part of it or, at the very least, affected by it. When the tactics are transactional, the results are often salutary. When they involve violence, they can be ruinous to entire generations (Moss, 2008).

SUBNATIONAL UNITS AND THEIR EVOLVING ROLES

The term "subnational unit" has come to designate any territorial entity below the level of state or country whose identity is defined in some significant way, either by delimited space (for example, a province or county or district) or by collective identity and conviction, which may transcend borders to create an informal but cohesive domain within the state. A subnational unit comes to international attention when its local administration is in serious discord with the national government, or when ideological or cultural forces threaten to enfeeble or destabilize the state. At that point the international community is likely to take action ranging from mediation to intervention: there is a global consensus that subnational units should not be enabled to fracture a state, barring exceptional and essentially uncontrollable circumstances, such as the collapse of the former Yugoslavia.

As a result, many a state survives on the map because a combination of external and centripetal forces overrides its historic and often growing divisiveness. The case of Belgium is illustrative: everyone knows that this is a culturally divided country in which the north speaks Flemish (Dutch) and the south speaks French, and that the geographic designation of Flanders represents the former while the name Wallonia depicts the latter. But, in fact, only two of Belgium's five Flemish-speaking provinces have Flanders in their names, and the city of Antwerp, the north's "primate city," does not even lie in either (figure 9.1). Still, the subnational designation of Flanders, defining not only a linguistic but also a particular political culture, is far more conspicuous than the collective name for the five dominantly French-speaking provinces. Flanders is a historic entity in the economic and cultural evolution of Western Europe; Wallonia is a construct to designate Belgium's poorer, landlocked interior. But this does not mean that Walloons have no wider aspirations. Following

Figure 9.1. Belgium's challenging geography.

Belgium's recent adoption of a federal system of government, the five French-speaking provinces embarked on a vigorous international advertising campaign proclaiming the regional, locational, economic, and social assets of Wallonia, "best for business in the heart of Europe." Nowhere in those advertisements and commercials does the word "Belgium" even appear, although subtle references to the prevalence of a "world language" are unmistakable.

Since the 1920s, not-so-subtle political discourse in the Flemish-speaking provinces of Belgium has often alluded to partition, and Belgium might indeed have fragmented along linguistic lines had it not been for the selection of Brussels, the national capital, as the headquarters of the European Union after World War II. As it happens, Brussels lies in its own tiny "region" comprising 162 square kilometers (63 square miles), a historically and still today dominantly French-speaking city encircled by the northern province of Flemish Brabant and still the seat of government of the Flemish-speaking north (figure 9.1). Now a thoroughly international and multilingual city, Brussels is a center of globalization, bringing Belgium—both the Flemish and Wallonian regions of it—enormous assets as a financial, administrative, corporate, operations, and service center. Thus the choice of Brussels as the EU capital created a vested interest in Belgium's political stability and survival in both Flanders and Wallonia, and the city's anomalous relative location makes partition appear so impractical that it is unlikely to occur. Two subnational units with an adversarial history are stuck together by international glue.

Belgium's bailout is, of course, in many ways unique. Even the EU itself has a compelling interest in Belgium's integrity, since the organization can hardly afford to be centered in a state that disintegrates around it. Belgium's survival is often compared to the former Czechoslovakia's breakup in 1993; had Prague been the EU capital, the argument goes, that collapse would never have happened. As it was, the "velvet divorce" between two subnational units anchored by Czech and Slovak cultures, respectively, occurred without strife in part because of the prospect of joint incorporation in the EU, to which both were admitted in 2004. But in the immediate aftermath of the separation, Slovakia's government was rife with incompetence, cronyism, corruption, and human-rights violations involving especially the country's Roma and Magyar minorities, casting doubt on the new country's future and precipitating a period of international isolation that did not end until more enlightened administration followed the 1998 elections. The EU's constructive engagement undoubtedly improved the lives of locals in Slovakia because of its economic benefits and subsidies as well as its scrutiny of domestic social conditions, and in that sense lowered barriers and enhanced transparency. But Czechoslovakia's partition is often cited by leaders in subnational entities elsewhere as a model for their own aspirations, which has the opposite effect.

Obviously the breakup of states runs counter to the "flattening" that speeds economic globalization and energizes globals. It complicates corporate access and penetration, requiring additional negotiations and perhaps compromise, should former subnational units be at odds following partition. One set of negotiations thus becomes two or more (in the case of the former Yugoslavia and following the most recent secession of Montenegro from Serbia, six—not counting Kosovo). The former Soviet Union in the 1990s gave rise to 15 independent countries, many of them, including Georgia and Kazakhstan, containing assertive subnational units. Former European dependencies in the periphery struggle with similar centrifugal forces. The cycle of political fragmentation is far from over; subnational units are taking on greater importance, and the map continues to change. "Flattening" would not be the term to apply to this process.

States take diverse steps to accommodate the associated pressures. Several of the larger member states of the European Union have reconfigured their administrative frameworks in ways that would have been unthinkable little more than a generation ago. Spain, still calling itself a kingdom, has gone from the highly centralized dictatorship of the Franco era, which endured until 1975, to an amalgam of 17 "autonomous communities" (ACs), each of which has its own parliament and administration in control of planning, public works, cultural affairs, education, environmental matters, and even, to a considerable extent, international trade and commerce. Each AC is authorized to negotiate its desired degree of autonomy with the central government in Madrid, a process still under way and expected to continue until 2012.

The Spanish model has promise in that it creates ways for local political, cultural, and economic pressures to be defused before they threaten the stability of the state, but it is also fraught with peril. One of the dangers is the "never enough" phenomenon, whereby each request, when met, is followed by more radical demands, with the obvious and ultimate goal the independence and secession of the entity involved. In Spain's case, a plebiscite in 1980 approved a higher level of self-determination for four of the country's "regions," a first step in the process still ongoing today. While all went well with three of these regions (Catalonia, Andalusia, and Galicia), and the voters in the fourth, the Basque "country," also approved the government's offer, a minority of Basques rejected it, and a terrorist element among them began a campaign of bombings and assassinations that has claimed more then 800 lives and may not be over. The Basque "nation," with its unique language (not a member of the Indo-European family and unrelated to Spanish) and its distinctive culture, amounts to less than 6 percent of Spain's total population. It inhabits but a small corner of coastal north-central Spain and southwest France (the separatist organization ETA claims a larger domain than Spanish maps acknowledge), yet its violent tactics have created an issue that in many ways dominates Spanish politics and affects relations between the Madrid government and its other ACs.

Another danger inherent in the Spanish model has to do with finances. Among the demands of the ACs is control over public spending, and the central government has been generous in allowing them to retain ever larger shares of tax money raised (in recent negotiations with Madrid, the Catalan government demanded to retain 50 percent of its income tax revenues, up from 33 percent in an earlier agreement). That satisfies the ACs, but government ministries in Madrid are dealing with shrinking budgets and, as a result, dwindling power and influence. Critics of the government argue that this is federalism run amuck, but the government consists of representatives from the ACs, and they are loathe to interfere with any diversion of funds to their constituencies. As a result, the relevance of the capital as the traditional center of power is waning, and the action is increasingly "subnational." Catalonia, the delta-shaped AC in Spain's northeast corner centered on Barcelona and containing about one-sixth of the population of 46 million, considers itself a discrete nation with its own language; on average, it produces a quarter of Spain's exports and 40 percent of its industrial exports. Such economic strength translates into political clout, and while each AC has its own charter with the government, none has the degree of self-determination Catalonia has secured. Barcelona has all the trappings of a political, cultural, and economic capital, and global corporations hardly need go through Madrid to establish their presence in Iberia. Notions of independence are never far below the surface in Catalonia, so the charter carefully steers a semantic course between Catalans asserting that they are a "nation" and Madrid stating that they form a "nationality"—meaning a Spanish nationality.

Thus the management of devolutionary forces is an exercise fraught with risk for both the center and the province. In the United Kingdom, the government's response to the rising tide of nationalism (prominent in Scotland, evident in Wales) had unintended consequences in the dominant "country," England. Scottish public pressure for greater autonomy (and, in the unbridled opinion of Scottish nationalists, independence) grew during the Thatcher-Major period of Conservative Party government, but that government rejected notions of devolution and resisted negotiating nationalist demands. Scotland is a stronghold of the Labor Party, then in opposition in London, but Scottish public opinion, as reflected by local media, transcended party politics. Support for independence was naturally strongest in the Scottish National Party, but significantly greater autonomy had support among other voters as well. Media commentaries proclaimed Scotland's distinctive culture, territorial and demographic dimensions (often comparing it to full-EU member Denmark), resources—including a "fair share" of revenues from North Sea oil and gas reserves—and historic role in science and technology, in which the "nation" produced early and significant leadership. When the Blair ("New Labor") government ousted the Conservatives in 1997, the stage was set for a new direction, and not only Scotland but also Wales was given the opportunity to decide on the installation of representative assemblies. In 1999, the first elections were held for a Scottish Parliament and a "National" Assembly in Wales, where devolutionary pressures were distinctly weaker. Scotland's Parliament acquired the wider range of powers, including taxation and law enforcement, but the overall effect was to defuse separatist tensions that had been building for decades.

The unintended consequences arose in England. In the first place, it seemed inappropriate to many in England that while the English had no vote or voice in the Scottish Parliament, Scots continued to participate as elected members in the British Parliament, thus making or affecting decisions primarily involving England (a Scot, Gordon Brown, became prime minister in 2007). Furthermore, if regions like Scotland and Wales could take steps toward self-government, what about recognized regions of England? In fact, there already is a regional map of England, authorized by the EU, dividing it into London (which already has its own assembly) and eight other regions, none of which displays much identity or desire to follow suit (figure 9.2). In 2004, the British government tried to launch a program to establish regional assemblies for each of these regions and put the idea to the vote in one of them, the "North East." The result was such—78 percent of the voters rejected it—that the whole idea was abandoned. Surveys showed, however, that this repudiation reflected a fear that local powers would be lost to regional bodies, and that the capacity of regional bodies to protect local interests was misunderstood. It was also clear that, Yorkshire and Cornwall apart, none of the English regions has much cohesion. No regional identities in the North West or South East have the strength of those in Scotland or Wales.

This does not mean that Scotland's autonomy and dual influence are not resented in England. The regional map has given rise to debate over options among which a federal system of twelve units is one: such a union would counter the perception (and reality) of

Figure 9.2. England's EU Regions.

monolithic England's dominating the rest of the United Kingdom. But the fact is that, with even embattled Northern Ireland now having an elected Assembly, the only UK subnational entity without its own parliament is the one that pays most of the bills—England. Devolutionary pressures in one British subnational unit have set in motion a sequence of events whose outcome is yet unclear.

In each of the cases just discussed, one or more subnational units has risen to prominence for reasons that range from outright rejection of central authority to moderate demands for increased autonomy. Other EU member states experience similar developments: France, for example, once the highly centralized prototype of the nation-state and its more than 80 *départements* dating from the Napoleonic era, now has a subnational framework of 22 historically significant provinces, groupings of *départements* called regions. These regions, though represented in Paris, have substantial autonomy in financial, developmental, and trade arenas, and their capitals have benefited as the seats of regional governments. The region called Rhône-Alpes and its capital, Lyon, have become a self-standing economic powerhouse with its own connections to the globalizing economy. But France has not escaped the strife faced by the Spanish in the Basque "country" and by the British in Northern Ireland: its large Mediterranean island of Corsica produced a rebel movement whose violent opposition to French control continued for decades and even touched the mainland. And while none of Italy's 20 regions or their numerous constituent provinces has sought independence, some in the north have become economic juggernauts (notably Piedmont and Lombardy), while others, mainly in the south, lag dangerously.

In these countries of Europe and elsewhere in the global core, the growing strengths, identities, and demands of subnational units have mostly been successfully accommodated by capable governments possessing the resources needed to channel the process. Canada's long-term adaptation to the cyclic challenges and demands from nationalists in its Francophone province of Québec (and French speakers outside the province) culminated in a provincial referendum in 1995, when Québec's voters narrowly defeated the independence option. Canada also experienced some associated violence, but given the scale and dimension of the issue—Quebec has nearly 8 million of Canada's 33 million citizens—its overall success in dealing with this subnational issue is exemplary. One of the most culturally plural societies on the planet with one of the highest proportional rates of legal immigration, Canada's response to aboriginal land claims has been to redraw its administrative map. In 1999, the most recent of these actions created the self-governing Inuit territory of Nunavut, incorporating a vast area west of Hudson Bay as well as all the islands from Southampton to Ellesmere and comprising about one-fifth of all Canadian land (figure 9.3).

Figure 9.3. Canada's map continues to change as Inuit and First-Nation interests are reflected by territorial and administrative adjustments. Substantially self-governed Nunavut is the product of a major aboriginal land-claim agreement between the Inuit people and the federal government. First-Nation reserves are far more numerous in Canada than in the United States, but individually much smaller in area. The scale of this map only allows a depiction of their wide distribution, but even the numerous reserves shown here as dots contain less than 50 percent of Canada's aboriginals; a slight majority now reside in urban and suburban areas. Modified from M. J. Norris and L. Jantzen (2002), "Aboriginal Languages in Canada, 1996" (Ottawa: Statistics Canada), from 1996 Census.

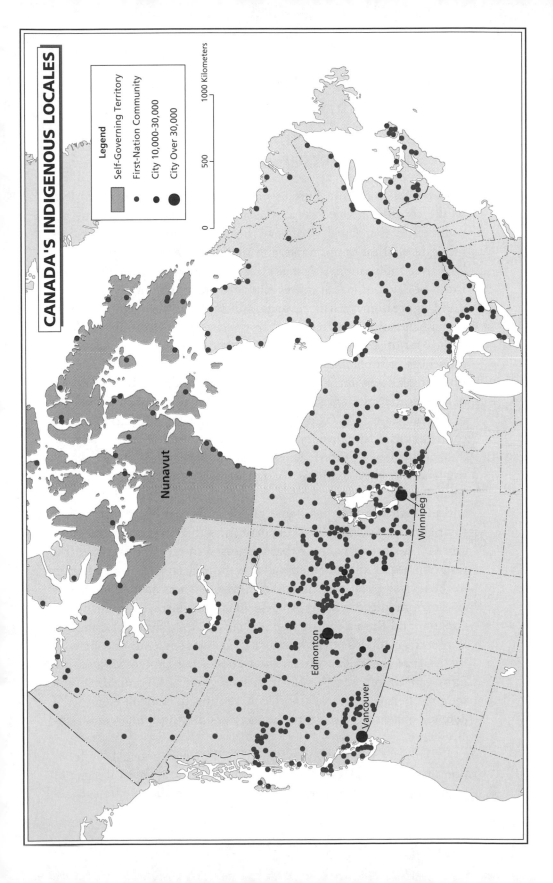

CANADA'S INDIGENOUS LOCALES

Legend

Self-Governing Territory
First-Nation Community
City 10,000–30,000
City Over 30,000

1000 Kilometers
0   500   1000

Nunavut

Winnipeg

Edmonton

Vancouver

Canada's federal flexibility has paid incalculable dividends in terms of social order, peace, and stability.

ROUGH TIMES IN THE CORE

Such success stories in Europe and North America should not lead to the conclusion that the most serious subnational problems are confined to the global periphery. Economic prosperity often does facilitate political compromise, and the involvement of stable neighbors and international agencies can constrain potentially violent forms of devolution, but power (the prospect of gaining or losing it), greed, aggression, racism, revenge, and other intense emotions leave no human culture unaffected when the circumstances allow. "Allow" is the operative word here, because the most serious and deadly consequences of subnational assertion occur when systems and institutions break down and collective action, usually driven by a minority of leaders and agitators, spins out of control. The catastrophic collapse of Yugoslavia in 1990 is only the most recent manifestation of this combination of circumstances, but it is all the more telling because it happened in a Europe whose nations had vowed "never again" to stand by while extremists committed crimes against humanity. That, however, is what happened as Yugoslavia's subnational units and numerous minorities, some of them abetted by cohorts across their borders, saw and seized opportunities to gain ground and settle scores. The orgy of violence that witnessed the revival of concentration camps and implementations of "ethnic cleansing"—an addition to the lexicon of all-too-human inhumanity—was abetted by odious succor from interested parties in Germany (in the case of subnational Croatia) and Russia (bolstering Serbia). That a quarter of a million Europeans could lose their lives in a crisis that spun out of control in the heart of the global core on the watch of the United Nations, the European Union, and the North Atlantic Treaty Organization, and required belated external (U.S.) intervention to control, evinces the potency of territorial-cultural imperatives driving human emotions anywhere.

The former Yugoslavia may have constituted an unusual combination of physiographic and cultural complexities, a physical stage of high relief and a social mosaic of 7 major and 17 smaller ethnic-cultural components, but its social fabric was no more intricate than that of many parts of the global periphery (figure 9.4). When the former communist dictatorship disintegrated into its subnational units, one complicating factor was that several of the subnational units themselves contained subnational entities harboring aspirations of independence. In the case of Muslim-Croat-Serbian Bosnia, such aspirations were assuaged by the 1995 Dayton Accords designed to functionally but temporarily partition the new country until reintegration of its subdivisions became feasible. That originally NATO-supervised process still is ongoing, and has a long way to go. In Macedonia, a Greek regional name appeared on the new map to designate a country whose population is about 30 percent Muslim-Albanian, a minority that is largely concentrated in its northwest. Macedonia's survival and stability, in the face of Greek objections over its name, rebel activity in its Muslim corner, and risky government efforts to limit minority rights, are a stroke of luck in a region bedeviled by misfortune. The peaceful secession of Montenegro from Serbia-Montenegro in 2006, the latest (but probably not last) shoe to drop, created another of Europe's still-growing cadre of ministates, an independent country with a population of about 625,000, two capitals, a territory half the size of Massachusetts, and full membership in the United Nations. Perhaps the most consequential result of Montenegro's newfound independence is that it landlocks Serbia, although no major port development had taken place on the Adriatic coast and Serbia has an alternate route to the sea via the Danube River.

And still the devolution of Yugoslavia is not at an end. While the former country's dominant component was named Serbia-Montenegro, two other subnational units formed part of it: the Hungarian-minority province of Vojvodina in the north and the Albanian-Muslim stronghold of Kosovo in the south. No serious separatist movement has arisen in Vojvodina, but Kosovo became the focus of a confrontation that required outside intervention to resolve. In 1998, Muslim Albanians in Kosovo launched a violent campaign to secede from Serbia, to which Serbia responded with a massive attack that, by early 1999, had driven about one-third of Kosovo's two million Muslims from their homes. Serbia's ethnic-cleansing policy in Kosovo drew unheeded warnings from NATO, resulting in a bombing campaign that inflicted major damage to Serbia's infrastructure and forced it to surrender. Serbian troops withdrew from Kosovo, and the stage

Figure 9.4. The still-evolving political geography of the former Yugoslavia and Albania. Landlocked, dominantly Muslim Kosovo is the current challenge.

appeared to be set for the province's independence. NATO peacekeepers and UN supervision and jurisdiction would provide time for a negotiated transition to sovereignty.

Geography and history conspire to make this transition difficult. As figure 9.4 shows, the tables are turned: the Kosovo Muslims were a minority in Serbia, but now Serbs remain as small minorities in Kosovo, where they have reason to complain of threats and mistreatment—this in a province where Muslims and Christians centuries ago fought epic battles that established Christianity's dominance.

Kosovo's independence hinges on Serbia's acquiescence, but Serbian nationalism recoils at the prospect of abandoning ethnic Serbs to a state that is 90 percent Muslim. In February 2008 Kosovo's leadership declared the territory independent, setting off celebrations in the Kosovar areas and angry and violent demonstrations in the Serb-majority corners of the new state. The international community was divided on the matter: the United States, Germany, France, and the United Kingdom recognized Kosovo's sovereignty, but China, Russia, and Spain were among the dissenters. With two permanent UN Security Council members holding veto power opposed to the move, the future for the new state was uncertain, and the risk that Kosovo's secession might precipitate renewed conflict in the region was real.

The map suggests a potential compromise: the boundary between Kosovo and Serbia could be redrawn to incorporate the northern corner of Kosovo, centered on Mitrovica, into Serbia while attaching small areas along their eastern and western borders, where some Muslim Kosovars remain on the Serbian side of the border, into Kosovo. Using new boundaries to channel territorial imperatives in Bosnia worked; it might work in Kosovo's case as well. As the search for a negotiated solution continues, Kosovo poses one final threat to the hard-won stability of this embattled part of Europe.

Even a casual glance at figure 9.4 reveals that the problems arising from the breakdown of the former Yugoslavia are not merely representative of a physically and culturally fractured Europe. The long-term rule of the Ottoman Empire over the Slavic populations in this area endowed the region with millions of Muslim converts who today form the majority population in Albania and strong minorities in Bosnia, Macedonia, and (pending Kosovo's future) Serbia. During the periods of violent conflict marking Yugoslavia's disintegration, Islamic extremists appeared from as far afield as Afghanistan, Iraq, Chechnya, and elsewhere to participate in what they saw as a *jihad*, but the jihadists and the locals had little in common, and the former never became a political factor. Islam in post-Ottoman Eastern Europe in general is far less rigid or dogmatic than it is in its Arab versions, and it is Western, not Eastern Europe that has taken the brunt of its extremism. It is governance and economics, not culture or ethnicity, that will slow the accession of the subnational units of the former Yugoslavia into the European Union. It is nevertheless still possible that the first inclusion of major Muslim populations into the EU will happen here rather than as a result of the still-uncertain accession of Turkey.

And herein lie several ironies. The subnational units of collapsed Yugoslavia are rising from comparative obscurity and marginality to full-fledged membership of the EU and UN—as Slovenia already has and Croatia soon will—when such economic and cultural powerhouses as Catalonia and Scotland have no such option. This would suggest that the foundering of a state enhances the prospects of its subnational units, a perilous notion in a world with numerous weak governments, not all of them in the periphery. A tragedy arising from Yugoslavia's collapse is that its largest and many ways leading constituent, Serbia, has seen its aspirations demolished by the actions initiated by its former president, Slobodan Milošević, who initially sought to take control over all areas inhabited by Serbs, including those in Croatia and Bosnia, and several of his generals, who are accused of war crimes. Milošević was turned over to the UN to face charges before the International Criminal Tribunal in The Hague, where he died in custody. But Serbia failed to arrest and extradite the most wanted of the Serb war criminals, resulting in the suspension in 2006 of the first-stage discussions leading to eventual EU membership. Add to this Serbia's loss of Montenegro, its reluctance to end its claim over Kosovo, and the potential for devolutionary pressures in its northern province of Vojvodina, and it is clear that this key component of the region still faces a difficult transition—and with it the region as a whole.

Thus the global core has been and remains the scene of predicaments more commonly thought of as problems of the periphery: restive provinces, separatist campaigns, boundary quarrels, ethnic and cultural conflicts, proxy contests, autocratic rulers, war crimes, fraudulent elections. The treatment of minorities, for example, the eight million Roma (Gypsies) in various EU member states, given their governments' comparative resources, is little if any better than that accorded to minorities in many countries of the periphery (de Blij, 2006). Some states in the global core may be older than many of those in the periphery, but their locals' attachment to territory and cultural landscape has not lost much—or any—of its intensity. Notions of a "more mature" view of their place on the planet are countered by the seemingly irrational parochialism that arises when local interests appear threatened. European Union treaty designers prefer to submit plans, programs, and agreements to parliaments for approval because voters tend to turn them down (as was the case with the first draft of the EU Constitution). The grand objective of the EU is a leveling of economic playing fields and a flattening of political barriers, and much has been achieved. But even in the global core, it can still be rough out there in the provinces.

IN THE PERIPHERY

Visit cities and villages so grievously damaged during the violent breakup of Yugoslavia, and the crisis seems to be far more distant than it really was. In Slovenia, it is difficult to find a trace of the bombings that followed its declaration of independence in 1991. Tourists flock to Croatian cities and towns where Serb militias roamed, crowding streets and filling sidewalk cafes. Bridges and roads in divided Bosnia have been repaired and homes rebuilt, and Sarajevo bears few scars of the conflict. Even Serbia is recovering rapidly from the enormous damage that the 1999 bombardment did to its infrastructure.

Perhaps even more remarkable is the emergence of representative government and civic institutions. Societies that for generations had lived under authoritarian regimes and repressive rule made unprecedented gains toward EU standards of governance and administration. Even formerly communist Albania has been touched by the spirit of modernization, not to say globalization, with the aid of World Bank loans. Construction in the CBD of its once-bleak capital, Tirane, reflects an optimism bolstered by the opening of first-stage membership discussions with the EU in 2006.

No such buoyancy marks places in the global periphery that have gone through (or are experiencing) similar transitions. Just imagine what the chances are that a sliver of territory in East Africa or South Asia inhabited by fewer than 700,000 people without significant international linkages could hold a referendum on independence, vote yes, become a full-fledged constituent of the African Union or ASEAN, and join the United Nations as a member, all within a couple of years.

It is not that inhabitants of subnational units in the postcolonial periphery have failed to make their case. The Ibo of what was then the Eastern Region of Nigeria and their allies in 1967 proclaimed a Republic of Biafra and fought a war of independence that lasted until early 1970. The African peoples in Sudan's southern provinces seek secession from the Islamic and Arabized north. The peoples of Indonesia's Aceh Province struggled for independence against Dutch colonizers as well as Indonesian rulers. The Kayin (Karen), Shan, Kachin, and other minorities in Myanmar's "States" have battled the ruling junta for decades. Inhabitants of India's Asom (Assam) State demand self-determination. Taiwan is China's subnational quandary. The periphery is no less vulnerable to devolution than is the core.

In the periphery, though, the prospects of success and recovery are weaker. Take the case of Somalia, the failed state in the "Horn" of Africa (figure 9.5). The Muslim Somali inhabit a region long dominated by others (Ethiopians and Europeans, who carved up their domain) and found themselves astride colonial borders when the Europeans, in this case the British in the north and the Italians in the south, withdrew. Centered on the south-coast capital of Mogadishu, the clan-riven, warlord-driven state lacked the institutions it needed. Soon, southerners were engaged in raids into Ethiopia's Ogaden region, inhabited by ethnic Somalis, and Ethiopian retaliation followed. Drought, starvation, refugee crises, foreign assistance gone fatally wrong, and recurrent clan warfare made Somalia emblematic of state failure.

But not in the far north, in the former British Somaliland (figure 9.5). There, Somalis proved that clan structure and sensible traditional leadership could produce stable and orderly society, and in 1991 the northerners gave political voice to their achievement by declaring independence as the Republic of Somaliland. In sharp contrast to the south, Somaliland's stability has been rewarded with relative prosperity: its capital, Hargeysa, bustles with commerce, and some overseas trade goes through the port of Berbera. Meanwhile, the political system evolved toward constitutional democracy. By 2006, all three levels of Somaliland's provisional government, including its president, were elected.

One might conclude that such spectacular achievements under the most difficult of circumstances would elicit favorable responses from the African Union in particular and from the "international community" generally, but this is not Montenegro. Appeals for recognition

Figure 9.5. The embattled Horn of Africa. In the 2000s, Eritrea was at war with Ethiopia over its border, Somalia had fragmented into three parts, Djibouti was a Western fortress at the entrance to the Red Sea, and Kenya suffered the violent aftermath of a disputed election that raised ethnic tensions.

HORN OF AFRICA

SAUDI ARABIA

Jiddah
Makkah (Mecca)

Port Sudan

Khamis Mushayt

Najran

Atbara

Jizan

Red Sea

YEMEN

ERITREA

Keren
Massawa

San'a

Al Mukalla

Kassala
Agordat
Asmara

Al Hudaydah

Omdurman

Khartoum

Wad Medani

Gedaref

TIGRAY

Mek'ele

Ta'izz

Adan

Bab el Mandeb Strait

Gulf of Adan

Sennar

Gonder

Assab

Kosti

Lake Tana

Weldiya

DJIBOUTI

Djibouti

Bahir Dar

Berbera

SUDAN

Debre Mark'os

Dese

Lake Assal

SOMALILAND
(Independence proclaimed 1991)

Blue Nile

Malakal

AMHARA

Dire Dawa

Hargeysa

Adis Abeba

Harer

ETHIOPIA

Garoowe

White Nile

Jima

Asela

OROMO

SOMALI

PUNTLAND
(Autonomy declared 1998)

Juba

Lake Turkana

S O M A L I A

Baidoa

GULU

UGANDA

SOMALI

Merca

Mogadishu

THE CONGO

Lake Albert

Soroti

Mbale

KALENJIN

Eldoret

K E N Y A

INDIAN

Kampala

Jinja

Kisumu

Meru

OCEAN

Entebbe

Nakuru

Mbarara

Lake Victoria

LUO

KIKUYU

KAMBA

Jamaame

Kismaayo

RWANDA

Nairobi

Mwanza

BURUNDI

Arusha

Moshi

Mombasa

Tabora

Tanga

TANZANIA

Lake Tanganyika

POPULATION

- • Under 50,000
- • 50,000–250,000
- ● 250,000–1,000,000
- ● 1,000,000–5,000,000

National capitals are underlined

OROMO Major ethnic group

0   200   400 Kilometers

were ignored, no diplomatic or corporate officers visited Hargeysa, and no invitations were issued to Somaliland's President Dahir Riyale Kahin to visit any foreign countries until 2006, when he toured five East African capitals. Members of the United Nations, falling over themselves to promise Kosovo recognition whether the Security Council approves or not, were silent on Somaliland. And the world is flat?

It is likely that the disregard of the "international community" will eventually have its costs. What keeps subnational units on course is their capacity to strengthen their own linkages to the outside world irrespective of the connections of their capitals; what keeps their politics open and transparent is the knowledge that the world is looking in. By isolating Somaliland and ignoring its outreach, foreign actors will make it far more difficult for Somalilanders to deal with economic setbacks and their political fallout than would otherwise be the case. Rather than watching Somaliland's success spread to Puntland (the intervening sector of the country, also with notions of autonomy) and perhaps even farther south, we may see the south's apparently incurable malaise infect the north. The plight of the periphery is on display here in the Horn of Africa.

Somaliland lies on the Muslim side of the "Islamic Front" that crosses Africa from Guinea to Tanzania and traverses Ethiopia just to its south, but Sudan straddles it, and that cultural contradiction is in the process of yielding a different outcome. North and South in Sudan are different worlds; colonial boundaries encircled peoples whose environments, economies, and traditions differed fundamentally. Incorporation into the state of Sudan upon independence (1956) did nothing to mitigate those differences. At the time of independence, Sudan was administratively divided into 10 provinces, of which the southernmost three contained the African, Christian-animist minority, with the northern seven (including the capital district of Khartoum) primarily Muslim. The Muslim North thus held the demographic majority, the seat of government, the coastal outlet (Port Sudan on the Red Sea), and the major irrigated agricultural zone where the White and Blue Nile converge.

It was a geographic recipe for trouble, but initially the turmoil was among Northerners themselves as a series of coups and military juntas destabilized the government. Before long, however, the conflict erupted that would come to rank among the world's costliest in terms of lives lost and people dislocated. Successive Khartoum regimes tried to exercise their authority over the Southern provinces, where resistance turned into rebellion. The promising decision in 1972 to award the southern provinces a measure of autonomy, however, was followed in 1983 by the fatal effort by the Gaafar Nimeiri regime to institute Islamic law throughout the country, turning simmering armed opposition into a full-scale war. In three decades, according to UN estimates, two million people lost their lives through violence and starvation; as recently as 2003, some four million Southerners were refugees in their own country. Meanwhile, the regime experimented with the country's administrative structure, first dividing it into "regions" and subsidiary "provinces" (and thus fragmenting the three Southern provinces into smaller entities), then scrapping this framework in favor of 26 States, and then grouping these States officially into 16 Northern and 10 Southern States. This awarded a formal subnational status to the South that was to become a basis for settlement of the civil war and the formulation of a federal Sudan.

Few students of Sudan's agonies would have predicted that the South would ever see the opportunity apparently at hand. The Sudan's Muslim rulers used famine as a weapon, denying relief supplies to starving refugees; they used their military superiority to inflict heavy casualties on the Sudan People's Liberation Army (SPLA) and were bolstered by the discovery of major oil reserves and resulting revenues. Even as stories of ruthless dispossession of villagers beneath whose land the oil was found caused some interested global companies to withdraw, Sudan's rulers had reasons to settle the bigger issue. Sudan had been added to the U.S. list of states that sponsor terrorism, the United Nations formally endorsed an accusation that Sudan sheltered Islamic militants trying to kill neighboring Egypt's president, a new crisis in Darfur heaped world criticism on the regime, and continued instability in and near the South would impede the exploitation of oil reserves because most of those that had been discovered lay very near the North–South border. In 2004, leaders of the North and South signed a remarkable agreement that gave Southerners direct representation in the transitional Khartoum government (the vice president would be a Southerner), awarded the South 50 percent of oil revenues, and committed Khartoum to allow the South to conduct a referendum on independence in 2010 and to abide by the result. Almost immediately, hundreds of thousands of displaced Southerners began moving back to their homeland, UN peacekeepers were being deployed, and the unofficial Southern capital of Juba, long cut off from the rest of the world, was coming to life. Even the sudden and accidental death of the SPLA's long-term leader, John Garang, who would have been Vice President in the new Khartoum government, did not derail the peace process. Meanwhile, oil revenues were changing the skyline of Khartoum, ushering in an era of modernization unprecedented in the ancient city's history.

Although Southern Sudan's referendum is still in the (now-near) future, its regional and indeed global implications are significant. Southerners constitute about one-quarter of Sudan's population of 44 million, so they will always have minority status. But Southerners themselves are not without their own cultural divisions, so independence would entail new relationships among locals. Independence would create a landlocked state larger than Botswana and more populous than Chad (larger than France, more populous than Belgium) with the weakest of external surface links and a skeletal economy. Depending on future relations with Khartoum, the South may need an alternative outlet to Port Sudan, which would require rail and/or road connections through Uganda and Kenya to the port of Mombasa. Even with oil revenues— again depending on Sudan—the new state would be born as one of Subsaharan Africa's poorest, wedged between the landlocked Central African Republic to the west and landlocked Ethiopia to the east.

Even as the secession of the South became a real possibility, another crisis deepened in Sudan's three Darfur Provinces in the west. Southern and Western Darfur (Arabic for "House of the Fur") are inhabited by Islamized ethnically African Fur. Northern Darfur is predominantly Arab. The Khartoum regime had for some time accused the Fur of sympathizing with the South during the long civil war, but other, more local stresses, including environmental issues in this parched area, also contributed to the tragedy that unfolded here. Camel- and cattle-herding northerners invaded the Africans' fields and villages, empowered by the so-called *janjaweed* militia and supported at times by the national army. As they killed locals, burned homes and crops, disabled wells, and laid waste to the countryside, the "international community" debated whether what was happening in this part of Sudan constituted genocide. By late 2007, an estimated 300,000 Fur had been killed, more than 2.5 million had been driven from their homes, and UN as well as other relief efforts fell far short of the growing need in this ruined region. Inevitably, voices arose proposing the separation of Southern and Western Darfur Provinces from Sudan and their attachment to the South (which, as the map shows, they border). It was not difficult to hear the echoes: will Sudan become the Yugoslavia of Africa?

But this is unlikely. Governments in the global periphery have resisted the kind of devolutionary compromise enabled by the North–South agreement in Sudan, arguing that any accommodation with separatists will serve to embolden others; thus, the African Union has withheld support not only from Somaliland but also Western Sahara, where a population of locals resists incorporation into Morocco. Opponents of secessionist initiatives often cite the case of Eritrea, which in its earlier history was the scene of Muslim–Christian contests and became part of the sphere of influence of Ethiopia. Italian colonialism in the 1880s had established holdings along the Red Sea and Indian Ocean coasts, and in 1890 Italy proclaimed Eritrea a colony. The boundary on the map today is the approximate border that the Italians and Ethiopian Emperor Menelik II negotiated in 1896, and the Italians soon began converting Eritrea into a base for later conquest of Ethiopia. In a frenzy of activity, they built towns, roads, bridges, ports, and airfields, but their campaign turned out to be short-lived. Allied with Nazi Germany and defeated in World War II, Italy was forced to yield its African possessions, and the United Nations stepped in to determine Ethiopia's future. After several UN commissions failed to come up with a blueprint, the General Assembly itself passed a resolution stipulating that Eritrea would be reattached to Ethiopia in a federal union. Ten years later, Emperor Haile Selassie altered these terms unilaterally, declaring Eritrea a province of Ethiopia and absorbing it into his empire. Now Ethiopia had reclaimed its window on the Red Sea, including the ports of Massawa (Mits'iwa) and Assab (Aseb), the former extensively modernized by the Italians. In Eritrea, a war of secession began almost immediately.

As a subnational unit of Ethiopia, Eritrea had little support in Africa at large for its quest, but the costly conflict dragged on and became part of the Cold War. For more than three decades, Eritrean separatists fought whoever was in charge in Ethiopia, beginning with Haile Selassie and continuing after Ethiopia came under Marxist rule. Not until after the collapse of the communist regime, and renewed efforts at a negotiated settlement, did Eritrea secure from Ethiopia the sovereignty it sought, promising "never" to interfere with Ethiopia's use of its ports. In 1993, when Eritrea proclaimed independence, prospects for cooperation in this fractious part of the Horn of Africa seemed good. But—and herein lies a lesson of secession—relationships between Ethiopia and Eritrea deteriorated, a bitter, costly, and seemingly pointless border war over their former colonial boundary cost tens of thousands of lives and millions of wasted dollars, the ports were closed to Ethiopian traffic, and a sliver of a former coastal province now landlocked one of Africa's largest and most populous states. The unintended consequences of devolution can be staggering.

Nor will Eritrea soon attract tourists or cruise ships. In the immediate aftermath of independence, hopes were high; unlike Sudan's South or Western Sahara, Eritrea's colonial infrastructure was essentially intact if in need of repair, its relative location appeared advantageous, its port functions promised profits, and its president, who had led the campaign for independence, promised representative government. With only five million citizens (compared to Ethiopia's 80 million), Eritrea seemed to have a bright future. But authoritarian rule and political repression, human rights violations, economic mismanagement, state control over the media, ethnic and religious tensions, and ongoing disputes with Ethiopia have ruined the country's prospects and, with them, those of a wider region beyond its borders. Devolution in the periphery can have perilous ramifications.

A LATENT THREAT

It is not surprising that, in a world dominated by geopolitical superpowers and corporate globals, locals in the provinces often see territorial secession as a panacea. Given the opportunity by wider conflict, by the breakdown of central authority, or by governments willing to accommodate their demands, they envision a better world in which they have stronger control over their own affairs. It may not be clear to such separatists that their fate, within new borders or without them, still is inextricably linked to the fortunes of those their secession is intended to reject. Nor is it always clear that their newly discrete status may entail new forms of encroachment on their autonomy. Organized crime, for example, is an expanding world industry with its own globalizing network. Weak ministates such as Montenegro and Moldova are favorite targets because their capacity for law enforcement is limited.

Nevertheless, frustrations of many kinds produce local restiveness that may arouse separatist notions ranging from spurious (such as Vermont's amusing "referendum" on independence that got media attention in 2007) to serious, for example, the sharpening regional divisions of Bolivia, where the prosperous east, centered on Santa Cruz, sees its economic objectives thwarted by a government dominated by a populist leader from the impoverished west. There, talk of autonomy and even secession roils a debate that has dangerous intimations. While it may be impossible to measure the intensity of such sentiments, they arise worldwide and probably affect almost all countries, even some ministates. The European Union stimulated local cultural consciousness even as it flattened economic playing fields, and globalization evokes similar responses from France to India.

Secessionist notions wax and wane as political and economic changes affect individual states. In South Africa, the largest constituent nation in the population is the Zulu nation, whose historic and traditional base is also a subnational unit of the modern state, the province of KwaZulu-Natal. As the apartheid era ended, the issue of KwaZulu-Natal's representation in the new national government provoked violence and intimidation, and for a short time the prospect of the province's secession appeared real, especially when the Zulus' leader, Chief Mangosuthu Buthelezi, hinted at it in public debate. But the essentially federal structure of the new state accommodated Zulu demands, and the fear of a breakup receded. In Brazil, a secessionist movement arose in three of its southern states in the 1990s, rooted in local discontent with economic, political, and cultural agendas of the country's federal government (Spears and de Blij, 2001). Proponents of the putative country, to be named the "Republic of the Pampas," attracted a good deal of vocal support as well as publicity and even flew a flag, but the campaign's racist overtones and unrealistic aspirations doomed it within a decade. In Venezuela, the westernmost province of Zulia, bordering Lake Maracaibo, is a comparatively wealthy area of oil reserves, cattle ranches, and conservative politics in a country ruled by a high-handed populist, Hugo Chavez. A pro-autonomy movement called "Our Way" responds to Chavez's economic policies by calling for the kind of devolution that has given Catalonia its special place in Spain. The U.S. Ambassador to Venezuela is accused of fanning the flames by having once referred to the "Republic of Zulia," and the movement alleges that the Chavez regime has blocked efforts to arrange a plebiscite on the issue (Dudley, 2006). Presidential politics have a way of exposing the fault lines in a state: in Ukraine, an east–west split between two candidates gave rise to fears that this territorially largest of all European states might go the way of Czechoslovakia, fragmenting it into a pro-European west and a pro-Russian east. No such fears arose in Mexico following the 2007 presidential election there, but the north–south division between the conservative and liberal candidates, respectively, revealed a fundamental contrast between two kinds of Mexico.

All over the world, local aspirations reveal that the landscape of political geography is jagged and still eroding. As Kwame Anthony Appiah and others have emphasized, humanity's great hope is that people have multiple identities and affiliations that ensure their having common ground across ethnic, religious, linguistic, political, and other borders. But when locals get caught up in campaigns of the kind still roiling the global core as well as the periphery, shared identities tend to be forgotten amid conflict and chaos. Always there will be those—profiteers, warlords, rebels, nationalists, preachers—whose interests are served by stoking the strife at or just below the surface. Stopping them from gaining traction should be an international objective, but all such agitators have their allies. When the surge of new states following the collapse of the Soviet Union and Yugoslavia was over (the second surge of the twentieth century after the earlier one precipitated by decolonization), it appeared that the global map would stabilize and that the boundary framework in place in 2000 would endure for generations to come. But the enormous demographic, cultural, and economic changes still ahead in the global periphery, coupled with the immaturity of the political framework left behind by European colonization, suggests that such stability is still a long way off.

10

LOWERING THE BARRIERS

Becoming conscious of one's cultural and physical environments early in life involves fast-developing recognition of circumstances malleable and immutable. By the time we are about six years old, our brain is about as big as it will be for the duration, but its maturation goes on for many years more. The language-learning ability of young children, the subject of numerous studies and much speculation, undoubtedly connects this process; youngsters are able to recollect facts and vocabularies but cannot match adults or even adolescents in conceptualizing context or relationships. While we quickly learn to use words to gain immediate objectives such as nourishment or affection, it takes much longer to begin forming an understanding of our place and its (apparently) fixed attributes.

Thus our perception of place changes over time, as do the opportunities to counter its formative impress. Bilingualism and multilingualism already are a key to upward mobility and will be more so in the future; exposing children in their earliest years of learning to a language other than the mother tongue will endow them with potentially immense advantages. Religious fanaticism is intensifying in many parts of the world; protecting children against it in their early years gives them the chance to develop their contextual abilities before being exposed to it. Religious leaders of all faiths would do well to consider the divine potential of pronouncements that assert the superiority of their particular beliefs and rituals over others. Pope Benedict in the spring of 2007 declared that Roman Catholicism afforded the only true route to salvation and that all other (Christian) approaches are "defective," a proclamation Christianity and the world could have done without. Drilling into children that "there is no god but Allah" closes young minds to the religious convergence that should be the hope of all believers. It may not be absolutely true that "religion poisons everything," the subtitle of an angry book on the topic, but religious males in medieval outfits do misuse their powers to erect barriers that last lifetimes.

The power of place defines an aggregate of circumstances and conditions ranging from cultural traditions to natural phenomena, into which we are born, with which we cope, and from which we derive our own multiple identities. It is human nature to assign to place (of birth, of upbringing) a large measure of blame for failure and to credit personal virtues, not place, for success, but for every "self-made man" there are thousands who *were* born in the right place at the right time, who owe their fortune to just that, luck, and who all too often have little sympathy for those less well-off. Their world is flat indeed, and for them place was always a matter of choice, not constraint. But such globals still constitute a small minority on this planet, and their proportion is shrinking as population growth over the next three generations swells the ranks of locals in the poorest areas of the periphery. For these locals, and even for a minority in the global core, place is a crucial element in the fabric of destiny.

As noted in chapter 1, the world in the broadest geographic sense may be divided into a prosperous and exclusive core and a periphery where conditions range from acceptable to abject, but all countries and societies have core–periphery dichotomies. It is a matter of scale: the United States has its own eastern megalopolitan core and its remote periphery, including Mississippi, but Mississippi in turn has its modern and commercial Gulf Coast and its interior rural "Deep South." Chile calls its heartland the *nucleo central*, a world apart from its mountain and desert periphery. Bangladesh epitomizes the global periphery, but the megacity of Dhaka anchors a core that breaks the rural sameness dominating its cultural landscape.

While it is noteworthy that the planet is crossing the threshold from minority to majority urbanization in this first decade of the new century, it is also remarkable that very nearly half the world's population still lives in rural environs after several historic episodes of globalization, all of which had an urbanizing dimension. The intricate and still evolving international boundary framework, coupled with multinational efforts to deter mobals from becoming transnational and intercultural migrants, served (and continues) to slow the urbanizing drive. But even where such obstructions were not in the way, urbanization has been inhibited by factors ranging from regulatory control to cultural inertia. That burgeoning China should still be well below the global average and India less than one-third urbanized when both countries offer huge domestic megacity magnets is all the evidence required. With less than 3 percent of the world's people residing in a country other than that of their birth, it is clear that, for all of migration's push and pull factors, the overwhelming majority confront the realities of the locale of their parents and grandparents. Undoubtedly, the computer age has fundamentally changed the interactive aspect of those realities for hundreds of millions of these locals. The flow of information and communication is unprecedented, although it is—again—the poorest of the poor who are being left behind. But this has not altered other challenges, for them or for the better-off. A place still is defined by cultural *milieus* and natural environs whose imprints on its inhabitants are durable and whose power ranges from the infusion of language to the transmission of disease and from the inculcation of belief to the delivery of natural disaster. The question, and the topic of this concluding chapter, is how that power can be mitigated.

PROGRAMS AND PROJECTS

Both sides in the ongoing debate over the impact of economic and cultural globalization on locals and mobals cite place-specific evidence to buttress their case. Those who point to rising material inequalities in globalizing societies tend to dismiss evidence that absolute poverty declines simultaneously. Those who decry the attrition of local cultures do not see wider choices as beneficial. The contradictions of globalization leave no doubt: even as its nodes and corridors impose a network of modernization and integration on the world, it also raises barriers and hardens the impress of place. In a sense, globalization is the ultimate megaproject, its urban corporate skylines and rural labor migrations symbolic of a future still to be defined.

Around the world, a significant majority has faith in that future. A 2007 worldwide Pew Global Attitudes Survey reported that international trade and business, globalization's signature, elicited positive responses from more than 45,000 respondents in 46 countries (U.S. respondents gave one of the world's lowest rates of approval); concerns over threats to local cultures, damage to natural environments, and problems arising from immigration did not override support for the globalization process. In general, approval was stronger in the global periphery, where it has been growing, than in the core, where it is declining in the face of job losses and perceived disadvantage. It is especially high in countries that rank among the poorest of the poor, such as Bangladesh, Ethiopia, and Nigeria, where foreign trade and related jobs are seen as the best hope for an escape from the problems locals face. It is equally strong in countries that have already witnessed the benefits outweighing the liabilities: international trade is seen as "good" by 91 percent of respondents in China and "bad" by 5 percent, and in India the score is 89 to 8 (Knowlton, 2007). Here, globalization is viewed as the great equalizer of opportunity, not primarily as the cause of growing inequities; many regard the latter as an inevitable but temporary symptom on the way to a richer society.

As globalization marches on, the immediate challenge is to alleviate those local circumstances that still trap billions in places of insecurity and violence, natural hazards, health threats, inadequate education, religious indoctrination, sexual discrimination, cultural brutality, and other conditions still associated with place. Numerous, indeed, countless programs, projects, schemes, and plans already operate worldwide to alleviate poverty, improve public health, enhance education, and promote development, and among these, the UN Millennium Project and its eight development goals (with 18 associated targets) first referred to in chapter 4 is the most global, comprehensive, and ambitious. The World Bank, also known as the International Bank for Reconstruction and Development, is affiliated with the United Nations and dispenses members' contributions and investment proceeds in support of projects large and small in needy countries. Individual states in the global core dispense foreign aid in a variety of ways: the United States has a federal agency, the Millennium Challenge Corporation (MCC), to help poor but well-governed countries in the periphery. At the other end of the continuum, hundreds of nongovernmental organizations (NGOs), including many with meager resources and very limited objectives (for example, helping just one African village install a few mosquito nets), try to make a difference at the local level, sometimes under threat from governments and regimes uncomfortable with their intrusion. Between, there is a set of assistance projects ranging from those managed by national governments under the foreign aid rubric to others funded by wealthy individuals, often through their personal or corporate foundations, usually in pursuit of specific goals in areas of health or education. The Gates Foundation and the Clinton Foundation are two such high-profile donors. In aggregate, these efforts have a significant impact, although the magnitude of the continuing need underscores the insufficiency of the collective remedy.

While critics of the "aid process" argue that there is no evidence that such infusions of grants and loans actually make things better in much of the global periphery, the question is how much worse things would be without it. Subsaharan Africa's continuing over-all slide, despite the approximately U.S. $600 billion in aid received there over the past five decades, masks numerous local achievements. Inevitably the failures, especially of ill-conceived megaprojects, make the news and bolster the naysayers' case. But evidence that trans-parency, accountability, and responsibility produce enduring and productive relationships between donors and recipients is clear to all governments and regimes, strengthening political institutions and local economies alike and brightening the future. In Burkina Faso, for example, the conditions for a large MCC national development grant included better education for girls (female literacy in this West African country is only 13 percent). Local school-age girls tend to find themselves taking care of their younger siblings, but the new schools the government built included day-care centers that allowed the girls to stay in school.

Of necessity, such aid projects tend to have national or regional goals, although local needs in countries or regions can vary quite con-siderably. Objectives are usually stated in general terms, as in the case of UN Millennium Development Goal 1: "Eradicate extreme poverty and hunger: reduce by half (by 2015 in the original version) the pro-portion of people living on less than a dollar a day" or Goal 6: "Halt [by 2015] and begun to reverse the incidence of malaria and other major diseases." In the operational stage, regional needs are taken into consideration, but the immensity of the challenge makes it impracti-cal to address all local variations. In high-relief tropical areas, villages and valleys in lowland areas tend to be at greater risk from certain infectious diseases than those at higher elevations, but the higher and steeper slopes may be more vulnerable to landslides and mudflows. Women in some of India's States are far worse off than those in oth-ers, and there are local variations in their well-being within the States themselves. The potential dangers from rising sea level to inhabitants of low-lying areas of rural Bangladesh are very different from those confronting urban parts of Pacific Rim China where resources needed for responses ranging from relocation to remediation are far more plentiful. Every place has its particular combination of challenges, but agendas for intervention and assistance tend to reflect the macro view of the core rather the micro needs of localities.

This is inevitable: the prevailing view of globals has been that people in places of all kinds will be helped by broad-stroke involvement in bureaucratic forms, that is, in the form of financial aid to governments, technological help, military assistance, trade policy coordination, and other agency-to-government initiatives. In the European Union, a combination of such policies, designed to reduce national and regional inequities, has had impressive results, funding needed infrastructure projects in poorer member states such as Portugal and Greece, and giving provinces, communities, regions, and States within member countries the opportunity to apply directly to Brussels for assistance with projects of a more local nature (as a result, the EU's cultural landscape is studded with small blue signs complete with the twelve-star flag stating that "this project was paid for by the EU" at rehabilitated town squares, museums, parks, and waterfronts). Even in the EU-doubting United Kingdom, there is plenty of evidence that local applications to Brussels had good results.

COMBATING COLLABORATIVE CORRUPTION

Such money transfers within the global core, however, cannot serve as a model for much of the periphery. Corruption is not unknown in the EU, but it would be difficult for a European leader to deposit millions of those aid euros into foreign bank accounts without being detected. The same cannot be said for numerous rulers and their hangers-on in the periphery: hundreds of millions of aid dollars wound up in their Swiss (and British and American) bank accounts, casting doubt on the whole foreign-aid enterprise and costing it much public support. Still, the globals who were involved in those financial shenanigans bear a large share of responsibility for this as well. Switzerland lies at the heart of the EU and is deeply entangled in EU economic affairs even though it is not a formal member, having chosen hitherto to stay outside of it, a decision reaffirmed in 2006 because "its national interests were best served by intensifying bilateral agreements in such sectors as transport, energy, and labor" (Kapp, 2007). No mention is made of banking or financial affairs, the key reason for Switzerland's continued non-EU membership, but surely the millions of dollars deposited into Swiss bank accounts by Nigeria's dictator Sani Abacha (and others like him) must have been recognized by bank officials for what they were: stolen aid money. Switzerland's identity-protected banking system is a nonpareil among globals, but facilitating corruption is itself corrupt; it is dispiriting to realize that respected financial institutions in the global core would allow themselves to be used this way. And Swiss officials' reaction to the exposure of Abacha's excesses must have been encouraging to other swindlers. Instead of expeditiously returning the funds to the Nigerian government, they used every delaying tactic in the book, forcing a court to rule in Nigeria's favor and then obstructing the transfer at ministerial levels. Such prevarication has additional ramifications in this time of terrorist activity: it took the Swiss Federal Tribunal four years to approve a 2002 U.S request to provide information on bank accounts that might be used for terrorist funding.

Swiss banks may be the favorite hideaway among corrupt and criminal elements for ill-gotten gains, but make no mistake: the Swiss are not the only bankers swayed by huge deposits. It is a widespread practice in the supposedly less corrupt global core to accept large hoards from known officials of low-income countries without raising questions or revealing details. Abacha's secret Swiss accounts were supplemented by "confidential" ones in the United Kingdom. A venerable name in American banking, Riggs National Bank of Washington, D.C., was sullied by the disclosure of its acceptance of enormous amounts of cash, skimmed from oil revenues, deposited by President Teodoro Obiang of Equatorial Guinea and senior officials of his regime. Numerous other "offshore" banking options facilitate such plunder.

In this way, the diversion of foreign aid and the theft of windfall revenues in the periphery are facilitated by turpitude in the core. "The opportunity creates the thief," a proverb common to several European languages, certainly applies to circumstances in which officials in low-income countries who would otherwise have difficulty stashing and safeguarding their ill-gotten gains can partner with rich-country financial institutions to deposit and invest them.

Not all recipient governments or regimes are equally culpable, of course, but the risk rises with the dimensions of the aid packages and windfall revenues. As a recent commentary on Equatorial Guinea stated matter-of-factly, "What did not go into the bank accounts of the leading politicians went mainly into infrastructure development" (Saunders, 2006). Media reports in South Africa in 2007 stated that Obiang's son Teodorin had spent, in short order following his arrival, about eight million U.S. dollars on houses and automobiles in Cape Town.

So numerous are accounts of stolen aid funds and diverted oil revenues that the excesses seem to be seen as an inevitable by-product of a transfer process that cannot be halted or controlled. In the case of foreign aid, the argument is that despite extremes of the Abacha variety, substantial amounts of it do reach their intended goals and, as such, make a significant difference. For every news-making scandal, there is a lower profile instance of smooth and transparent disposition that goes unnoticed. Well, perhaps not for every one of them, but there are indeed low-income countries in the periphery that use their foreign aid frugally and mostly efficiently. Ghana depends heavily on outside aid but is considered a model of economic recovery as well as political reform. In 2006 President John Kufuor, on a state visit to America, received a $547 million aid package from the U.S. Millennium Challenge Corporation for projects designed to expand commercial agriculture, improve infrastructure, and alleviate poverty.

Only the third of these initiatives, however, goes to the heart of the issue: the betterment of the circumstances of those people most severely suppressed by the stultifying power of stagnant place. The growth of commercial agriculture and the enhancement of infrastructure are laudable long-range objectives (Ghana hopes to fulfill former President Kwame Nkrumah's ambition to remake itself as the gateway to interior West Africa), but by many measures the most urgent need is for reliable fresh water, electricity, clinics, classrooms, insect nets, waste disposal, and other basics in Ghana's villages. Increased farm exports and rising overall economic growth rates signal general improvement for the long term, but locals' needs are urgent and immediate. Women's literacy in 2007 stood at barely more than 60 percent compared to men's at 80 percent; women's life expectancy (58 years) was only one year higher than men's, and the rate of population growth (2.3 percent) was nearly double the world average. In spite of its progress, Ghana's local needs mirror those of much of the global periphery.

RESPONSIBILITIES AND OPPORTUNITIES

The world may not be flat, but in some regions the gap between rich countries and those less prosperous has been shrinking, a process economists refer to as convergence. The European Union is the most often cited example of this process, and Ireland, the "Celtic Tiger," as its most striking proof. With a colonial history and lacking significant domestic resources, Ireland joined the EU, then called the European Economic Community, in 1973 with a stagnant economy and creaking infrastructure. Subsidies from the EU addressed the latter, but it was Ireland's well-educated, English-speaking, comparatively low-salaried workforce that attracted European and American telecommunications and high-tech industries. Soon its booming, service-based economy was the fastest growing in all of the EU. Mushrooming industrial parks, burgeoning cities, bustling traffic, and fast-rising real estate prices transformed the country as never before, and workers of Irish descent who had taken jobs elsewhere returned to take the opportunities the new economy offered. Other mobals discovered Ireland as well, arriving from Africa and Asia and posing unfamiliar social problems for this closely knit, long-isolated society. No economy can grow so fast without a slowdown, and Ireland experienced this in the early 2000s; but growth has resumed, and Ireland remains an EU frontrunner rather than an also-ran. Meanwhile, it is remarkable how secular this country has become, the domination of its dreaded parish priests mostly history, the children safer, the cultural landscape more cosmopolitan.

The EU, however, is not the only instance of convergence in the globalizing world. Figure 1.1 displays a global core of high-income states, but there are many countries outside this core whose economies outrank some of those within. Based solely on gross national income (GNI) per person, Botswana ranks ahead of both EU members Bulgaria and Romania, but in other ways Botswana remains far more typical of the periphery. Saudi Arabia's GNI is higher than Poland's, but lacks governmental and institutional norms common to the core. Convergence is also a matter of geography, however, and from this perspective the most significant developments are taking place in South America. These are revealed less by GNI than by other indicators, such as urbanization, female literacy (nearly 90 percent across the realm), fast-declining population growth now barely above the world average, and reductions in the number of people living in extreme poverty. The dozen countries clustered on the continent, led by Brazil, appear poised to further narrow the gap between this corner of the periphery and the global core. Potent developments in parts of Southeast and East Asia confirm that the global periphery is in transition there as well, although no South American country is as poor as East Timor and none as rich as Singapore, signaling far wider and persistent divergence in a crucial corner of the world.

With nearly 50 percent of the world's population—and a much higher percentage in the periphery—still living in rural villages, and hundreds of millions of city dwellers living in urban poverty, what options are there for those trying to make the best of their particular circumstances of place? It is likely that the still-small percentage of mobals leaving their domicile in search of better opportunities internationally will increase exponentially in the decades ahead. Although the governments of countries with stable or declining populations try encouraging their citizens to have more children, the real answer to their immediate as well as long-range economic challenges is immigration; the domestic demographic trend they seek to reverse is inexorable. Coupled with this problem (still essentially characteristic of the core) is the reality that the human population today is still increasing by more than 75 million per year and that the poorer parts of the periphery, long before the population of the planet as a whole stabilizes, will grow by about one billion (and the entire periphery as now defined by more than double and possibly triple that). In the near future, the lure of the richer world will thus tempt far more would-be mobals than is already the case, but no global organization to coordinate migration policies and practices exists. The UN monitors international migration but cannot codify it, and even within the converging EU, immigration policies, definitions of asylum, and other regulations not only differ but also cause disputes.

Few if any issues arouse xenophobia, nationalism, isolationism, and racism as easily as unregulated immigration does. The ugly manifestations of social and economic fears demarcate the margins of the global core from the Rio Grande to the Mediterranean Sea. And yet the migration stream continues: North America, the European Union, and Australia form the dominant destinations, while Mexico, China, India, Iran, Pakistan, Indonesia, and the Philippines are only some of the leading sources. From Sudan to Bangladesh and from Peru to Sri Lanka, virtually all countries in the periphery are losing citizens to the core (and to oil-rich, labor-short autocracies on the Arabian Peninsula).

But their numbers, in absolute terms, remain small. According to U.N. Population Division data, in the first five years of this century, only 270,000 mobals left India and 380,000 emigrated from China, countries with a combined population of 2.5 billion. The 800,000 Mexicans who legally moved to the United States during that period represent 0.7 percent of Mexico's population. While the United States is currently the world's leading destination by far of unregulated migrants, the EU and, to a lesser degree, Australia also confront this growing problem, whose exact dimensions are, of course, unknown. By some estimates, more than 10 million and perhaps as many as 12 million mobals have made their way illegally from Mexico and Central America to the United States, perhaps a harbinger of times to come for other areas of the core, although no core-periphery border presents comparable opportunities for similar numbers of potential mobals. If the higher estimate is accurate, that population of undocumented mobals constitutes less than 4 percent of the population within U.S. borders. By the turn of the century, Hispanics had become the second-largest ethnic component of the U.S. population, overtaking the African-American minority.

At a time of occasionally bitter debate over immigration in the United States and elsewhere in the global core, is it possible to discern any positives in this course of events? Many mobals' work ethic, as exemplified by millions of Southeast and East Asian immigrants to the United States and Canada, challenges locals and globals alike. (Even as the United States faces a glut of immigrants, Canada is in need of foreign workers willing to take on the low-skilled jobs in its expanding industries.) Their annual remittances of more than $150 billion help sustain source-country economies from Mexico to the Philippines. Many of their cultural traditions enrich those prevailing in their destinations. Their presence, especially that of the well educated, can engender international links and networks that enhance intercultural understanding. (It is an excruciating tragedy that the influx of Muslim mobals into Europe has coincided with the criminal activities of terrorists using Islam as their pretext, because that cultural infusion might otherwise have been mutually reinforcing.) If the world is to avoid a repeat of the catastrophes of the twentieth century, it will be because international, interregional, and intercultural linkages make global conflict over local issues purposeless and futile. Mobals are crucial in the dispersal of the seeds of understanding.

But such hopes tend to get lost among the disputes the current wave of illegal immigration has generated. From the daily "broken borders" refrain on a cable news network to the "lost jobs" argument of opportunistic politicians, the issue has become a litmus test for a people many of whom (or whose ancestors) benefited from their own American "amnesty" in one form or another. Some transnational mobals reacted to the power of an initiative-stifling place by leaving it, often risking their lives in the process; others saw scope for their talents not evident at home. All who succeeded found themselves in new places presenting novel and unfamiliar challenges, but not all managed to adjust to these environs. Even the best-intentioned efforts by locals to accommodate transnational mobals can have unanticipated consequences, as European governments experimenting with various multicultural models discovered. In the case of the United States, virtually all illegal immigrants who entered over the past decade arrived with conforming cultural baggage (Christian religious background, Hispanic traditions, a language already widely dispersed in the country) and without motivations to engage in the kinds of retribution Europeans have endured from Muslim immigrants.

For the United States, this combination of circumstances spells significant good fortune. The Mexican and Central American immigrant stream has no built-in ideological or cultural baggage incompatible with American norms. This country has always assimilated its immigrants into local and national economies, and this is the largest part of the challenge now being faced; the current debate is nothing new. On the other hand, there is no point in pretending that the current Mexican immigration is just the latest in America's melting-pot experience. This is a transformative invasion, and it will put unprecedented pressure on American institutions (Rodriguez, 2007). It will create stresses between Hispanic and African-American minorities that will pose new and difficult challenges.

CONFRONTING THE ISSUE

There is no denying that the arrival of 10 million or more undocumented immigrants over a short time span challenges even the world's largest and richest economy. In the process, the costs of accommodation and integration already are not being borne equally, and any future system involving an element of amnesty must entail a budgetary apportionment obligating all 50 States to contribute in some proportional way. The brunt of the invasion is borne by the States bordering Mexico, and while many migrants tend to disperse to nonborder states over time, most stay in the southern areas of the country. The causes of the massive influx can be attributed to several factors; the U.S.–Mexican boundary used to be called the only border separating the First World from the Third World in the days when such nomenclature was still appropriate. Today, it is in many ways the most conspicuous divider between core and periphery, creating pull factors perhaps unmatched in the world and powerful push factors in an economy marked by mismanagement and gross inequities. NAFTA has been blamed for it, drawing countless workers to the *maquiladora* factories near the border and then denying them job security. NAFTA also has been faulted for putting Mexican farmers out of business through its agricultural clauses. Some see globalization as the ultimate reason: corporations using and then abandoning Mexico in search of higher profits discard labor as so much waste.

The more immediate question is how to address the issue north of the border. To many Mexican and Central American immigrants, place in America consists of a combination of substandard and overcrowded housing and few if any of the amenities available to legal immigrants. The power such places have over daily life is daunting: the risk of detection, the absence of recourse in case of medical or other emergency, the lack of schooling. To use the old terminology, third-world existence in a first-world country is not unique to migrants in, say, the Los Angeles area—there are plenty of locales with periphery-like conditions elsewhere in the United States—but the absence of policy adjustment risks the rapid emergence of a Hispanic underclass whose deficiencies will become entrenched and take generations to undo.

Meanwhile, the argument over costs and benefits rages on. Those who assert that undocumented migrants will do jobs spurned by Americans tend to minimize the employment impact of these immigrants, arguing that they may even have a positive effect by spurring the upward mobility of locals. Others fear not only that low-skilled workers will lose their jobs to immigrants willing to work for less, but also that the effect of their arrival will be to reduce wages overall, giving employers an opportunity to circumvent minimum-wage regulations. This, in turn, affects taxation and thus budgets of individual States, while policing employers entails further costs.

Obviously, it is not reasonable to expect U.S. States located in the immediate path of the unregulated immigrant influx to fund the resulting expenses without federal assistance. This is a national problem, not just a regional or local one, and it is not enough for the government to build walls and fences to keep would-be migrants out. Since it will be impossible to close the border and impractical to repatriate all or even most illegal migrants, the ultimate policy compromise will have to contain a measure of the amnesty so despised by its opponents and a circulatory system of some kind to ease the continuing pressure. Meanwhile, illegal-immigrant families cannot be excluded from essential services for reasons already cited, and this, too, is in the national, not just the local, interest. This will definitely entail significant costs. Yet it will be a better investment than waging war to install democracy in foreign countries.

One method for both American locals and illegal mobals to confront the power of culture-divided place is to promote the teaching of English, and of American ways of doing things, by requiring it as part of the amnesty, without risk of arrest and deportation for those who participate (what a fine way this would be to use the time that churches stand empty, and classrooms on weekends). A massive campaign marshaling all available resources and attracting learners of all ages, but especially children, would counter the drift toward Mexicans' and Central Americans' underclass status and equip youngsters for school when normalization is achieved. Here lies an opportunity for locals to offer their talents as native speakers of the prevailing language in free and informal classes organized for adults as well as youngsters. Indeed, it would be salutary policy for the United States to engage in a cooperative campaign with Mexico in support of the teaching of English in Mexican schools, as well as other venues such as adult-education classes. If Beijing can promote the teaching of Chinese in Zimbabwe, then surely Washington can make a case for English in Mexico—and thereby flatten the cultural terrain of the future.

Language teaching by those able to commit to the responsibilities involved constitutes only one example of the help individuals can give to those whose cultural baggage weighs them down in new surroundings. On a personal note, as an immigrant myself I spoke heavily accented English that corrected itself over time, but I should have been compelled to learn much more than I initially did about the way the American state functions and how its institutions evolved. Had it not been for Roland Young, a professor of political science at Northwestern University in the 1950s whose impromptu dinners for foreign graduate students invariably segued into discussions ranging from the Bill of Rights to the Electoral College, I would not have passed the stringent test when my turn came to apply for citizenship. When I see television images of hundreds of new citizens being sworn in, waving little American flags and reciting the Pledge of Allegiance, I wonder how many of those new Americans, legal though they are, have a comprehensive sense of the rights and responsibilities with which they have just been endowed. When it comes to undocumented mobals, don't ask.

For all its capacity for assimilation, America stands at the threshold of the first real challenge to the primacy of its version of the English Language. No other previous immigrant stream was large or persistent enough to counter that dominance; it is one of this country's great good fortunes that the African-American community became and remained English-speaking. Historically, Hispanic immigrants (from Cuba, for example) speak Spanish, their children are bilingual, and the third generation speaks mostly English. But the numbers of Spanish-speaking mobals arriving legally in America, their regional distribution, and their growing political influence make it likely that demands for formal recognition of Spanish as an official language will arise. Those who counter with demands for English-only legislation would find that a far more effective way to defuse this pressure is by learning Spanish themselves, to better persuade their fellow citizens that one common language has been, and will be, and incalculable American asset even as bilingualism opens doors to the hemisphere and the world.

Here is an opportunity for PBS Television in search of relevance: a late-afternoon or early-evening hour of Spanish language instruction using the modern, entertaining and rewarding methods that have transformed that kind of education in recent times.

CONFRONTING DISORDER

Compared to places swept up in recurrent violent conflicts among ethnic groups, subnational entities, and even nations, the problems of excess immigration seem minor indeed. Certain areas of the world, and not only in the periphery, experience cycles of strife seemingly without end, driving millions from their homes, destroying local economies, causing death and disease. Scenes of burning homes and general devastation in Bosnia during the collapse of Yugoslavia are tragically similar to those in Darfur in strife-torn Sudan, except that the Fur are even poorer than the Bosniaks and were left with much less surviving infrastucture than Bosnia was. The mass emigration of Armenians in recent years is only the latest surge in a region from which millions have fled over centuries of endemic strife and resulting social and economic breakdowns. But many would-be migrants never have the chance to make their move. The Korean Peninsula has witnessed upheavals without end, the latest episode producing unprecedented prosperity in the south while rapacious regimes in the north abandoned millions to famine and death in their villages or in desperate attempts to cross the sealed border with China. The cultural shatter belt between China and India in mainland Southeast Asia, centered on Myanmar (Burma), generates conflict and human dislocation of massive dimensions, the latest of which, in 2007, pitted the Burman military against the Buddhist monks. Afghanistan and Kashmir suffered from endemic strife since long before the area's modern borders were drawn. In all these disorders, villagers and farmers are worst off. When already-fragile agricultural systems are disrupted by war and crops fail, it is the locals who pay with their lives. The tragedy in Sudan's Darfur caused no casualties in the oil-boom capital of Khartoum.

As noted earlier, some areas of the world are historically more severely afflicted by such violence than others. In east-central Africa, the human toll is the highest on the planet since World War II, approaching four million. There is no preparing for the kind of paroxysms that repeatedly devastate the interior of this remote region, and no way for most locals to leave before the next crisis arises. Nor can private initiatives mitigate the mayhem. That is why a growing number of specialists are calling for a significant expansion of international intervention and peacekeeping capacities and more efficient diplomatic and logistical mechanisms to facilitate their operations.

Other objectives that can help break the cycle of violence include restricting the flow (and thus sales) of weapons in conflict-prone areas and limiting the export (and thus purchase) of quick-money commodities such as gemstones that fill the coffers of combatants. Such efforts are costly, and require member support of UN-sponsored campaigns. Despite the usual—and at times justified—criticisms of UN performance, the organization's peacekeeping projects, which tend to attract little media attention, are among its considerable successes. Congressional representatives who vote on UN appropriations need to hear from their constituents on the matter. Such comments carry surprising weight and form another way to counter the power of, in this instance remote, place.

One way to enhance international peacekeeping is through the involvement of far more women in such operations than has hitherto been the case. Public opinion in many countries reflects a general unease when it comes to women serving in the armed forces, but were they to serve in large numbers in peacekeeping missions that discomfort may be allayed. We have no way of knowing; some women have risen to high responsibility in logistical settings, but almost none serve on the ground. And yet sexual violence perpetrated by males adds incalculably to the damage done during violent political upheavals; in some instances even male peacekeepers themselves have been charged with such offenses. Female peacekeepers in greater numbers would protect women and children caught in the mayhem more effectively than all-male forces; they can be expected to understand the needs of locals better and they might even act to constrain the behavior of less responsible male peacekeepers.

Among the options not sufficiently explored in the matter of international intervention in areas of endemic conflict is boundary adjustment. This is invariably a highly sensitive issue; during the debate over the putative partitioning of Iraq following the American-led military campaign there was much discussion, but no (because potentially incendiary) cartographic representation of the model. Nevertheless, boundaries have been erased, established, and repositioned in a sufficient number of instances, in both the core and the periphery, to merit more consideration. In the core, the EU project in effect is a boundary-mitigation program, although boundaries between subnational entities escalated to international status as well (between, for example, the Czech Republic and Slovakia). In Europe the most effective use of boundary delimitation involved Bosnia, where many lives were undoubtedly saved by a judicious and, it is hoped, temporary partition. A similar though more marginal modification of Kosovo's political geography, assigning a special status to the northern corners of Kosovo, which would require territorial delineation on both the Kosovo and Serb sides of the border and a renegotiated status for both Serb- and Kosovar-minority areas, may be part of a solution to the issues created by Kosovo's declaration of independence. But it is in the periphery where the use of boundary renegotiation may hold the greatest promise. Especially in tropical Africa there may be ways to use Bosnia-model accommodations to defuse persistent ethnic conflicts and perhaps even to mobilize territorial exchanges.

Some critics argue that such intervention, by any means or methods, is simply another version of wasted foreign aid in societies that are incurably fractious and of no consequence to countries of the core. Apart from the obvious humanitarian aspect of multilateral intervention, though, the issue has taken on another dimension. States plagued by this kind of endemic disorder are vulnerable to failure, and failed states constitute a strategic risk in a world challenged by terrorist movements and imperiled by an unprecedented diffusion of weapons. Furthermore, there is ample evidence that cycles of destabilizing violence can be broken—but this requires investments the international community has not always been willing to make. Conceivably, the next challenge (mainly to NATO) will involve still another brick to fall in the devolution of Yugoslavia as Kosovo declares independence.

DANGERS NEW AND OLD

The geography of risk is changing. The United States got a foretaste of what may lie ahead when, during the height of the Cold War, American planners advised citizens to build provisioned bomb shelters in their basements and positioned grain supplies across the Midwest in locales of maximum accessibility. That threat is history, but the era of nuclear weapons proliferation it presaged is here. Even before the end of the Cold War, the inevitable dissemination of nuclear arms technology was under way, and it now threatens to spin out of control. Efforts by the original "nuclear club" to constrain expansion of the in-group were thwarted by North Korea, Pakistan, India, China, and Israel, in part because of ideological alliances among members of the club. Successes in curbing the nuclear ambitions of Iraq (by Israel in 1981), South Africa, Libya, Syria (allegedly in 2007, again by Israel), and potentially North Korea must be weighed against the difficulties in securing consensus on Iran and the rising dangers of nonstate (terrorist) acquisition of the means to produce or acquire such weaponry. Consider how Pakistan's possession of these weapons has changed the image as well as the reality of that place's power: from an Islamic state a step ahead of Afghanistan to a force capable of initiating nuclear war—and of selling the required technology. Pakistan's political instability might once have merited a footnote; now it is a matter of global concern. Israel's unconfirmed possession of nuclear weapons converts its image from that of a ministate with a powerful military to a place among forces capable of changing the world in an instant. This is a convergence of another sort: no place on the planet now lies beyond the reach of nuclear-capable missiles controlled by national governments or regimes.

Is this a brink from which, as in the Cold War, the parties will retreat? It would appear that the answer lies in the degree of success that nonstate actors will have in acquiring the means to deliver a nuclear weapon to a target. As long as nuclear arms remain in the control of governments aware that any first use would result in annihilation, the likelihood of nuclear attack remains low. But such disincentives do not affect terrorist organizations, and al-Qaeda's leaders have proclaimed their desire and intent to acquire such weapons as a "religious duty" (Richardson, 2006). So much in the way of technology, logistics, tactics, and strategy would have to fall into place for a terrorist group to succeed in a nuclear attack that the prospect is remote, but it is not inconceivable. Nor is there a way to effectively prepare for it, except in the broader national context. Accommodating unprecedented loss of life would have to be accompanied by restoration of infrastructural functions to limit the material damage, but for such an eventuality no emergency preparations could suffice.

PLACE AND NATURE

Of more immediate and increasingly urgent concern is the power of nature over the fortunes of populated space, a rubric that ranges from the impact of climate change to the danger of earthquakes, and from the resurgence of tropical diseases to the incidence of hurricanes. The environmental transition in which we find ourselves entails abrupt changes in regional climate as well as local and short-term fluctuations already evident in the daily record of heat waves, floods, droughts, storms, fires, cold snaps, and other extremes. The question for residents of the global core is how to best prepare for such contingencies; for the periphery it continues to be a matter of post-emergency assistance.

The current cycle of global warming has raised awareness of direct and dramatic threats to coastal places urban as well as rural, but rising temperatures are having less spectacular implications as well. Medical as well as general scientific journals are reporting that several infectious diseases are now making a comeback in areas where global warming is expanding the range as well as the number of maladies to which populations outside the tropics are vulnerable. Of particular concern is the resurgence of two "supervector" tropical mosquitoes, between them capable of transmitting more than 20 viral diseases, that have made a reappearance in Europe as far north as the Netherlands; their North American range is likewise expanding. Warmer conditions have biological effects on lakes, ponds, and streams, and other vectors undoubtedly are also extending their ranges. A recent report chronicles the first known transmission of a little-known disease, chikungunya, a dengue-like malady, outside the tropics (Enserink, 2007). In India in 2006, this infection sickened more than 1.2 million people; later it was recorded in Italy. Public health authorities will increasingly stress the need to control mosquito breeding places, and hitherto little-known diseases are likely to become more familiar concerns.

Not only is the range of "tropical" diseases expanding into extra-tropical areas (West Nile has become a public health matter in parts of the United States), but global warming is having an ecological impact within the tropics as well. Higher temperatures accelerate biological processes, lending even greater urgency to campaigns to defeat malaria and other scourges in equatorial regions. Such campaigns are conducted by international organizations as well as private groups, even individuals "adopting" a family or village in Subsaharan Africa or South Asia, and they were never more vital.

The most dramatic and widespread manifestation of the power of nature in this time of climate change, however, is the fierce tropical storm in one incarnation or another. The question as to whether global warming (actually, regional warming raising the global average) directly influences hurricane intensity remains open. But the capacity of hurricanes—or typhoons or cyclones, as they are called in other parts of the world—to inflict death and destruction on coastal and even interior locales is beyond doubt. The fate of New Orleans in the wake of Hurricane Katrina is fresh in memory, and the massive collapse of artificial defenses against the storm's onslaught was followed by a titanic failure of human intervention. While the combination of circumstances at that particular place was in many ways unique, it serves as a warning that historic precedent and scientific projection portend a future marked by extremes of climate and weather for which much of the planet is unprepared. The early manifestations of those extremes already are a matter of record, from severe droughts and floods to intense heat and cold. Behind the conceptual construct of global warming lie regional climatic variations that will confront inhabited places with nature's power in ways not seen since the glaciers last receded thousands of years ago. Cities and towns in the core as well as the periphery with hundreds of millions of inhabitants lie on coastal plains and deltas where land meets sea— along temporary, mobile shores. Others in river basins or on desert margins will learn the irrelevance of environmental averages such as "thousand-year events."

What can locals do when confronted by such exigencies, in the core as well as the periphery? Globals and globalizers, who are hitherto the major contributors to the anthropogenic dimension of global warming, also have the greatest capacity to mitigate the human factor. While a growing portion of future greenhouse-enhancing pollution will undoubtedly come from China, India, and other industrializing and mobilizing economies in the periphery, most of what already exists has come from core countries. These countries can best lead by behavioral example and by technological innovation, examples including a sensible carbon tax and innovations focusing on alternative energy sources. Making one's views known to congressional representatives, especially relating to the U.S. failure to ratify the Kyoto Protocols, is one action locals in North America can take. But even the most optimistic projections suggest that climate change will remain a crucial challenge for a long time to come, and that associated environmental crises will hit communities in the periphery, who are least capable of dealing with them, the hardest.

As to the global core, where resources and remedies are more readily available, the lessons already learned are valuable, but all too often go unheeded. Long-term preparation obviously is crucial. The post-Katrina rescue operation was a fiasco, but even an efficient intervention could not soon have reached or sheltered many who were in urgent need. One of those urgent needs was drinkable water, ironically a most difficult delivery in times of flood. In gigantic emergencies of this kind, government cannot be relied upon to deliver well-organized relief in short order. In practical terms, every urban household capable of it should store a three-week supply of fresh water for each family member. This is more crucial than food, which can be stocked in various non-refrigerated forms for emergency consumption, and of which a week's supply should be held and rotated. In this time of uncertainty, the possibility of a prolonged power outage should be contemplated as well, with battery-operated equipment and hand-crank charge systems where alternatives such as portable generators are impractical. The need for such planning may be self-evident, but from television reports of last-moment rushes on grocery and hardware stores when storms threaten it is clear that it is also rare. The optimal time to plan, obviously, is in the absence of an emergency, not when it threatens.

Individual and family preparedness is therefore crucial. Against the sudden and unexpected onslaught of nature in the form of tsunamis, typhoons, or tornadoes, another, more collective form of preparation is needed. The best defense against manifestations of such destructive power of nature is early warning. Many tens of thousands of lives would have been saved, studies indicate, had historic and repeated warnings regarding the potential for a disastrous tsunami in the Indian Ocean resulted in the creation of a regional alert system for which the technology was already available. As it was, nearly two hours after the first of three destructive mounds of water had hit northern Sumatra, "the first wave barreled into Phuket [Thailand]....It was a Sunday morning; most government offices were closed....Staff in a meteorological office in Thailand saw the seismic report but had no idea a tsunami might be imminent....After striking the Nicobar Islands...it took another 90 minutes for the tsunami to travel across the Bay of Bengal [but] no one sounded an alarm, and the waves claimed 15,000 in India and 31,000 in Sri Lanka" (Stone and Kerr, 2005). In the 2004 tsunami's aftermath, an international effort began to create the early-warning network that would have saved countless lives, initially a loose web of deep-ocean sensors, tide gauges, and land-based seismic stations connected by a system for sharing data and issuing public warnings. In Thailand, where nearly 6,000 people were lost, this takes the form of dozens of siren towers along the coast, much like those alerting Midwestern Americans of approaching tornadoes. By mid-2007, the beginnings of a basic Indian-Ocean early-warning system were in place, with improvements still in progress. Meanwhile, planners were beginning to look at the potential risks on low-lying shores along the Atlantic Ocean, vulnerable to tsunami events originating in the Mid-Atlantic Ridge but without adequate alert systems.

Predicting nature's onslaughts, from the timing of earthquakes to the eruptive cycles of active volcanoes, is a science still in its infancy. From Vesuvius to Merapi, millions live at risk from forces whose destructive powers have at times changed the course of history. But no matter how evident the hazard or how devastating the toll, people continue to cluster in such locales, abandoning their homes only under the direst of threats. It is a power of place that seems to defy common sense, and while the science of vulnerability is maturing, the number of potential victims keeps growing.

In any case, even alerts and warnings will not persuade some habitants to leave their familiar places when threats arise. And when disaster does strike, these victims in the first instance depend on each other for survival. During the calamitous 1953 storm in the Netherlands described in chapter 5, hundreds of lives were saved by neighbors, and in New Orleans in 2005 many neighbors helped each other as well. But in truth the dispersal of suburbanization has loosened the bonds of neighborhood, and we are less likely to know our neighbors well, even in more proximate circumstances. In the global core, close-knit neighborhoods may be fading from view, but if neighbors can organize a crime watch, as often happens in response to joint security concerns, they should be able to form an emergency self-help alliance. We may have social differences, but when it comes to environmental crises we are all in it together. In this respect, the power of nature is the great equalizer.

TOWARD A FLATTER WORLD

The Earth is one small planet, but its seven billion people still inhabit vastly different worlds. The time will come, if we do not destroy ourselves over our inevitable differences or suffer the fate of the dinosaurs, when the core-periphery contrasts with which this book opened are a thing of the past. By then, the power of place will have diminished and the barricades of exclusion will be no more. At its best, globalization gives us a glimpse of that future. At its worst, globalization facilitates some of our least desirable behaviors, from xenophobia to exclusivity. And yet the rewards of accessibility, inclusion, and participation under the rules are self-evident. America has no stronger champions than can be found among those who arrived as immigrants, attained citizenship, and achieved well-being. The same is true in other societies of the global core, and in many in the periphery. Still today, the lives of globals in the core and locals in the periphery have too little in common; social canyons still separate rich from poor; women and men have divergent destinies; and, as Amartya Sen puts it, "Depending on where they are born, children can have the means and facilities for great prosperity or face the likelihood of desperately deprived lives" (Sen, 2006). In the aggregate, we are born into natural and cultural environs that may either demand our every effort to survive or give us space and scope to make choices and decisions of which others can only dream. Such contrasts persist worldwide, confirming the variable and durable power of place; confronting that power through lowering barriers and creating opportunities will make this a better—and flatter—world.

WORKS CITED

Ahmad, E, 2003. "Knowledge, Place, and Power: A Critique of Globalization." In A. Mirsepassi et al., eds., *Localizing Knowledge in a Globalizing World: Recasting the Areas Studies Debate*. Syracuse, N.Y.: Syracuse University Press.

Alley, R. B., 2004. "Abrupt Climate Change." *Scientific American*, 292 (11):62.

Altman, L. K., 2006. "Scientists Trace Link between Chimp Virus and H.I.V." *New York Times*, May 26.

Arnold, W., 2007. "Mosquitoes Have the Edge in Singapore's Dengue War." *New York Times*, June 27.

Barone, J., 2005. "(Laki Volcanic Eruption)" *Discover*, 24 (2):9.

Bauer, P., 2006. "Cataclysm in Kashmir." *2006 Book of the Year*. Chicago: Encyclopaedia Britannica, 442.

Best, A. C. G., and H. J. de Blij, 1977. *African Survey*. New York: John Wiley & Sons.

Bhagwati, J., 2004. *In Defense of Globalization*. New York: Oxford University Press.

Bloom, A., 1987. *The Closing of the American Mind*. New York: Simon & Schuster.

Botkin, D. B., 2007. "Global Warming Delusions." *Wall Street Journal*, October 17.

Bouazza, H., 2002. "Nederland Is Blind Voor Moslem Extremisme." *NRC Handelsblad*, February 20.

Bradsher, K., and D. Barboza, 2006. "Clouds from Chinese Coal Cast a Long Shadow." *New York Times*, June 11.

Budiansky, S., 2002. "Mosquitoes and Disease." *Science*, 292:82.

Carter, J., 2007. *Palestine: Peace Not Apartheid*. New York: Simon & Schuster.

Cavalli-Sforza, L.-L., P. Menozzi, and A. Piazza, 1994. *The History and Geography of Human Genes*. Princeton, N.J.: Princeton University Press.

Chowdhury, A. M. R., 2004. "Arsenic Crisis in Bangladesh." *Scientific American*, 292 (8): 86.

Cohen, J. E., 2003. "Human Population: The Next Half Century." *Science,* 302:1172.

Collier, B., 2007. *The Bottom Billion.* New York: Oxford University Press.

Coogan, J., 2007. "Summerless: The Year of Eighteen Hundred and Froze to Death." *Cape Cod Times Summerscape 2007.*

Corbridge, S., and J. Harriss, 2000. *Reinventing India: Liberalization, Hindu Nationalism and Popular Democracy.* Cambridge University Press (Blackwell).

Crystal, D., 2003. *Cambridge Encyclopedia of the English Language,* 2nd ed. Cambridge: Cambridge University Press.

Dawkins, R., 2006. *The God Delusion.* New York: Mariner (Houghton Mifflin).

De Blij, H. J., 1996. *Human Geography: Culture, Society and Space,* 5th ed. New York: John Wiley & Sons.

De Blij, H. J., 2004. "Africa's Unequaled Geographic Misfortunes." *Pennsylvania Geographer,* 42:1.

De Blij, H. J., 2005. *Why Geography Matters: Three Challenges Facing America.* New York: Oxford University Press.

De Blij, H. J., 2006. "Europe at the Crossroads." *Eurasian Geography and Economics,* 47:698.

De Blij, H. J., P. O. Muller, and R. S. Williams, Jr., 2004. *Physical Geography: The Global Environment,* 3rd ed. New York: Oxford University Press.

Dennett, D., 2006. *Breaking the Spell: Religion as a Natural Phenomenon.* New York: Viking.

Diamond, J., 1997. *Guns, Germs, and Steel: The Fates of Human Societies.* New York: Norton.

Diamond, J., 2001. "Deaths of Languages." *Natural History,* 4(1):30.

Diamond, J., 2005. *Collapse: How Societies Choose to Fail or Succeed.* New York: Viking.

Domingo, V., 2004. *South Africa.* Philadelphia: Chelsea House.

Dudley, S., 2006. "More Self-Rule Sought for Oil-Rich Texas of Venezuela." *Miami Herald,* April 6.

Dunavan, C. P., 2005. "Tackling Malaria." *Scientific American,* 293(6):75.

Easterly, W. R., 2006. *The White Man's Burden: Why the West's Efforts to Aid the Rest Have Done So Much Ill and So Little Good.* New York: Penguin.

Economist, 2004. "After Babel, a New Common Tongue." August 7:41.

Economist, 2007a. "They All Speak English." December 16:55.

Economist, 2007b. "Thailand's Buddhists: Monks on the March." May 5:56.

Economist, 2007c. "Dengue Fever: A Deadly Scourge." April 21:42.

Economist, 2007d. "The Unbearable Weight of Shinzo Abe." July 7:41.

Economist, 2007e. "A Little Less Purity Goes a Long Way." July 7:47.

Ember, M., 1982. "Statistical Evidence for an Ecological Explanation of Warfare." *American Anthropologist*, 84:645.

Enserink, M., 2005. "Is Holland Becoming the Kansas of Europe?" *Science*, 308:1394.

Enserink, M., 2007. "Tropical Disease Follows Mosquitoes to Europe." *Science*, 317:1485.

Fenwick, A., 2006. "Waterborne Infectious Diseases—Could They Be Consigned to History?" *Science*, 313:1077.

Fernandes, E., 2006. *Holy Warriors: A Journey into the Heart of Indian Fundamentalism*. Delhi: Penguin Viking India.

Fischetti, M., 2001. "Drowning New Orleans." *Scientific American*, 285(4):78.

French, H. W., 2005. "Uniting China to Speak Mandarin." *New York Times*, July 10.

Friedman, T. L., 2005. *The World Is Flat: A Brief History of the Twentieth Century*. New York: Farrar, Straus & Giroux.

Fung, V. K., W. K. Fung, and Y. Wind, 2008. *Competing in a Flat World: Building Enterprises for a Borderless World*. Upper Saddle River, N.J.: Pearson Education/Wharton School.

Gallagher, T., 2007. "Britain: A Radical Stronghold for European Muslims." *2007 Book of the Year*. Chicago: Encyclopaedia Britannica.

Garfield, K., 2007. "Is There a Genetic Basis to Race After All?" *Discover*, 26(3):21.

Gould, P. R., 1993. *The Slow Plague: A Geography of the AIDS Pandemic*. Oxford: Blackwell.

Graddol, D., 1997. *The Future of English?* London: British Council.

Graddol, D., 2004. "The Future of Language." *Science*, 303:1329.

Grant, R., and J. Nijman, 2002. "Globalization and the Corporate Geography of Cities in the Less-Developed World." *Annals of the Association of American Geographers*, 92(2).

Greenberg, J., 1963. *The Languages of Africa*. Bloomington: Indiana University Press.

Greenberg, J., 1987. *Languages of the Americas*. Bloomington: Indiana University Press.

Hansen, J., 2004. "Defusing the Global Warming Time Bomb." *Scientific American*, 291(3):68.

Hanson, S., and G. Pratt, 1995. *Gender, Work and Space*. New York: Routledge.

Harris, S., 2004. *The End of Faith: Religion, Terror, and the Future of Reason*. New York: Norton.

Homer-Dixon, T., 2006. *The Upside of Down: Catastrophe, Creativity and the Renewal of Civilization*. Washington, D.C.: Island Press.

Howland, C. W., 2001. *Religious Fundamentalism and the Human Rights of Women*. New York: Palgrave.

Huntington, E., 1940. *Principles of Human Geography*. New York: John Wiley & Sons.

Huntington, S. P., 1996. *The Clash of Civilizations and the Remaking of the World Order*. New York: Simon & Schuster.

Jefferson, M., 1939. "The Law of the Primate City." *Geographical Review*, 29:226.

Johnson, S., 2006. *The Ghost Map: The Story of London's Most Terrifying Epidemic—and How It Changed Science, Cities, and the Modern World*. New York: Riverhead Books.

Kapp, C., 2007. "Switzerland." *2007 Book of the Year*. Chicago: Encyclopaedia Britannica.

Kerr, R. A., 2007. "Mammoth-Killer Impact Gets Mixed Reception from Earth Scientists." *Science*, 316:1264.

Kiefer, P., 2007. "Organized Crime Takes Lead in Italian Economy, Report Says." *New York Times*, October 22.

Knapp, G., ed., 2002. *Latin America in the Twentieth Century: Challenges and Solutions*. Austin: University of Texas Press.

Knowlton, B., 2007. "Global Support for Trade, Mixed with Some Doubts." *New York Times*, October 5.

Kurlantzick, J., 2007. "Sometimes, Sightseeing Is a Look at Your X-Rays." *New York Times*, May 20.

Landes, D., 1998. *The Wealth and Poverty of Nations: Why Some Are So Rich and Some So Poor*. New York: Norton.

Legassick, M., 2007. "South Africa." *2007 Book of the Year*. Chicago: Encyclopaedia Britannica.

Leroi, A. M., 2005. "A Family Tree in Every Gene." *New York Times*, March 14.

Lim, M., R. Metzler, and Y. Bar-Yam, 2007. "Global Pattern Formation and Ethnic/Cultural Violence." *Science*, 317:1540.

Lloyd, B. S., A. C. Rengert, and J. J. Monk, 1982. *Women and Spatial Change*. Dubuque, Iowa: Kendall-Hunt.

Luce, E., 2006. *In Spite of the Gods: The Rise of Modern India*. New York: Little, Brown.

Mackinder, H. J., 1904. "The Geographical Pivot of History." *Geographical Journal*, 23:421.

Mandela, N., 1994. *Long Walk to Freedom*. Boston: Little, Brown.

McArthur, T., 1998. *The English Languages*. Cambridge: Cambridge University Press.

Meade, M. S., and R. J. Earickson, 2005. *Medical Geography*. New York: Guilford Press.

Moss, W. G., 2008. *An Age of Progress? Clashing Twentieth Century Forces*. London: Anthem Press.

Murray, W. E., 2006. *Geographies of Globalization*. New York: Routledge.

Nagourney, E., 2007. "Skilled Ear for Music May Help Language." *New York Times*, August 11.

Nijman, J., 2004. "De Analyse van Mondiale Stedelijke Netwerken: Observaties vanuit Miami." Personal communication in response to a query, manuscript of a 2004 paper attached to letter dated October 4, 2007.

Opdycke, S., 2000. *The Routledge Historical Atlas of Women in America*. New York: Routledge.

Oppenheimer, S., 2003. *The Real Eve: Modern Man's Journey Out of Africa*. New York: Carroll & Graf.

Prothero, R. M., 1963. "Population Mobility and Trypanosomiasis in Africa." *Bulletin of the World Health Organization*, 28:615.

Richardson, L., 2006. *What Terrorists Want: Understanding the Enemy, Containing the Threat*. New York: Random House.

Rodriguez, G., 2007. *Mongrels, Bastards, Orphans, and Vagabonds: Mexican Immigration and the Future of Race in America*. New York: Pantheon.

Rosenberg, N. A. et al., 2002. "Genetic Structure of Human Populations." *Science*, 298:122.

Rushdie, S., 2005. "India and Pakistan's Code of Dishonor." *New York Times*, July 10.

Sachs, J. D., 2002. "A New Global Effort to Control Malaria." *Science*, 298:122.

Sachs, J. D., 2005. *The End of Poverty: Economic Possibilities for Our Time*. New York: Penguin Books.

Sachs, J. D., 2006. "Ecology and Political Upheaval." *Scientific American*, 295(1):37.

Sapolsky, R., 2005. "Are the Desert People Winning?" *Discover*, 24(8):42.

Sassen, S., 1991. *The Global City: New York, London, Tokyo*. Princeton: Princeton University Press.

Saunders, C., 2006. "Equatorial Guinea." *2006 Book of the Year*. Chicago: Encyclopaedia Britannica.

Savage, T. M., 2004. "Europe and Islam: Crescent Waxing, Cultures Clashing." *Washington Quarterly* 27(3):25.

Scarth, A., 2002. *La Catastrophe*. Oxford: Oxford University Press.

Sen, A., 2006. *Identity and Violence: The Illusion of Destiny*. New York: Norton.

Sengupta, S., 2006. "Report Shows Muslims near Bottom of Social Ladder." *New York Times*, November 24.

Short, J., et. al., 2000. "From World Cities to Gateway Cities." *City*, 4:317.

Sivard, R. L., 1985. *Women: A World Survey*. Washington, D.C.: World Priorities.

Sowell, T., 1994. *Race and Culture: A World View*. New York: Basic Books.

Spears, E. K., and H. J. de Blij, 2001. "Political Geography of Devolution in the Americas: The Case of Brazil's South." *Pennsylvania Geographer,* 39(1):3.

Stamp, L. D., 1964. *The Geography of Life and Death*. Ithaca, N.Y.: Cornell University Press.

Stone, R., 2004. "Iceland's Doomsday Scenario?" *Science,* 306:1602.

Stone, R. and R. A. Kerr, 2005. "Girding for the Next Killer Wave." *Science,* 310:1602.

Taylor, P. J., 2004. *World City Network: a Global Urban Analysis*. London: Routledge.

Thomas Jr., L., 2007. "A Fragile Foothold: The Ranks of Top-Tier Women on Wall Street Are Shrinking." *New York Times,* December 1.

UNAIDS, 2006. *2006 UNAIDS Epidemic Update*. Geneva: Joint UN Programme on HIV/AIDS.

United Nations, 2000. *The World's Women, 2000*. New York: UN Press.

United Nations, 2006. *Report on Migration*. New York: United Nations.

Vogel, G., 2005. "Will a Preemptive Strike against Malaria Pay Off?" *Science,* 310:1606.

Wellems, T. E., 2002. "*Plasmodium* Chloroquine Resistance and the Search for a Replacement Antimalarial Drug." *Science,* 298:124.

Winchester, S., 2003. *Krakatoa: The Day the World Exploded*. New York: HarperCollins.

Wolpert, S., 1999. *India*. Berkeley: University of California Press.

Woodman, J., 2007. *Patients Beyond Borders: Everybody's Guide to Affordable, World-Class Medical Tourism*. Chapel Hill, N.C.: Healthy Travel Media.

World Bank, 2007. *Maternal Mortality in 2005*. Washington, D.C.: World Bank.

Yardley, J., 2006. "A Spectator's Role for China's Muslims." *New York Times,* February 19.

INDEX

The letter *f* following a page number denotes a figure.